Receptor-Oriented Communication for Hui Muslims in China

American Society of Missiology Monograph Series

Series Editor, James R. Krabill

The ASM Monograph Series provides a forum for publishing quality dissertations and studies in the field of missiology. Collaborating with Pickwick Publications—a division of Wipf and Stock Publishers of Eugene, Oregon—the American Society of Missiology selects high quality dissertations and other monographic studies that offer research materials in mission studies for scholars, mission and church leaders, and the academic community at large. The ASM seeks scholarly work for publication in the series that throws light on issues confronting Christian world mission in its cultural, social, historical, biblical, and theological dimensions.

Missiology is an academic field that brings together scholars whose professional training ranges from doctoral-level preparation in areas such as Scripture, history and sociology of religions, anthropology, theology, international relations, interreligious interchange, mission history, inculturation, and church law. The American Society of Missiology, which sponsors this series, is an ecumenical body drawing members from Independent and Ecumenical Protestant, Catholic, Orthodox, and other traditions. Members of the ASM are united by their commitment to reflect on and do scholarly work relating to both mission history and the present-day mission of the church. The ASM Monograph Series aims to publish works of exceptional merit on specialized topics, with particular attention given to work by younger scholars, the dissemination and publication of which is difficult under the economic pressures of standard publishing models.

Persons seeking information about the ASM or the guidelines for having their dissertations considered for publication in the ASM Monograph Series should consult the Society's website—www.asmweb.org.

Members of the ASM Monograph Committe who approved this book are:

James R. Krabill, Global Ministries at Mennonite Mission Network in Elkhart, Indiana

Michael A. Rynkiewich, Retired from Asbury Theological Seminary

RECENTLY PUBLISHED IN THE ASM MONOGRAPH SERIES

Matthew Friedman, *Union with God in Christ: Early Christian and Wesleyan Spirituality as an Approach to Islamic Mysticism*

Megan Meyers, *Grazing and Growing in Mozambique: Developing Disciples through Contextualized Worship Arts*

Receptor-Oriented Communication for Hui Muslims in China

With Special Reference to Church Planting

Enoch Jinsik Kim

American Society of Missiology Monograph
Series vol. 34

☙PICKWICK *Publications* · Eugene, Oregon

RECEPTOR-ORIENTED COMMUNICATION FOR HUI MUSLIMS IN CHINA
With Special Reference to Church Planting

American Society of Missiology Monograph Series 34

Copyright © 2018 Enoch Jinsik Kim. All rights reserved. Except for brief quotations in critical publications or reviews, no part of this book may be reproduced in any manner without prior written permission from the publisher. Write: Permissions, Wipf and Stock Publishers, 199 W. 8th Ave., Suite 3, Eugene, OR 97401.

Pickwick Publications
An Imprint of Wipf and Stock Publishers
199 W. 8th Ave., Suite 3
Eugene, OR 97401

www.wipfandstock.com

PAPERBACK ISBN: 978-1-5326-0205-4
HARDCOVER ISBN: 978-1-5326-0207-8
EBOOK ISBN: 978-1-5326-0206-1

Cataloguing-in-Publication data:

Names: Kim, Enoch Jinsik, author. | Sunquist, Scott W., foreword.

Title: Receptor-oriented communication for Hui Muslims in China : with special reference to church planting / by Enoch Jinsik Kim; foreword by Scott W. Sunquist.

Description: Eugene, OR: Pickwick Publications, 2018 | Series: American Society of Missiology Monograph Series 34 | Includes bibliographical references and index.

Identifiers: ISBN 978-1-5326-0205-4 (paperback) | ISBN 978-1-5326-0207-8 (hardcover) | ISBN 978-1-5326-0206-1 (ebook)

Subjects: LCSH: Muslims—China, Northwest. | Islam—China, Northwest. | Hui (Chinese people)—China, Northwest—Religious life and customs. | China—Church history—21st century. | Christianity—China.

Classification: LCC BR1285 K58 2018 (print) | LCC BR1285 (ebook)

Manufactured in the U.S.A.   04/17/18

To my wife, Sarah Hyaeran Ko,
for her sacrificial love and support

To my children, Joy Chanhee, Timothy Heeseung,
and Josephine Kim

Contents

List of Tables | xi
List of Figures | xiii
List of Abbreviations | xv
Foreword | xvii
Acknowledgments | xix

1. **Thesis Design** | 1
   Background of the Study | 1
   Significance of Research | 2
   Central Research Issue | 3
   Research Questions | 3
   Delimitations | 3
   Definitions | 4
   Field Research | 5
   Data Analysis | 6
   Overview of the Study | 6

PART ONE: A CULTURAL STUDY OF THE HUI AND YEU-HUI

2. **The Cultural Background of the Hui** | 9
   Defining the Hui | 9
   Historical Background of the Hui | 10
   Religious Background of the Hui | 11

Worldview and Cultural Study | 15
Summary | 19

3 The Impact of Modernization upon the Hui | 21
The Impact of Modernization in the Islamic World | 22
The Impact of Modernization and the Hui | 25
Modernization's Impact upon Hui Interethnic Dynamics | 28
Summary | 31

4 The Sociological Identity of the Urban Hui | 33
Theoretical Foundation of Urbanization | 33
China's Urbanism and the Hui | 36
The Hui Social Network | 41
The Hui New Network Models | 48
Summary | 53

5 YEU-Hui Identity | 54
The YEU-Hui | 54
Modernization and the YEU-Hui | 57
Early Adopter and Innovators | 59
Field Research Purpose and Goals | 61
Sampling Plan and Data Collection | 61
Demographic Data | 62
Research Limitation | 77
Interpretation | 77
Summary | 79

6 Biblical Teachings That Relate to YEU-Hui Cultural Themes | 80
Biblical Definition of Power and Pride | 81
Power and Pride for Marginal Groups in the Bible | 86
Issues of Biblical Messages about Power and Pride
    in Muslim Context | 88
Seven Messages as Bridge of Communication | 91
Summary | 103

7 Necessity of a Contextual Church among the YEU-Hui | 105
Precedent Theories to Contextualization | 105
Current Situation of YEU-Hui Church Planting | 118

Criteria for YEU-Hui Contextualized Church | 120
Summary | 131

PART II: COMMUNICATION PRINCIPLE AND STRATEGY

8   Communication Principles | 135
Lessons from the Bible | 136
Communication Process | 140
Receptor-Oriented Communication | 145
Summary and Reflection | 150

9   Media and Signals | 151
Signals | 151
Media | 152
Mass Communication and Interpersonal Communication | 154
Media Description | 156
Media Preferences and the YEU-Hui | 162
Summary | 164

10 Christian Virtual Community in China | 166
Defining Virtual Communities | 166
Virtual Community's Mode of Communication | 170
Virtual Community's Membership Structure | 171
Virtual Community Types | 172
Direction from Field Research | 173
Data Report to China's Current Internet User Situation | 175
Analysis of Chinese Christian Website and
    Virtual Communities | 179
Sample Case Sites | 186
Interpretation | 190
Summary | 192

**11 Developing Strategies for Church Planting among
    the YEU-Hui** | 193
Defining Strategy | 194
Selected Theories of Communication Strategy | 195
Developing Strategies | 204
Summary | 209

12 Propositions for Receptor-Oriented Communication Strategies for the YEU-Hui | 211

13 Future Challenges | 219

Appendix A: Questionnaire to YEU-Hui and Their Media Preference | 221

Appendix B: Questionnaire for Chinese Christian Websites | 227

Appendix C: Pearson Correlation Coefficient and Each M-Factors Contribution to MM-Scale | 231

Appendix D: Analyzing E-Group's Background | 233

Appendix E: Background Analysis: Conservatives versus Liberal and Open E-Groups | 236

Bibliography | 239
Index | 249

Tables

Table 1: Comparison of Real Concerns between Islamic Fundamental and Non-Fundamental Groups | 74

Table 2: Favorite Themes of YEU-Han and E-Group | 76

Table 3: YEU-Han's Real Concern | 77

Table 4: YEU-Han and E-Group's Media Preference | 163

Table 5: YEU-Han and E-Group Program Preferences | 164

Table 6: The Percentages of Web Page Content Forms | 176

Table 7: High and Low Tendencies for Forming Virtual Communities | 180

Table 8: Goal of Sites | 181

Table 9: Primary Recipients | 181

Table 10: Cultural Theme of the Sites | 182

Table 11: Evangelism Methods | 183

Table 12: Attraction to Newcomers | 184

Table 13: Feedback Systems | 185

Table 14: Readiness for Offline Community | 186

Table 15: A Summary of Conversation on a Chinese Christian Website | 189

Table 16: A Sample of Chinese Christian Website Bulletin | 190

Table 17: Each M-Factors Contribution | 232

Table 18: E-Group and Residence Period | 233

Table 19: E-Group and Residence Environment | 233

Table 20: E-Group and Working and Schooling Period | 234

Table 21: E-Group and Mosque Attendance | 234

Table 22: E-Group and Contact with Western Culture | 234

Table 23: E-Group and Influence of Western and Hong Kong Fashion | 235

Table 24: E-Group and Muslim Friends | 235

Table 25: Residence Environment of the Two Groups | 236

Table 26: Urban Preferences among the Two Groups | 236

Table 27: Reasons for Urban Preference among the Two Groups | 237

Table 28: Child Education among the Two Groups | 237

Table 29: Mosque Attendance among the Two Groups | 237

Table 30: Contact with Global Media among the Two Groups | 238

Table 31: Influence from Western and Hong Kong Fashion among the Two Groups | 238

Table 32: Muslim Friends among the Two Groups | 238

Figures

Figure 1: Conceptual Model of Traditional Secondary Networks | 48

Figure 2: Conceptual Model of Expanded Secondary Networks beyond the Ethnic Boundary | 49

Figure 3: Three Major Urban Components in Traditional Community | 50

Figure 4: Changed Three Major Urban Components in Modern Community | 51

Figure 5: Gender Ratio | 62

Figure 6: Age Categories | 63

Figure 7: Urban Residence Periods | 63

Figure 8: Residence Environments | 64

Figure 9: Schooling Background | 65

Figure 10: Q Number Comparisons between YEU and Non-YEU | 66

Figure 11: Relations between Q-Scale and Age | 67

Figure 12: Relation of Q-Scale to Urban Residence Period | 68

Figure 14: Classification of the YEU-Hui by M Number | 69

Figure 15: MM-Scale | 70

Figure 16: Identifying E-Group among the YEU-Hui | 72

Figure 17: Conservative Groups in the MM-Scale | 73

Figure 18: A Paradigm of Thematic Dissonance | 89

Figure 19: H-H Ratio vs. Contextualization Scale | 123

Figure 20: Step 1: Process of Launching Hui Church from a Multiethnic Church Model | 126

Figure 21: Step 2: Process of Launching Hui Church from a Multiethnic Church Model | 126

Figure 22: Step 3: Process of Launching Hui Church from a Multiethnic Church Model | 127

Figure 23: Step 4: Process of Launching Hui Church from a Multiethnic Church Model | 127

Figure 24: Step 5: Process of Launching Hui Church from a Multiethnic Church Model | 128

Figure 25: Søgaard's Communication Model | 144

Figure 26: Number of Internet Users in Previous Survey | 176

Figure 27: Internet User's Age Situation | 177

Figure 28: Internet User's Education Level | 178

Figure 29: Internet User's Occupation Situation | 178

Figure 30: Internet and Mobile Phone User's Location | 179

Figure 31: Søgaard's Two Dimensional Model with All Media Penetration Project Example | 203

Figure 32: Overall Mission Strategy and Søgaard's Two Dimensional Model | 204

Figure 33: Local Church-Driven Virtual-Supported Offline Church-Planting Model | 209

Abbreviations

C-Group	Conservative Islam group among the E-Group
E-Group	Entrance group among the YEU-H
H-H Ratio	Hui and Han ratio
High 30%	A group that marks higher 30% grade in M-Scale
LOE-Group	Liberal and opened E-Group
M-Group	A group of people whose M-Scale grade is higher than 30%
MBB	Muslim background believer
MM-Scale	More modernization scale
M-Scale	Modernization scale, a tool for measuring the degree of modernization
Q-Scale	*Qingzhen* scale
YEU-Han	Young, Educated, and Urban Han
YEU-Hui	Young, Educated, and Urban Hui

Foreword

IN THE WORLD OF Christian mission a major shift took place in the 1970s when mission agencies and missionaries began to focus not on mission in general, and not even on mission in certain countries, but on reaching out to unreached people groups (UPG). This new approach and focus, pioneered by the ever-creative Ralph Winter, has been the foundation for a new stream of literature that looks specifically at ethnic groups that are less responsive to the gospel. Many are less responsive because there are few people reaching out to them, and those who are reaching out are not taking the time to study how best to communicate. Studies focused on UPGs followed the pattern of earlier church growth studies by using the social sciences, both quantitative and qualitative research, to discover the most efficient methods of communicating the gospel and then of growing churches among these newer groups.

In this volume, Enoch Kim focuses on a largely unreached group of Muslims in China, the Hui people. To be exact, he has focused his study even more carefully on the "young, educated and urban" Hui living in cities such as Xian. This is what he calls the "YEU-Hui" people. Thus, this study is focused upon a very important group that has the connections and ability to reach the larger population of their own Hui people. Close to 11 million Hui people live in China and, as Kim has identified, newer technologies, migration and newer relationships are variables that need attention if Christian witness is to be effective. Enoch Kim has carefully interviewed, collected data, and analyzed the data to discover what might be effective means of outreach, and what might be the form of church that would develop among the Hui people.

I believe that this book is an excellent example of anthropological research, in the hands of a Christian scholar, in service of the unreached. I have often said that one of the greatest injustices in the world is that for all of these centuries there are still whole cultures who have not had an opportunity to hear, understand, and respond to the good news that Jesus Christ brought to humanity. As a result, many other injustices germinate in these unreached cultures. Enoch Kim shows us, through his attention to detail as well as his continued academic persistence, what it means to be a missionary scholarly for the twenty-first century. In this study he is aware of the impact of social media and the internet on ancient Muslim cultures in China. He recognizes the need to be aware of communication patterns, fears and hopes of a people.

It would be wonderful if many people involved in mission strategy as well as mission theology would pick up this book as a guide to careful and compassionate thinking for those who are still unreached.

Scott W. Sunquist

Dean of the School of Intercultural Studies and
Professor of World Christianity in Fuller Theological Seminary

Acknowledgments

I WANT TO EXPRESS my deep felt thanksgiving to my mentor, Viggo B. Søgaard, director of Asian Institute of Christian Communication and senior professor of communication at Fuller School of Intercultural Studies. His tireless encouragement and counsel enabled me to complete today's product.

I also want to thank my committee members, Timothy Park and Dudley Woodberry, who have taken time to guide me through continual inspiration and academic expertise. I appreciate the comments and input from Mary Kay McVicker, who was gracious enough to take the time to be my external reader.

I thank Scott Sunquist, my supervisor and dean of the School of Intercultural Studies in Fuller Theological Seminary, for helping me thrive in my early scholar days. He willingly wrote the foreword for this publication without hesitation.

I thank Sebastian Kim and his leadership team who pours his energy and passion for building up Korean Studies Center in Fuller Theological Seminary. Korean Studies Center was a good umbrella, safeguard, and energy center for this product. I am deeply grateful to the faculty of Fuller Theological Seminary, including Charles H. Kraft, Wilbert R. Shenk, R. Daniel Shaw, Dean S. Gilliland, Charles E. Van Engen. Roberta King, and Elizabeth Glanville, the former doctoral program advisor and a current colleague. Their insights and passions encouraged me during my whole time of study.

I express my gratitude to Rev. Joseph Min, Kim Taejung, Joo Youngchan and the staff at HOPE Missions, who served me while I was serving and researching in China. Furthermore, I will not forget the grace of David Tai Woong Lee, Felipe Jin Suck Byun in GMF, and Joo Youngchan in HOPE, who constantly mentored and cooperated with me. I will not be able to forget the leadership of the Frontiers leaders, Greg Livingstone, Patrick Lai, Rick Love, Bob Peckham, Tim Lewis, missionary Hyun Soo Lee, and especially my former team leaders, J and Iv,[1] for helping me perceive the Chinese Muslims with respect, and as creations of God.

This research would not have been successful without the help and generosity of foundations and people. Among them are pastor Taehyung Kim and Amos Park, elder Jungmin Suh, Paul Woo, Mrs. Sunny Chang, deacon Hoseung Lee, missionary Robert Lee, and Grace Foundation.

Thanks to my parents, Won Seop Kim and Hae Nyuh Shim for their encouragements. I would like to say thanks to my wife, Sarah Hyaeran Ko, who always trust me and support my studies with prayers. I also sincerely thank to my children, Joy, and Josephine Kim, especially to Timothy Heeseung Kim, for being my personal editor.

I thank K. C. Hanson, the editor-in-chief of Pickwick's staff, and Brian Palmer for the publication of this book. I also give a big thanksgiving to James R. Krabill, Michael A. Rynkiewich and other American Society of Missiology Monograph Series Committee members who evaluated and decide to publish this product.

I hope this research project can help all the workers, expatriates and locals, who have sacrificed their lives and family to serve Chinese Muslims. All glory, honor and thanks be to God, who allowed me to know true love, sacrifice, and divine friendship. God's blessing is beyond my measure, and he has given me his wisdom and passion whenever I needed it.

Pasadena, California, 2017

---

1. These are not their real names, to protect their privacy.

1

Thesis Design

THE HUI IS A Chinese Muslim minority with a population of about 10.7 million[1] and an annual growth of 2.4 percent.[2] They are the largest group among all Chinese Muslims, and have very limited exposure to the Christian message. Notably, in the countryside most Hui are farmers, shop owners, and laborers, yet they traditionally work as merchants. In the city, most of them work as laborers, although some of them run small businesses—mostly Muslim restaurants or shops. Today, the Hui live throughout China, but they are highly concentrated in the northwestern Chinese provinces. There are very few Christians among the Hui.

This research studies communication strategies for the establishment of culturally relevant churches among the Hui. This research limits its study to young, educated, urban Hui (YEU-Hui) in northwestern China.

BACKGROUND OF THE STUDY

I came to personal faith in the *Bulgwangdong* Bible Baptist Church in Korea, and God formed the root of my faith there. Sixteen years ago, God called me to be a missionary among the Hui people. I worked with two mission organizations: HOPE and Frontiers Mission. HOPE stands for Helping Overseas Professional Employment, and it primarily works with peoples and nations who are communist and Muslims. Frontiers Mission exclusively works with Muslims.

---

1. Hattaway, *Operation China*, 219.
2. Gladney, *Ethnic Identity in China*, 12.

2   Thesis Design

In Frontiers Mission, my team and I focused on reaching Hui students and young couples. During my furlough, I studied missiology at Fuller Theological Seminary. This study opened my eyes to the need for further study regarding the Hui and developing a mission strategy for them. Through several Islamic courses and behavioral science classes, I became aware of God leading me to focus on communicating the gospel with the Hui. Therefore, my decision to study further has led to this present research.

I have seen that there are relatively high possibilities of openness among the young, educated, and urban Hui people (YEU-Hui). I believe this study will be an important tool for Hui evangelism and will expand and cultivate new missiological areas.

Purpose

The purpose of this study is to identify conceptual issues for the development of receptor-oriented communication strategies among young, educated, urban Hui Muslims in China's northwestern cities in order to achieve culturally relevant churches.

Research Goals

1. To understand the cultural issues that need to be considered when presenting the gospel to young, educated, urban Hui Muslims in China.
2. To discover cultural themes among young, educated, urban Hui Muslim and suggest biblical illustrations that can serve as bridges for evangelism and church planting.
3. To identify relevant communication channels among young, urban, educated Hui Muslims in China.
4. To describe the type of church that would be relevant for young, educated, urban Hui Muslims in China.

SIGNIFICANCE OF RESEARCH

The significance of this research is threefold:

1. This study guides me in how to fulfill my personal calling from God to be a missionary to the Hui. This research provides an academic

basis for better understanding the Hui and YEU-Hui, which helps me to fulfill my vision.
2. This study helps Global Missionary Fellowship, Frontiers Mission, and my sending church to reach their mission goals. One of Global Missionary Fellowship's goals is reaching people in communist and Muslim countries, while Frontiers mission is mainly working to reach Muslims. My church has also educated and formed me to have a burden for people who are rarely exposed to the gospel.
3. This study will expand missiological viewpoints as well. Very few scholars have studied the Hui from the Christian perspective. This research will include historical data, an anthropological study, cross-cultural communication strategies, a mission strategy, a sociological study, a biblical study, and Chinese Islamic studies. This multidimensional approach to intercultural communication studies will contribute to developing the missiological basis for planting churches among the Hui.

CENTRAL RESEARCH ISSUE

The central research issue to be addressed in this study is to identify the conceptual issues of receptor-oriented communication strategies that will lead to establishing culturally relevant churches among young, educated, urban Hui Muslims in China's northwestern cities.

RESEARCH QUESTIONS

1. What are the cultural issues that need to be considered when presenting the gospel to young, educated, urban Hui Muslims in China?
2. What are biblical answers that serve as bridges for evangelism and church planting among the young, educated, urban Hui?
3. What relevant communication channels can be used to reach the young, educated, urban Hui Muslims?
4. Which type of churches would be the most relevant for young, educated, urban Hui Muslims in China?

DELIMITATIONS

The study delimits the condition of young, educated, urban Hui Muslims in China as following: Among the Chinese Muslims, they must be from the Hui people, born after the beginning of the Cultural Revolution (1965), have a post-high school education, and live in the capital city of their province. This study does not research non-Muslim Hui who consider themselves atheist, nor people from other people groups who became Hui in order to receive social benefits.

This study only researches Hui anthropological, historical, and socioreligious data that may be used as basal data regarding communication patterns and contextualization. The research is focused mainly on the communication theory that will become the basic data for contextualization.

Research question 1 deals with the culturally relevant variables in the problem statement. Therefore, this study is limited in its area to cultural background, the current situation of modernization, and urban ethnic dynamics.

Research question 2 deals with cultural themes and their biblical studies. It is related to the receptor-oriented variable in the problem statement. This research limits this area to biblical studies that can serve as a bridge of communicating the gospel by dealing with cultural themes.

Research question 3 deals with communication strategies among young, educated, and urban variables in the problem statement. Therefore, this study limits its area to communication theory, channels, and strategy.

Research question 4 is related to variables regarding the establishment of relevant churches, as mentioned in the problem statement. This question deals with cross-cultural church-planting strategies and local Muslim evangelism within a contextualization study.

DEFINITIONS

1. YEU-Hui: This is an acronym for young, educated, urban Hui.

2. The Hui people: The Hui population is one of fifty-five Chinese minorities. This research defines the concept of Hui as people who satisfy two conditions. The first condition is that the people are called the Hui *minzu* by the People's Republic of China (PRC). The second condition is that the people understand themselves to have Islamic background and, at least partially, practice Muslim cultural activities.

Methodology

The data collection consists of literature research and field research. The literature research has been in libraries, on the Internet, and through the resources of the Chinese Muslim society. The field research has been done through survey research, participant observation, and interviews.

Literature Research

This study largely depends on literature research using research tools at Fuller Theological Seminary's McAlister Library, at the library at UCLA, through the Interlibrary loan system, and on Internet search engines.

FIELD RESEARCH

There were four major areas of field research. These were surveys, case studies, participant observation, and personal interviews. The researcher and his coworkers have both lived in or near to the Hui community. Therefore, the data collection was completed through personal contacts and the help of coworkers.

First, the researcher and coworkers collected data from cases. They visited missionaries and obtained information from them and their records. Other information was collected from Muslim background believers (MBB), as well as potential converts. This data lays the groundwork for finding the answers to research questions three and four. This field research includes several ministry cases involving Hui expatriate missionaries.

Second, the researcher used the participant observation method. The researcher participated in Hui rituals, ceremonies, and activities and even visited homes to observe their worldview, patterns of behavior, customs, and relationships. The researcher took an *emic* approach in order to experience how and why they understand, feel, and behave the way they do.

Third, the interview method was used. The researcher interviewed people already known by the researcher or other coworkers. The researcher used this interview method as a supplementary method of questionnaire, too.

Fourth, two kinds of questionnaires were primary tools of data collection. The first questionnaire had twenty-four questions and was mainly used for identifying the YEU-Hui group and their media preference. The second questionnaire was used to better understand the Chinese Christian website situation. For this second questionnaire, the researcher used indirect case study, interview, and participant observation methods to researches virtual community members' patterns.

DATA ANALYSIS

To summarize the results of the questionnaire, there were 229 respondents in the sample for tabulation. The main computer program used for analysis was the SPSS, version 13. With this program, the researcher was able to analyze and tabulate the results.

The second questionnaire has twenty-six websites as samples, which were screened out of sixty sites. The SPSS program and Microsoft Excel, version 2003, were the main programs used for this analysis.

The collected information was used to answer the four research questions. The researcher evaluated and analyzed the data, and then assessed it for a communication theory for establishing culturally relevant churches.

OVERVIEW OF THE STUDY

This study consists of two parts: propositions and conclusions. The first part studies the culture of the Hui and, in more detail, a social class known as the young, educated, and urban Hui. The main areas of study are their background and current issues, as well as biblical messages that are relevant to their culture. The second part is communication and strategy for reaching out to the Hui people. There are fifteen propositions with future challenges that come from the cultural study and communication strategy in the final part.

PART ONE

A Cultural Study of
the Hui and YEU-Hui

2

The Cultural Background of the Hui

IN 2002, PAUL HATTAWAY wrote, "The Hui are probably the largest people group in the world without a single known Christian fellowship group."[1] This provides a crucial motivation for this research. To plant a church requires the Christian missionary to have a cultural understanding about the people group. For designing a mission strategy to the Hui, therefore, understanding their background is necessary. Before the background study, the Hui people group should be well defined in order to lay down significant guidelines for future research.

Therefore, this first part of this study examines the cultural background of the Hui in order to fulfill the first research goal of this dissertation: to understand the cultural issues that need to be considered when presenting the gospel to young, educated, urban Hui Muslims in China. Their historical and religious background will provide crucial knowledge and basal data for setting up mission strategies.

DEFINING THE HUI

The Hui is a people group among the fifty-six Chinese people groups. Among them, the Han are the majority group, and fifty-five people groups are regarded as minorities. Though they are categorized as a people group in China, the Hui people are actually hard to define. *Minzu* (民族) [minju] is the Chinese term for "people."[2] However, Chinese politicians, scholars, and others use different criteria for defining *minzu*. Some define *minzu* as race, religion, or people. Maris Boyd Gillette says,

---

1. Hattaway, *Operation China*, 219.
2. English transliterations such as this appear in brackets throughout.

"Through the first 50 years of the twentieth century, 'Hui' was primarily a religious category."[3] However, when the PRC (People's Republic of China) dispatched a series of ethnological missions, they categorized the Hui as "no longer dependent on Islamic observance," but rather as a "'people' a 'race.'"[4] Therefore, the *minzu* as a race is larger than the Hui as a people group.

This research will exclusively regard Hui as people who satisfy the following two conditions: (1) they are called Hui *minzu* by China, and (2) they consider themselves to be from an Islamic background and practice at least some Muslim cultural activities.

HISTORICAL BACKGROUND OF THE HUI

The Hui people have lived in China for about 1,300 years and have mingled with many different cultures. Their ancestors are not just one single group, but represent a variety of people, including soldiers, peasants, merchants, and nomads. The collective cultural influences on the Hui also originate from a variety of geographic regions: Central Asia and Middle Eastern regions, including Persia, Pakistan, Turkey, and even Mongolia and Uygur.[5] Since the Hui have mainly lived among Mongolians, Tibetans, Han Chinese, and Uyghur in northwestern China, their Muslim culture, architecture, economic systems, worldview, and cultural habits have been continually influenced by the diversity that surrounds them.

Ancient Muslims used two main routes into China from the Arabic world. Some of them came by sea and arrived in Guangdong province on China's southeast coast. However, a significantly larger numbers of Muslims came by the Silk Road, which is "an interconnected series of routes connecting China and Asia Minor."[6] Marshall Broomhall, who summarizes the historical origins of the Muslim Chinese, asserts that the rise of this group dates back to the seventh-century Tang Dynasty.[7] Another possible link to the origin of this people comes from the expeditionary forces that were occurring "during the fourth Caliphate, with Arab forces consisting of some four thousand cavalry" to help the reigning emperor

---

3. Gillette, *Between Mecca and Beijing*, 11.
4. Ibid., 13.
5. Kim, "'Us' or 'Me'?," 90.
6. *Wikipedia*, s.v. "Silk Road."
7. Broomhall, *Islam in China*, 64–68.

of China "in his warfare against the Tibetans."⁸ From the seventh century onward, large numbers of Arab traders came "across the Indian Ocean, and began to introduce their new faith in the coastal cities of China."⁹ Then, over "the next 200 years, Islam spread through the interior too as other Muslim traders traveled along the old Silk Road."¹⁰ After the Hui settled in China, they dispersed throughout China following the channels of international trade.¹¹

Later, according to Donald Leslie, during the Ming and Qing dynasties, the Hui writers began the "sinicization and assimilation of Muslims in Confucian China," and they even "attempted to accommodate with Confucianism."¹²

From the Ming Dynasty (1368–1644), both the Hui and the Han saw each other as competitors who caused hegemony as well as economic, social, and religious conflicts.¹³ In 1862, a serious reaction prompted actions to defend Muslim communities rapidly spreading from southern Shansi westward. These rival sect conflicts grew into warring factions against the Qing Dynasty government.¹⁴ The most recent collision was in 1975 in the Yunnan Province. The conflict began as the red army closed down the religious activities of the Hui during the Cultural Revolution.¹⁵

RELIGIOUS BACKGROUND OF THE HUI

Throughout history, the Hui Muslims have renewed and changed their religious colors and diversified them. Today, Hui Islam has diversified its Islamic mysticism from indigenous mystical roots, as well as both Sunni and Sufi traditions.

Sunni: Gedimu Traditional Chinese Islam

Between the seventh and fourteenth centuries, Muslims from Arabia, Persia, and Central Asia, as well as Mongolian Muslims, moved into China's

---

8. Findlay, *Crescent in North-West China*, 14, 15.

9. Lawton, "Muslim in China," 4.

10. Ibid.

11. Gao, "民族教育于甘肅少數民族地區的補貧問題," 37–40 (my translation).

12. Leslie, *Islam in Traditional China*, 115, 119.

13. Such conflicts were in 1450–1456, 1476, 1504, 1533, 1575, 1582, 1595, 1599, 1603, and 1612. Ibid., 129–30.

14. Lipman, "Ethnic Violence in Modern China," 71–73.

15. Dillon, *China's Muslim Hui Community*, 164.

northwest and southeast coastal regions, generally residing in independent communities around central mosques. They usually did not mingle with diverse Chinese people but lived independently. The Hui called their independent community *gedimu* (community-based mosque), which comes from *qadim* in Arabic terminology. Quoting Robert Ekvall, Dru C. Gladney explains that, "due to different cultural, ritual, and dietary preferences that sometimes lead to open conflict, the communities preferred physical separation."[16] They regarded themselves as orthodox Sunni Muslims who followed the *Hanafi* school of law. This group became the *Lao Jiao* (老教) [laojiao], or the "Old Teachings." The history of the "New Teachings," or *Xin Jiao* (新教) [sinjiao], and even the "New-new Teachings," or *Xinxin Jiao* (新新教) [sinsinjiao], began as Sufism continued to influence China since the seventeenth century.[17]

Most of the Hui are Sunni Muslims. In the past, when Westerners and Christian missionaries had met the Hui Islam believers, these outsiders misunderstood the *Lao Jiao* (Old Teachings) as Sunni, and that the new religion governed the *Shi'a*. However, recent scholars have found that China has very few *Shi'a* Muslims. The "New Teaching" and the "New-new Teaching" sects are actually Sufi. Dillon explains, "It is now generally accepted that the New Teachings and even the New-new Teachings were not *Shi'a* sects but Sufi and *Ikhwani* organizations."[18] Therefore, we do not include *Shi'ism* in our study of China, for it does not relate much to the Hui people.

Under the communist government during the 1950s, this Hui *gedimu* was disrupted. To survive, the communities dispersed throughout China. Because of the calamity and impoverishment, the Hui moved around for trade purposes. Today, Hui *gedimu*s are spread all over in China's big cities.

There is a new sect in *gedimu*, called "*Xidaotang*." Its theology was created from some parts of the Chinese Qur'an, and they call it "Han ketabu." This sect is known as the non-Arabic and compromised sect.

Sufi Communities and a National Network

The history of Chinese Sufism began in the seventeenth century when the Ming Dynasty governed China. Like the other Sufi throughout the

---

16. Ekvall, *Cultural Relations*, 19; Gladney, "Qingzhen," 16.
17. Ibid.
18. Dillon, *China's Muslims*, 20.

world, the Chinese Sufi movement began with the descendants of early Sufi saintly leaders. They also built socioeconomic and religious-political institutions around the schools. That institution became known as the menhuan (門宦) [munhwan], which means "saintly lineage."[19]

The impact of Sufism was enough to promote renewal in traditional Chinese Islam. Today Chinese menhuan have four major sects: Qadariyya, Khufiyya, Jahriyya, and Khubrawiyya menhuan.[20]

Khoja Abd Alla brought Qadrihi Sufism to China in 1674, and Chinese Muslims call it the Qadriyya sect. Khoja Abd Alla preached in several places: Guangdong, Guangxi, Yunnan, and Linxia in Gansu. The early priest's tombs are in the Linxia's da gongbei ("great tomb") shrine complex, which became the center of Qadariyya Sufism in China.[21]

Next, there is Khuffiyya Sufism in Chinese Islam. Khuffiyya Sufism and Jahriyya Sufism have the same origin: Naqshbandi tariqa. Today's Khuffiyya has about twenty kinds of subsects. Most of them are dispersed in northwest provinces: Gansu, Qinghai, Ningxia, and Xinjiang. The Khuffiyya seek inspiration at tombs and Dhikr.[22]

Third, Jahriyya Sufism is a sect of Hui Islam and was raised by Ma Mingxin (1719–81). He studied Sufism in Yemen and then came to China. Jahriyya Sufism tried to be more militaristic and fundamentalist in its reforms. Unfortunately, in wars with the Qing Dynasty, about a million Jahriyya followers died. Today, Jahriyya Sufism has two subsects with about one hundred thousand followers altogether. One of the sects is the Shagou order of which the followers are mainly located in Southern Ningxia, Xinjiang, and Gansu. The other one is called Banqaio, which has about twenty-five thousand followers.

Historically, the Naqshbandiyya in China take active participation in worldly affairs. They emphasize self-cultivation and formal ritual, as well as withdrawal from social activity. Unlike Qadariyya Sufis, the Khufiyya and Jahriyya Sufis enjoy family life and material wealth.

Kuhbrawiyya is the fourth main Sufi order among Chinese Muslims. An Arabian Mohidin is said to have introduced Kuhbrawiyya to China in the 1600s. Many followers of the Kuhbrayya sect are now concentrated in the Muslim minority area of Dongxiang.

19. Ibid., 21.
20. Gladney, "Qingzhen," 18–28.
21. Ibid., 21.
22. Fletcher, "Brief History," 38; Schimmel, *Mystical Dimensions*, 122, 366; Gladney, "Qingzhen," 22.

At the end of the *Qing* Dynasty—during the late eighteenth and nineteenth centuries—there were several large-scale confrontations between the Hui and *Qing* Dynasty. The traditional *gedimu* community leaders have been generally inactive within the society, and they isolated themselves from participating in nonreligious activities. In contrast to this, the Sufi leaders participate with people and their societies. They provided active leadership among the whole Hui society in order to protect and maintain it. Like Sufism in other countries, Chinese Sufis tried to give religious renewal to traditional Muslims.[23] Sufism and its beliefs continue to maintain a crucial influence among those in Hui society today.

Shrine, Baraka, and Mysticism

Sufists believe that they can get spiritual power from the saints' shrines and tombs. They call the activity to receive and encounter this spiritual power a *"baraka."* The saints' tombs and graveyards have significant social, political, economic, and religious meanings for the Hui. The Hui call these *"tu-gongbei."*

The meaning of the *tu-gongbei* is very different to northwestern and southeastern Hui people. Some of the Hui ancestors came to the mainland by sea and arrived in a southeast port—Guangdong province—and the others came through the northwestern Silk Road. The southeastern Hui are the descendants of Arab merchants. The *tu-gongbei* tombs tangibly demonstrate the genealogical bond between these Hui communities and their foreign ancestors. Therefore, the role of the tomb in southeast is a center of ethnic division from the Han Chinese.[24]

Northwestern Hui see the *tu-gongbei* more as a medium of spiritual empowerment than as symbol of ethnic identification. The northwesterners believe that they can receive power from a saint's tomb, *tu-gongbei*, because they believe that the *tu-gongbei*s, or saints, are directly connected with Muhammad. The northwestern Hui daily seek power to overcome their social and economic problems.

Scriptural Concerns and Modernist Reforms

At the end of the Qing Dynasty, many of the Chinese Muslims began *Hajji*, a pilgrimage to Saudi Arabia. Between 1923 and 1934, about 834

---

23. Horrie and Chippindale, *What Is Islam?*, 139.
24. Gladney, "Qingzhen," 516.

Hui went on the journey. In 1939, about thirty-three Hui studied at the *Al-Azhar* University in Cairo.[25] Increased contact with the Middle East led Chinese Muslims to reevaluate their traditional notions of Islam. Through frequent meetings, *Wahhabism* entered China and established a more fundamentalist Muslim brotherhood, *Ikhwan* [*yihewan*] *al-Muslim*. These sects transformed traditional Chinese mosque architecture into their own style of mosque. The *Yihewani* mosque does not have any paintings or sculptures, only white walls with Arabic architectural style. The Sufi Muslims draw pictures on the wall.

Comparison of Chinese Muslims

Gladney gives the percentage breakdown and comparison of Chinese Muslim sects, directly quoting from Tong Ma's research: "Out of a total of 6,781,500 Hui Muslims, Tong Ma records that there are 58.2% *Gedimu*, 21% *Yihewani*, 0.5% *Xidaotong*, 1.4% *Qadriyya*, 7.2% *Kuhiyya*, 10.9% *Jahriyya*, and 0.7% *Khubrawiyya*."[26]

Even though more than 58% of the population is *Gedimu*, the Sufi have influenced the Sunni *Gedimu* since the seventeenth century. This historical and religious background contributes a crucial role in forming the Hui traditional worldview. Through this background, like other Hui, the Hui in the northwestern cities have many religious divisions and have formed a general and common Hui ethnic spirit.

WORLDVIEW AND CULTURAL STUDY

Understanding their worldview provides profound knowledge of the Hui. Each cultural zone uniquely expresses its behavior, emotion, and manners, which often causes misunderstandings between people from different cultures. The source of the difference is a difference in worldview. In order to analyze the Hui worldview, a useful definition of worldview is important. Several scholars define worldview in a variety of ways.

In his book *Creating Understanding*, Donald K. Smith illustrates the basic model of culture with the example of an onion. The outer shell represents the "behavior level." The second level represents the "social authority level." The third is the "experience level." The core level represents

---

25. Ibid., 28–29.
26. Ma, *Zhongguo Yishiland Jiaopai Yu Menhuan Zhidu Shilue*, 477–82.

the worldview.[27] Therefore, a worldview governs the behavior, mindset, and belief system of a culture.[28]

Charles Kraft defines worldview as culturally structured assumptions that "underlie a people's perception of reality and their responses to it."[29] Therefore, worldviews "are accepted uncritically and unquestioningly by most members of the culture."[30]

Paul G. Hiebert describes worldview as a "certain assumption" that lies "behind the observable patterns of human culture." It is "a people's total response to their universe."[31] Louis J. Luzbetak's general notion about worldview is described as "the deepest questions one might ask about the world and life and about the corresponding orientation that one should take toward them."[32] He categorizes worldview into four areas: supernature, nature, human beings, and time.[33]

Understanding worldview helps cross-cultural workers to see the receptor's culture as an integrated system and also enables them to analyze the culture more effectively. With this worldview concept, cross-cultural communicators can "look at the world around us in an ordered way," then "look at it through learned concepts and categories with regard to both material things and abstracts."[34]

D. Smith's description of worldview as several layers seems to be a good tool to understand how Hui worldview, cultural background, and current socio-behavior pattern are all interrelated.[35] These are backgrounds to their current behaviors, and backgrounds are continually influenced by worldview. Hui historical and religious experiences and worldviews are correlated and have formed the Hui culture. From this co-relationship, the Hui people have their own cultural themes, and they create signals and symbols to express the themes.

There are six cultural items that seem to express Hui cultural themes. Those items are collected through observation and literature

27. Smith, *Creating Understanding*, 251–60.
28. Ibid., 257.
29. Kraft, *Anthropology for Christian Witness*, 52.
30. Walsh and Middleton, *Transforming Vision*, 72.
31. Hiebert, *Cultural Anthropology*, 356.
32. Luzbetak, *Church and Cultures*, 252.
33. Michael Kearney also offers a similar definition to the worldview, in *World View*, 41.
34. Jorgensen, "Role and Function of the Media," 49.
35. Smith, *Creating Understanding*, 257.

studies. First, the concept of *qingzhen* [chingjun] is an example of Hui symbolic terms. *Qingzhen* means "clean and truth." More than a symbolic term, *qingzhen* is representative of a concept's integration into the Hui way of life.

The meaning of *qingzhen* is more than what the character means; it is also tied to the idea of Hui ethnic superiority over the Han.[36] Therefore, the concept of *qingzhen* is an important value among the Hui. *Qingzhen* gives the Hui a feeling of superiority over the Han, as well as senses of belonging and ethnic pride.

Second, the Hui ethnic enclave is a symbol of Hui cultural themes. There are two types of enclave among the Hui: *gedimu* for the Sunni, and *menhuan* for the Sufi. On the urban front, most Hui live in their own communities. In many cases, those communities have religious systems and social networks within boundaries that overlap poor urban areas. These enclaves provide a convenient system within Hui life, like Muslim restaurants, affection, and reliable ethnic trade networks.

Third, ethnic restaurants and mosques are also cultural symbols. Hui mosques and ethnic restaurants are centers for socioreligious activities and information networking. It is used as a religious and educational center, as a shelter for the poor and migrants, and as a philanthropic institution where any who are sick may rest until they recover.[37] The Hui have education, counseling, and community activities in the mosque.[38] It is the center of their community.[39]

Fourth, community ceremonies and festivals are cultural symbols. The Hui *ahong* is not only a religious leader, but also a schoolteacher, judge, counselor, political leader, and sometimes even a war leader.

The Hui have developed their own rituals, ceremonies, and life-cycle ceremonies. Those ceremonies are Ramadan, *Korbanjie*, Mohammed's birthday, a boy's circumcision, weddings, funerals, and so on. For the most part, these social practices are community activities with religious overtones added to the rituals.[40]

---

36. Gladney, "Qingzhen," 14.
37. Bethmann, *Bridge to Islam* 98.
38. Brislen, "Model for a Muslim-Culture Church," 357.
39. Gladney, "Qingzhen," 18.
40. For example, the Hui celebrate a wedding ceremony as a community and religious activity. Hai, "Tradition and Rule of Linxia Baifang," 57.

Funerals are a significant part of Muslim community life. The people believe that one's ethno-religious identity is as crucial in death as in life.[41]

The funeral is a communal and religious ritual. The Hui can build ethnic unity, a sense of belonging, and even religious revival, through these religious and cultural rituals.

Fifth, seeking power-oriented religion shows a cultural signal. The Hui, especially the Sufist, believe that *baraka*, or spiritual power, comes from saints' shrines and tombs, in addition to mosques.[42] Muslims go to shrines and tombs to be empowered. They believe that religious ancestors as well as mosques have powers.

Sixth, endogamy tradition shows important aspects of the Hui cultural system. This endogamy tradition naturally contributes to sociocultural control and the preservation of their ethnic identity and pride.[43]

The above-mentioned six significant cultural symbols have the meaning of self-protection, unity for survival, opposition to the majority, ethnic pride, power for daily survival, and a sense of belonging. Meanings derived from these terms can be abstracted into two categories: power and pride, which together reflect a cultural theme. The Hui community has expressed these themes by developing many signs and forms.

The Hui express their cultural themes through many different ways. First, the Hui are good at portraying two different faces: anger and happiness. As in the case of many Asian groups, the Hui rarely express their antagonism or anger. The Hui are kind to the Han, at least superficially, with ready-made smiles and greetings. However, this does not imply that the Hui are satisfied. The two people groups' biases, conflicts, and ethnic superiority and inferiority complexes still remain.

Second, by maintaining their traditions, the Hui defy Chinese government policy. For example, it is illegal for people less than eighteen years old to get married. I observed many married Hui who were less than eighteen, and a friend of mine had a sixteen-year-old daughter who was married. Many of the Hui seem to be more influenced by their tradition than social policy.

Third, the Hui have adapted and lived in multiple situations. The Hui are Muslim on one hand, but on the other hand, they are Chinese as well. Hui individuals have learned how to adjust themselves to and

41. Gladney reported his observation of Hui funerals, in *Making Majorities*, 142–43; *Ethnic Identity in China*.

42. "Qingzhen," 516.

43. *Ethnic Identity in China*, 249.

even benefit from this multicultural situation. This kind of individuality reflects a manner of assuming and asserting power and pride. In their modern situation, the Hui show this seeking of power and pride in a little bit of a different way. For example, today's young urban Hui parents move out of their communities to seek better schools through the Han system on behalf of their children. Since this social class is attempting to elevate future opportunities through education, they tend to more readily identify with modern Chinese society. However, when returning to the Hui community, these families will settle into the familiar environment and teach their children to do the same.

Finally, the Hui value Chinese pragmatism, which is crucial in gaining power and pride. For instance, for thousands of years, the Hui have understood how to earn Han money, but not be controlled by the government. Therefore, they know how to maintain a cultural distance from the Han—not too close and nor too far.

Through their history, the Hui have sought power and pride for survival and prosperity. Their cultural symbols and social system are well developed for expressing and keeping this ethnic power and pride.

SUMMARY[44]

The Hui is a Muslim people group in China. *Minzu* is a Chinese concept referring to people, and the current *minzu* concept is based upon race. From the earliest days of the Hui, they have been motivated to maintain their independence from, yet coexistence with the Chinese majority group, the Han.

Hui ancestors moved to China from the Arab world via the Silk Road and merchant sea routes. Since the Ming Dynasty, the conflict between the Hui and the Han has increased because of the Hui quest to survive among the majority.

Inside and outside influences split the Hui religions into several groups. *Gedimu* is Sunni community and has the longest history among the Hui sects. The Sufi came to China beginning in the seventeenth century, and this created a great impact upon traditional Hui Islam. Today's major Hui Sufi sects are diversified into many subsects. Their special relationship with the majority through history, the Sunni doctrine, and the Sufi power-oriented traditions are deep factors influencing the Hui worldview. This historical and religious background forms variety

---

44. Kim, "New Entrance Gate," 355.

among the broadly spread religious sects, as well as a general, yet profound Hui ethnic spirit. These phenomena contribute to the formation of the Hui background.

In order to introduce the gospel to the Hui and plant Hui churches, a mission strategy should be receptor-oriented. The receptor-oriented mission strategy necessarily requires an understanding of this Hui worldview, so a background study is necessary. Throughout their history, the Hui have sought power and pride.

In addition to their traditional backgrounds, Hui are facing a new trend: modernization. Though it appeared not long ago, this modernization strongly influences Hui lifestyle. Without an understanding of both the tradition and the new trend, designing a mission strategy will be greatly limited. The next chapter will study the impact of modernization on the Hui.

3

The Impact of Modernization upon the Hui

UNDERSTANDING THE IMPACT OF modernization upon the Hui is important for an understanding of current Hui. Modernization challenges Islamic societies to connect with the global village. It asks Islamic societies to be part of world networks, and challenges every corner of the Islamic traditions from an outsider's view. This section studies how the Hui, as a part of Islamic society, have changed under the influences of modernization, and their consequential reactions.

Modernization impacts the whole world.[1] Since "modernity is breaking up the fabric of all that is structured," people begin to ask questions in the name of reason that they have never asked before.[2] The questions that reason asks can shake up and even break up the roots of religions such as Hinduism, Judaism, Buddhism, Christianity, and Islam. Thus, Richard T Antoun says, "Modernization shifts traditional society into societies that prize consumer-oriented capitalism, competition, specialization, and mobility while repudiating hierarchy."[3]

J. Dudley Woodberry sees that our twenty-first-century world, including Islamic societies, is experiencing a bipolar phenomenon. The two different aspects of this phenomenon are secularization and resurgence in religious affiliation.[4]

---

1. David Lyon explains the power of modernization that challenges traditions, in *Postmodernity*, 27.
2. Hitching, *McDonalds, Minarets and Modernity*, 24.
3. Antoun, *Understanding Fundamentalism*, 3.
4. Woodberry, *Current Trends in Islam*, 37.

Since the late eighteenth century, Western colonialism has changed traditional Muslim societies culturally, economically, and politically. After World War I, despite national independence, foreign influence has originated from mainly Western sources causing a lot of tension with the Islamic tradition. Woodberry classifies those tensions into three categories: traditional tension, (post)modern issues, and globalization with multi-polar conflicts. A detailed explanation of the tensions are as follows:

- Traditional tension: This includes spiritual tension, ideological or theological tension, cultural and sociological tension, and political/historical tensions.
- Modern/postmodern issues: In contrast to the modern values of secularization, liberation, and the future, traditional Islamic values focus on purity, authority, and tradition. Postmodern values "intensify the Muslim backlash, since it processes secularization and suspects any universal authorities."
- Globalization conflicts: These are issues that have led the Islamic world "to pluralism."[5]

Like other traditional societies, modernization introduces Islamic societies to new issues and conflicts because modernization challenges traditional systems and values that are fundamental to religious societies.

THE IMPACT OF MODERNIZATION IN THE ISLAMIC WORLD

As they receive modernization, many traditional societies have been shaken and have restructured their values and social structures. Modernization does not allow the Islamic world to be isolated, but challenges them to be a part of global village. This new challenge naturally brings up many different reactions from Muslim groups. Identifying and categorizing the different reactions to modernization is important for designing mission strategy. A group that is positive toward modernization seems to be a group that will be more open to adopting change early on.

---

5. Ibid., 21–22.

Muslim Reaction Types to Modernization

Scholar Mahmood Monshipouri believes that the "separation between religious and other aspects of people's lives is not distinct."[6] Muslims' lives cannot be separated from the Islamic religion. "Islam is special" because, as Dilip Hiro says, "it is more than a religion. It constitutes a complete social system that embraces all Muslims, all those who have accepted Islam."[7] Therefore, as modernization impacts Muslim society, it not only impacts their religion, but an entire cultural system. Naturally, all kinds of reactions regarding modernization are rising from the Muslim society.

Then, what kinds of reactions do Muslims have toward modernization? Several scholars have categorized the reactions. Woodberry categorizes the reactions in three groups: adaptionists, fundamentalists, and conservatives.

> The adaptionists have continued to adapt their faith with modern ideas and have become liberals or even secular in their orientation. The fundamentalists believe the answer to all problems is a return to the fundamentals of their faith—the Qur'an and the example of their prophet Muhammad and the early Muslim community. And the conservatives in turn believe the answer is a return to Islamic law as developed in its various forms during the first 200 years of Islam. Islamists include both fundamentalists and conservatives [8]

John Obert Voll's views are similar to Woodberry's with regard to these categories, except that he adds one more: "a more personal and individual aspect of Islam," which is an "individualized spirit."[9]

Andrew Rippin's classification identifies three categories that he labels traditionalist, Islamists, and modernist.[10] Charles Kurzman also conceptualizes three categories: customary, revivalist, and liberal Islam.[11]

To summarize these academic categorizations, there are at least three perspectives that each one falls under: opposed, conservative, or receptive with respect to modernization. Using these categories, the next

---

6. Monshipouri, *Islamism, Secularism, and Human Rights*, 21.
7. Hiro, *Holy Wars*, 1.
8. Woodberry, "Islam and Grantmaking."
9. Voll, *Islam*, 23.
10. Rippin, *Muslims*, 181–82.
11. Kurzman, *Liberal Islam*, 5–6.

sections will examine the portion of the Islamic population that is most open to modernization.

Five Processes in Modernization

The changing of a society is a kind of ongoing process with procedures and stages. As Bob Hitching says, "Modernity can be described as both the process of change and the consequence of change that is brought about in society by the influence of what sociologists call carriers."[12]

The phenomena of modernization have influenced Islamic societies' receptivity to change. Hitching introduces five consequences of modernization that a society usually experiences: urbanization, secularization, globalization, religious pluralization, and privatization.[13] Identifying the Hui's changes by these five consequences of modernization provides theoretical frameworks for field data collections and means to examine the situation of young, educated, and urban Hui.

The first consequence is the urbanization that Muslims are facing. A city's role as change agent is stronger whereas an individual's relational ties are looser than in the rural context.[14] By this, urbanites "become socially-alienated by the sheer size of the urban centers. As a result, citizens or migrants lose touch with their roots and their traditions."[15] Often, people migrating to urban areas come from rural towns, where they preserve their traditions and ethnic heritage in enclaves of housing, which could be poor ghettoes. Therefore, as Roger S. Greenway and Timothy M. Monsma describe, "The urban poor constitute the largest unclaimed frontier Christian missions has ever encountered."[16]

The second consequence is secularization. Modernization forces people to move from their traditions and sometimes secularizes them. This force of secularization produces many "nominal believers."[17]

The third consequence is globalization. As Samuel P. Huntington says, the source of conflict shifts from ideology, economic, religious, or ethnic reasons to cultural division.[18] Through globalization, whether it is

12. Hitching, *McDonalds, Minarets and Modernity*, 11.
13. Ibid., 13–22.
14. Conn, "Urbanization and Its Implications," 69–72.
15. Hitching, *McDonalds, Minarets and Modernity*, 14.
16. Greenway and Monsma, *Cities*, 68.
17. Hitching, *McDonalds, Minarets and Modernity*, 17.
18. Huntington, "Clash of Civilizations?," 3–4.

wanted or not, Islamic societies all over the world increase their mutual influences. The influences of media, online culture, global thinking, and economic pressure have forced Muslims to embrace globalization.[19] This creates a new global horizontal generation. Hitching says, "It appears that all over the world, young people, irrespective of nationality or religious background are adopting similarities in dress, language and values which form them into a cultural entity."[20] This new generation enjoys MTV, blue jeans, McDonalds, and a new enormous cultural highway.

The fourth consequence is religious pluralization. Both urbanization and industrialization force people of different faiths and traditions to live and work together in the same places: factories, schools, or other urban junctures.[21] Greenway explains, "Truth claims become both relative and situational in the face of a growing number of alternatives."[22] Therefore, some Muslims become aware that Islam is one of many religions.

The fifth consequence is privatization and anonymity. Modernization gives power to individuals and the middle class. An absolute religion becomes relative and privatized. The traditional beliefs and religions that led whole communities become private matters through this following process.[23] Naturally, urban Muslims live in anonymity. These situations force young urban Muslims to decide many new things that their traditional culture has not considered.

As the Hui have been influenced by the impact of modernization, the Hui who are living in larger cities have been exposed to these five consequences. Those categorizing the Muslims' reaction and the identifying consequences of modernization provide important theoretical foundation to Hui mission strategy. The following section will study the detailed research of this.

THE IMPACT OF MODERNIZATION AND THE HUI

There are similarities and differences between the reactions of the Hui and the rest of the Islamic world, as they each face modernization. The geographical, religious, and ethnic situations have caused the Hui to learn how to coexist with other ethnic groups, and to protect themselves

19. Hitching, *McDonalds, Minarets and Modernity*, 20–21.
20. Ibid., 36.
21. Ibid., 16.
22. Greenway, *Discipling the City*, 76.
23. Ibid., 39.

from Chinese Han acculturation, known as *sinification*, in which there is pressure for minorities to acculturate into the Han culture. Through their history, the Hui have compromised with this sinification, and sometimes sinification has led the Hui to recreate their identity. Today, the Hui are struggling with how to understand modernization, and some see this as another sinification trial. Hui individuals each have different views about modernization.

Sinification (汉化) and Coexistence

In China, though the Hui developed their own ways of living and tradition, like other ethnic minorities, they also have been forced to accept the Han's so-called superior culture.[24] This acculturation is "one of the most common terms applied to the Hui and their relationship with the rest of Chinese."[25]

When the pressure for sinification was too strong, the Hui became rebellious and even began militant riots.[26] For example, when the Hui had conflicts with the Qing Dynasty in 1780 and 1895, the Hui perceived ethnic threats. A number of villages participated in the riots, which expanded into historical massacres of the Hui, and later against China's Red Army in Yunnan province in 1975 during the Cultural Revolution.[27]

The relationship between the two peoples was confrontational, but they have also developed a corporate relationship, as well. Throughout their history, the Hui have learned how they "could benefit from closer ties with China."[28] "There was an interdependence between the two, the Muslims depending on the Chinese market for their basic needs, such as food, and the Chinese depending on Muslim traders and artisans for certain commodities."[29]

Given the communist's evolution theory and Chinese racism, Gillette says this sinocentric and Chinese-centric civilization has influenced the government party's view and position on the Hui. The modern Han government views the Han as a race, which is also an older brother, in a sense, which should guide other less advanced races, or minorities.

24. Lipman, *Familiar Strangers*, xxi.
25. Dillon, *China's Muslim Hui Community*, 4.
26. Winters, *Mao or Muhammad*, 39; Israeli, *Muslims in China*, 29, 122.
27. Lipman, *Familiar Strangers*, 69–72; Wang, *Concord and Conflict*, 11, 15.
28. Lipman, "Border World of Gansu," 283.
29. Israeli, *Muslims in China*, 29, 120.

As they proceed into modernization, this traditional older brother syndrome has influenced the Chinese government in finding ways to civilize and modernize minorities.[30]

Traditional Hui may interpret today's modernization campaign as a new face on sinification.[31] As long as the Chinese government holds such racist evolutionary views, the traditional sinification policy with regards to the Hui will continue under the misnomer "modernization," although the form of the campaign has changed.

Fundamentalism, Arabization, and Chinese Muslims

Sometimes, the impact of modernization creates conflict internally and externally. Traditionally, the Hui had to filter outside influences in order to balance two interests: maintaining tradition and developing community. Historically, the Hui have exercised militant opposition to outside forces, which has included the current modernization movement. The Hui often view sinification as a threat.

As the Hui feel the threat seriously, their ethnic spirit tends to be militant for survival, and religious trends become more fundamental. There are two major factors that provoke the Hui to militancy. First, the perception of a threat, such as the confrontation with the late Qing Dynasty, as well as the Cultural Revolution, which drove the Hui to militancy, on occasion. The second factor is their quest to gain political position and power. Not only in Hui history, but also in other Islamic history, Muslims tend to solve the crisis by initiating militant actions in order to gain power. There are several main factors causing the Hui to take up arms: the nature of Muslims; internal crises of religious corruption and conflicts between sects; outside cultural threats, via signification, to their seeking purity as Muslims; and social, economic, and politic threats to their ethnic survival.

Compared to Middle Eastern Islamic fundamentalism, Hui militants, or fundamentalists, have several similarities and differences. Their similarities include a shared quest for purity and renewal. The main differences are that the Hui principal fight is on a rather ethno-fundamentalism plain.[32]

30. Gillette, *Between Mecca and Beijing*, 8–14.
31. Ibid., 53.
32. Tibi, *Challenge of Fundamentalism*, 22–23.

The Hui involvement in fundamentalism is prompted by three factors: the Han government's racism and nationwide pressure for modernization directed at the Hui, and the Hui connection to an Islamic heartland—the Middle East and Central Asia. The reconstruction and scattering of the traditional community, as well as individualism, urbanization, consumerism, and the media revolution, create the feeling of crisis among Hui conservatives.

Arabization is another trend influencing the Hui under the pressure of modernization. The dilemma here is that they do not want to be limited to traditional exclusivists, but neither do they want to submit to Western modernism without any critique. To this end, some Hui create the third way between the two ways.[33]

This Arabization brings the Hui mental and emotional satisfaction because the Arabized modern goods allow them to believe that they have retained their religious atmosphere while not falling behind the Han in modernization.

MODERNIZATION'S IMPACT UPON HUI INTERETHNIC DYNAMICS

Foreseeing the Hui ethnic identities as continuing or changing is a very important topic for mission strategy. For an understanding of this process, it is helpful to compare several sociologists' analyses and their views to the ethnic changing.

First, in his book *Pluralism and Islamic Perspectives on Cultural Diversity*, Voll says that three factors in the twentieth century dissolve inter-group boundaries: openness to differences, encouraging diversities, and the development of media. With this, the world slowly learns how to tolerate cultural diversity and build trust among groups. The world creates an "undiversified mass society" through mass media and rapid mass production processes.[34] As individuals find commonness within proximity groups of other cultural zones, they can freely share ideas and have the sense of belonging there. Voll believes that the spreading of openness and diversity will dissolve traditional social borders and create new

---

33. Gillette explains this Arabization process in a Hui village in Xian city, in *Between Mecca and Beijing*, 233.

34. Voll, "Pluralism and Islamic Perspectives," 121–22.

subculture groups. Through these modern trends, different groups try to find common ground and cultivate coexistence.[35]

Second, Raphael introduces what Louis Wirth classified as four ultimate objectives of the minority group among the majority group: pluralistic, assimilation, secessionist, and militant.[36]

Since the two people groups—the Hui and the Han—have independently developed their own networks, they can independently coexist without active interethnic interaction. Israeli calls this type of Hui ethnic boundary "voluntary membership," which means members can easily shift to counter-members if they want to.[37] The Hui always worry about this, because there always is the possibility of assimilation. Considering Wirth's four minority goals, Israeli conceptualized where this voluntary membership moves. The voluntary membership creates superiority, and it promotes confrontation with counter-majority groups. As the confrontation goes further, it is developed into a rebellion, and finally, the minority secedes from the majority.

A continual sense of crisis produces ethnic superiority and causes confrontation, rebellion, and then finally arrives at secession. However, the twenty-first century's modernization usually does not allow secession to any subculture group. Unfortunately, Israeli's view does not seem to consider much of the current modernization impact upon China, because most of the data were collected before the time of modernization. However, his view is still valuable because political and cultural situations can always change, and the Hui ethnic community can choose any of those four choices.

Third, in his book *China and Its National Minorities: Autonomy or Assimilation?* German anthropologist and political scientist Thomas Heberer says Chinese minority assimilation into Han society is unavoidable. He gives the massive number of Han's inland immigration to the former minority territory, and its support from government policy, as an example of this.[38] According to Heberer, since the Han's size is incomparably larger than any one minority's, the assimilation policy will result in sinification.

---

35. Ibid., 121.
36. Wirth, "Problem of Minority Groups," 354–63.
37. Israeli, *Muslims in China*, 29, 120.
38. Herberer, *China and Its National Minorities*, 130.

Fourth, Barbara Kinne Kroll Pillsbury, who researches ethnic changes and persistence among Taiwanese Hui, said that within the interethnic boundary, there are both integrative forces that draw the community together and disintegrative forces that dissolve community identity. Both of these forces have external and internal factors. Three emergence factors contribute to the integrative forces: (1) the etymologic origin of the "Hui," (2) clear distinctions of occupation between the two peoples, (3) many other social reasons. By quoting Charles Wagley and Harris Marvin's idea, Pillsbury says that the four boundary disintegration factors are: new governmental mitigated policy, increased commonness, common goals, the minority's changes.[39] In Taiwan's history, all of the people groups have unified against Japanese invasion, and it created a huge common spirit between the Hui and the Han.[40]

Pillsbury's theory foresees that the Hui will choose pluralistic or assimilation among Wirth's four minority-chosen goals. The mitigated political and social pressure enables the Hui community to untie the bond between ethnicity and religion. Thus, without being under community pressure, Taiwanese Hui individuals can see Islam as just one of many religions, not as an inherited and predestined ethno-religion.

Of course there are several different factors on the mainland, as well. However, during the last two decades, the political and social atmosphere on the mainland of China has changed, and is one step closer to Taiwan's social mitigation. According to Pillsbury, these changes may contribute to disintegration factors.

Fifth, in his books *China's Minority Cultures* and *China's Ethnic Minorities and Globalisation*, Colin Mackerras summarizes dynamics of both integration (change) and identity (continuity).[41]

According to Mackerras, there is a higher tendency for integration under the current policies for several reasons: current Chinese policies are quite soft and less authoritative toward minorities; the minorities are satisfied with the current situation; the impact of modernization contributes to ethnic integration; and a growing Chinese infrastructure encourages minorities to participate in governmental integration efforts.[42]

---

39. Pillsbury, "Cohesion and Cleavage," 227–34.

40. Ibid., 234–36.

41. Mackerras, *China's Minority Cultures*, 214–15; Mackerras, *China's Ethnic Minorities*.

42. Mackerras, *China's Minority Cultures*, 217–19.

Though there are both integration and identity factors, according to Mackerras, integration will be the overall trend for several reasons: the current Chinese government is quite stable, minorities do not want to break free and establish an independent state, the minorities maintain their own recognizable cultures in modernized China.[43] Mackerras sees that the Hui may become more easily assimilated than the Uyghur, Tibetans, and Koreans, for these ethnic groups have former ethnic symbols: territories, language, and characters.

To summarize these scholars' views, as Pillsbury and most of other scholars admit, the Hui interethnic border has both changing and continuing forces. Charles Wagley and Marvin Harris's suggestion of "pluralism and assimilation" gives insights to foresee the Hui future.[44] Wagley and Harris say that the modern situation usually does not allow minorities to secede or become militant, but rather to be pluralistic or assimilated situation.

Therefore, the conclusion of this discussion is that if the Chinese government maintains the current mitigated policy regarding their minorities, continually prospers in economic development, and spreads the impact of modernization, the Hui will continue stepping toward pluralism and assimilation. Since the Hui people consist of many subculture groups, each of the groups will have different rates of change.

SUMMARY

Modernization changes traditional Islamic societies, along with the lives and values of individuals. Muslims have at least three responses to the modernization movement: opposed, conservative, or receptive.

The receptive group has at least five consequences of modernization: urbanization, secularization, globalization, pluralization, and privatization. The Chinese government has asked the Hui to be sinified, and modernization can be seen as a part of the sinification process in the Hui people's eyes. When the Chinese government forces Hui sinification, the Hui usually began to unite in order to strengthen their Islamic and ethnic identity. These days, the Hui seek a third way of modernization: Arabization.

The impact of modernization will empower both the assimilation and continuation of force exerted at ethnic borders. In spite of these two

43. Ibid., 221.
44. Wagley and Harris, *Minorities in the New World*, 287.

forces, if the impact of modernization continues, if the international atmosphere does not seriously stimulate the ethnic and Islamic separatism, and if the Chinese society and economy continually grows, the general trends will move toward assimilation.

Second, these changes and continuity dynamics will become more complicated in the future because both individuals and subgroups will individually decide how to react to modernization.

Third, the YEU-Hui will discern the difference between the modernization and traditional sinification. In contrast to the Chinese government's militant and authoritative use of assimilation, modernization is more indirect, materialistic, international, and individualistic. As a result, the YEU-Hui may regard modernization as Westernization instead of sinification.

The modern Hui are facing changes, and this is a very important point as strategists set mission strategy. The traditional communication theories believe that the receptors do not change, but the speaker needs to be receptor-oriented.

However, modernization requires many Muslims to move away from tradition and toward international common ground. Since the Hui are changing, traditional missionary images of the Hui, who are ethnically biased, religiously fundamentalist, poor in education, and resistant to modernization, may lead inappropriate mission strategies. Therefore, addressing their degree of change enables Christians to engage in receptor-oriented communication.

In spite of this, since the Hui have a long history and many different subculture groups, it is not realistic to expect that all the groups will have the same amount of change. Therefore, strategists need to think about two things. First, each subculture group will have a different reaction to modernization. Second, because of their deep-rooted cultural background, though some of them are changed, they may be still strongly influenced by their traditions. Addressing changed, unchanged, and changing is crucial for setting a strategy.

For this, researching the sociological identity of the Hui lays a profound theoretical basis for mission strategy. In many cases, expatriates meet locals in urban situations. At the same time, most of modernization's influence starts in urban areas. The study of the sociological identity of urbanites is necessary for setting up mission strategy to the Hui. The next chapter will study the urban Hui, and how information flows to the Hui in urban situations.

4

The Sociological Identity of the Urban Hui

NO MATTER WHAT PEOPLE group they come from, people in urban areas have quite different sociological dynamics and identities than those in rural areas. Especially as they are influenced by the impact of modernization, the two groups may change in different ways, so rural and urban areas each have a different density of modernization's impact. Identifying the urban Hui is a part of my research goal. Urbanized Hui social networks and culture may differ from those of the traditional Hui in rural areas. Since China is rapidly urbanized, understanding urbanization is crucial to setting up a mission strategy to reach the Hui.

THEORETICAL FOUNDATION OF URBANIZATION

There are three major urban theories that help us understand urbanism. Those theories are determinist theory, composition theory, and subculture theory. Each of them provides a different perspective about urbanism.

First, determinist theory began with Robert Ezra Park's paper "The City: Suggestions for Investigation of Human Behavior in the Urban Environment."[1] Louis Wirth's "Urbanism as a Way of Life" is another pioneering article in determinist theory.[2] Determinists say that urbanism produces social disorganization and personality disorders—being alone or suffering physical deterioration.[3]

---

1. Park et al., *The City*.
2. Wirth, "Urbanism as a Way of Life."
3. Ibid., 1.

Those determinist theorists describe that urbanization brings anomy phenomena, depersonalization, and isolation. Bryan R. Roberts reports examples of disorganization, disorders, and anonymity in a city of Guatemala. He said one of the most important social changes is "that which occurs when the basis for group organization shifts from stable face-to-face relationships to interdependence relationships where people fulfill specialized and related tasks."[4] Determinists believe that weakened social cohesion and the loneliness of people create high psychic stress. This determinist theory provides a helpful tool in understanding the anomy and disorganization phenomena among the urban Hui.

Second, the term "compositional theory" was established by Claude S. Fischer in his book *The Urban Experience*. This theory denies the effects of urbanism. It says the attributes of city and rural systems define and form the characteristics of their lives, but the systems themselves do not cause particular ways of life or personalities.[5] In his article "Urbanization without Breakdown: A Case Study," Oscar Lewis introduces a case study in Mexico in which some migrants' original lifestyles did not break down as they lived in the city. He said that "there is little evidence of disorganization and breakdown, of culture conflict, or of irreconcilable differences between generations."[6]

Compositionalists describe the city as a "mosaic of social worlds" because they think that each part of the city maintains their own homogeneousness.[7] Nathan Glazer and Daniel P. Moynihan in "Beyond the Melting Pot" support this idea. As an example of the limitation of urban assimilation, they introduce the continuity of immigrants' lifestyles as they settle in America.[8]

A pioneer of this compositional theory, Herbert J. Gans critiqued determinist theory by pointing out the phenomenon that most immigrant Americans go back to their original pattern of life as soon as they can. He says those phenomena that Wirth observed occurred only "during a time of immigration acculturation . . . and an era of minimal choice."[9] Herbert Kotter, who tried to prove the rural-urban continuum,

---

4. Roberts, *Organizing Strangers*, 11.
5. Fischer, *Urban Experience*, 32.
6. Lewis, "Urbanization without Breakdown," 40–41.
7. Fischer, *Urban Experience*, 33.
8. Glazer and Moynihan, *Beyond the Melting Pot*, 40–41.
9. Gans, "Urbanism and Suburbanism," 644–45.

says that "many city-country contacts have a continuing, periodic, rhythmic character e.g., people may not move from the original milieu but they have intensive communication through different channels."[10] Richard Dewey also points out the problem of sociologists' failure concerning the rural-urban continuum.[11]

Third, Fischer, who introduced subculture theory, combines the urban characteristics that determinists and compositionalists introduced. Fischer sees that cities consist of many subcultures. In his book *To Dwell among Friends*, Fischer defines urban life as building up plural community and a diversity of cultural groups.[12]

Fischer said that, though urbanism presents many influences to subcultures, the subcultures neither disorganize because of urbanism nor ignore its influences, but instead react to it. Urban effects are changing, reinforcing and weakening the subculture and creating new groups. Subculture theory said that urbanism produces a "mosaic of little worlds which touch but do not interpenetrate," and subcultures have inter-subculture relationships. Fischer described urbanism as synthesized mosaic of subcultures and developed subculture theory as following.[13]

Each of those three theories has different views on urban interethnic dynamics. Determinists said that ethnic groups would "ultimately be destroyed by the force of rationalization."[14] They foresaw that ethnic groups would first shrink into personal and local activities, and then they would be completely diminished. The compositionalists foresaw that each ethnic group would be strengthened and unified by creating their own jobs and lifestyles. Ethnic conflict would stimulate ethnic unification.

Subculturalists said that persistence and change factors would weaken and strengthen the ethnic boundaries.[15] First, Fisher introduced three persistence factors: (1) emphasizing social ties (friends and kin, marriage, clubs, and associations), (2) maintaining the old identity (old animosities against other groups and voting for their own ethnic candidates), and (3) maintaining ethnic customs and values.[16] Second, urban

10. Kotter, "Changes in Urban-Rural Relationship," 22.
11. Dewey, "Rural-Urban Continuum," 82.
12. Fischer, *To Dwell among Friends* 194.
13. Fischer described urbanism as a synthesized mosaic of subcultures and developed subculture theory, in *Urban Experience*, 39.
14. Ibid., 145.
15. Ibid.
16. Ibid., 146–52.

ethnic change factors create: disruption and family separation through migration, changes in language and occupation, and increased chances for interethnic activity opportunities. These cross-ethnic contacts create the adoption of selected lifestyles, beliefs, or objects from the other group. Ethnic culture and customs are also developed, changed, and altered by the insider subgroup.[17]

CHINA'S URBANISM AND THE HUI

After the Open Door Policy from the 1970s, China has become dramatically urbanized. Minzhi Zho spoke about Chinese urbanization in the following way:

> China is rapidly advancing towards its goal of being a modernized country, and industrialization is undoubtedly the driving force behind this move. . . . All the excitement and conflict in China today demonstrate that the country has begun the process of urbanization and social modernization.[18]

Of course, China's urban population has also been growing.[19] The Library of Congress website reported the dramatic increase of China's urban population since 1982.

> According to the 1953 and 1982 censuses, the urban population as a percentage of total population increased from 13.3 to 20.6 percent during that period. From 1982 to 1986, however, the urban population increased dramatically to 37 percent of the total population.[20]

According to analysis by the Library of Congress, the reasons for the dramatic increase in population are "the migration of large numbers of surplus agricultural workers," and "broaden[ing] the criteria for classifying an area as a city or town."[21]

Urbanism and Urban Anthropology

A city's infrastructure, buildings, or transportation is not very important when we study the urban Hui, but rather mission strategists need to know

---

17. Ibid., 152–55.
18. Zho, *Urbanization*, 10.
19. World Bank, "Urban Population," China section.
20. *Wikipedia*, s.v. "Urbanization in China."
21. Ibid.

about Hui individuals, their society, and their relationships. Therefore defining urbanism and having an urban anthropological view is necessary when mission strategists set up urban strategy.

Urbanism is a perspective into urbanites' lives, patterns, relationships, networks, and behavioral dynamics. Therefore, urbanism concerns the lives of citizens.[22]

Urban anthropology is an important tool for studying the Hui, because it is concerned about small social groups in contrast to traditional urban study, which is concerned with macro, industrial, impersonal sample surveys. Urban anthropology is more concerned with small scales of urban life, relationships, and behaviors.[23] Since urban anthropology integrates the lives of urbanites, it becomes an interdisciplinary study with sociology, anthropology, psychology, etc. John Gulick characterized that urban anthropology is more concern to humanity of city, so he says that urban anthropology is integrated "with small scale immediacies of everyday life with massive, large-scale realities that impinge on city dwellers' daily lives."[24] It is crucial to understand the lives of Hui individuals and their relationships with other individuals and societies.

Magnitudes and Unit of Integration

Magnitude and critical mass concepts tell us that the various cities' sizes give different influence to different groups. Scholars give different magnitude levels by the city's size. Urban anthropologists found that the different magnitudes give different influences to urbanites. The bigger cities have higher possibilities of gathering homogeneous subculture groups. As their numbers grow, the subcultures in the bigger cities easily outnumber their critical mass. Once this happens, the subcultures create and import cultural symbols, ceremonies, rituals, religions, institutions, and governing systems, which provide them with pride, power, and tradition.

These critical mass and magnitude concepts offer ideas for strategists when they set up mission strategies to reach the urban Hui. This enables us to figure out the most strategic degree of magnitude of cities for starting a mission to the Hui in China's urban areas, and helps us determine which cities are most effective for meeting strategic social groups. For example, Beijing and Shanghai are both big cities and their

22. Anderson, "Aspects of Urbanism and Urbanization," 2.
23. Gulick, *Humanity of Cities*, 1–21.
24. Ibid., xv.

magnitude is a high degree. All kinds of Chinese ethnic groups live in these cities, but the number of Hui is not guaranteed to outnumber its critical mass because there is a low density of Hui. Xian or Lanzhou cities are not as big as Beijing or Shanghai, but it has higher Hui density because they are close to high Hui-populated rural areas, and it has a traditional Hui ghetto. Furthermore, Xian and Lanzhou are quite modernized cities, which lead to openness and new trends among the Hui. Last, though their Hui densities are huge, Pinglang and Xining are smaller cities and have a relative lack of modern influences. Though they have plenty numbers of the Hui, there is a relatively low possibility that cities will outnumber the critical mass that is consistent with strategic social class.

Urban integration junctions provide connection and common ground between ethnic groups and subcultures. Urban junctions are strategic places for reaching the Hui, for it provides contact points with others. The Hui people have lived in ethnic ghettoes; therefore, very limited numbers of people have made contacts outside of their groups. In addition, the Hui taboo for eating pork prevents them from building deep relationships with the Han people who enjoy pork. However, the impact of modernization has forced the Hui to come out to urban junctures for social activities. Edwin Eames and Judith Granich Goode categorized these units of integration into: public places, temporal events, structural formation, networks as linking mechanism, and the city as a whole and rural-urban linkage.[25] Among them, the following three selected areas are quite relevant to the Hui situation.

The first unit, public places, consists of: eating and drinking establishments; leisure time places, like parks; marketplaces; service institutions like schools, hospitals, and government agencies; and transportation. These areas are very common to both the Hui and the Han Chinese, but, as determinists say, the relationship dynamics are very impersonal and functional. However, in the case of hospitals or schools, people can better develop trustworthiness. Therefore, some places remain very strategic places for interethnic reconciliation or mission strategy.

The second unit is temporal events like sports or festivals like Halloween. Hui traditional ceremonies are quite religious; therefore, they cannot be interethnic junctures. Furthermore, the Hui will regard a Han ceremony as *tamun de jieri* (他们的节日), or "their ceremony" and have no interest in them. However, I have observed some young Hui beginning

---

25. Eames and Goode, *Anthropology of the City*, 215–54.

to celebrate Han rituals. These cross-ethnic celebrations sometimes create generational conflicts. I observed a young Hui couple urgently hide a Chinese New Year red lamp when their Muslim parents visited their house from rural China.

Sports can be a more effective urban juncture. In my observation, different ethnic groups watch the same TV sports, creating a common spirit. They become one when a Chinese team runs against other nations; many of the Hui cheer for the Chinese team. It seems that the Hui believe that they are true members of the Chinese nation.

The third and final unit is virtual/modern space. Though Eames did not mention this, these areas have become tremendously important in urban juncture. These places are video shops, Internet cafés, shopping centers, etc. People receive and share much modern and high tech information from these places. Ethnic differences are not an important matter while sharing the information. Western food courts and foreign restaurants are also new urban junctions because, using traditional Hui concepts, these new food places cannot be categorized as either Muslim or Han. Western and imported soap operas or movies are new mental spaces and offer new junctions. For example, in most cases, Hong Kong superstars and Korean movie stars are very familiar and popular, so they provide easy conversation topics when my family visits Hui youngsters and wives.

The Ghetto Dynamics and the Hui

The ghetto is one subculture. Since the Hui usually live in the urban ghetto, understanding the ghetto will help us to better know the nature of urban Hui. The Hui ghettoes, just like other ghettoes, are challenged by changes brought on by modernization.

The ghetto has generally applied to the Jewish quarter of the cities. The origin of this term is unclear. The traditional image of ghetto was the poorest and most backward group of the Jewish. Nowadays, the image is of immigrant towns in America where foreign immigrants tentatively stay.[26] Today, the main reason for maintaining the ghetto is poverty.[27] The shantytown is generally formed by migrants, and the migrants try to enter into mainstream society, as they are ready. The newly formed Hui

---

26. Wirth, *The Ghetto*, 4.
27. Parker, *Urban Theory and the Urban Experience*, 90.

ghettoes are similar to shantytowns. Many migrants from countryside stay there to get ready to move into mainstream society.

In contrast to shantytown communities, the traditional Hui community is closer to a ghetto. The Hui communities have stably maintained their memberships for several hundreds of years because they believe the ghetto to be a domestic safe zone. Gulick also proves that there is stability in the ghetto.[28] While modernization acts as a centrifugal force to drag Hui members out of the ghetto, at the same time, the ghetto's stability works as a centripetal force to hold members in the ghetto.

As the Hui are influenced by urbanization and modernization, some young and educated people try to move out from their traditional ghetto and get into mainstream society. To this group, the ghetto slowly takes on the characteristics of a shantytown, but slow movers are still in the ghetto.

Several scholars have analyzed subgroups inside the ghettoes. Understanding the characteristics of the subgroups will give insights for identifying the Hui ghetto. Three different scholars and their associates have researched the ghetto community members in different contexts. Ulf Hannerz researched Winston Street's poor black community in Washington; Joan W. Moore researched a Mexican-American ghetto in Los Angeles; and Shirley Achor researched Mexican Americans in a Dallas barrio.[29] They all categorized their ghetto members into four different sects. Though three of the scholars used different terminology, most of the four sects are identified using similar concepts. Hannerz categorized the black community as street corner men, street family, swingers, and mainstreamers.[30] Moore categorized the Mexican-Americans as new immigrants, native, barrio-oriented deviant, and those who have entered the dominant Anglo system.[31] Finally, Achor's categories are insulation, accommodation, mobilization, and alienation.[32] The later groups in each of categorization were more assimilated with majority and mainstream people, and the earlier groups were more familiar with ghetto or local culture.

---

28. Gulick, *Humanity of Cities*, 152–56.
29. Hannerz, *Soulside*; Moore et al., *Homeboys*; Achor, *Mexican Americans*.
30. Hannerz, *Soulside*, 38–57.
31. Moore et al., *Homeboys*, 157–60.
32. Achor, *Mexican Americans*, 116–28.

Achor's categorization is quite close to the Hui situation because it is urban and deals with a minority people under the influence of the majority people driven by modernization. She gives the details of her categorization. An isolationist group is isolated from the external culture, is biased against those outside of their own culture, receives poor social benefits, and has mainly internal resources and culture.[33] Examples of this group among the Hui are those who are uneducated or from older generations.

An accommodation group consists of people who eagerly try to enter into the mainstream, but have not yet achieved it.[34] Both young Hui couples who have children and Hui college students are good examples of this accommodation group. They want to earn a higher public education for themselves and their children than would be possible by studying in the Hui ethnic education system.

A mobilization group involves people who move between two groups in order to mobilize the minority community.[35] Good examples of this type of group are either the Hui who seek Arabization and have an Islamic fundamentalist tendency, or a few Hui politicians in government systems.

Finally, alienation categorizes a group of people who never get into the dominant culture or the minority community. Actually, many young educated Hui are very Han-icized, which means their worldview and lifestyles are similar to the Han. They do not want to mingle with traditional society, but cannot truly mix with the Han society. I met Hui college graduates who work in a bakery. They said that they do not want to go back to the Hui ghetto and most of the customers are Han. At the same time they do want to retain their Hui identity on their identification cards because it gives them many social benefits, and they can have a government license for running their Muslim bakery.

THE HUI SOCIAL NETWORK

Like other societies, the Hui society has a variety of social networks. Social network theory helps us understand the urbanites' interpersonal relationship dynamics. Social networking is a conceptual metaphor that figures out and tracks a person's relationships. William G. Flanagan

33. Ibid., 116–21.
34. Ibid., 121–26.
35. Ibid., 128.

defines a social network as "a set of social relationships that encompass the individual's various group memberships (e.g., family, peers, work, and formal group memberships)."[36]

A scale is a unit of an actor's, or individual's interpersonal relationships. An actors' scale expands as his or her relationships increase. Scholars generally agree that small-scale refers to close and natural relationships, like kin, family, coworkers, neighbors, and friends. Actors in the small-scale group usually have face-to-face contact and share large amounts of emotion, time, and energy. However, large-scale relationships are said to be more impersonal, business-centered, and distant relationship.

Scholars categorize social networks into primary and secondary networks by their densities of relationship. The following section will deal with these.

The Primary Social Units

Primary social units are generally predestined and unconditional relationships. Fischer defines primary groups as "social networks that typically do involve individuals intimately, with which they are fully identified, and that are ends in themselves—ethnic groups, friends, and kin."[37] Eames limits the primary unit into direct bloodline—for example, family, kin, and domestic units. Additionally some friends seem to be a primary unit because some Asians have stronger relationship to friendship than relationship to family.[38]

KINSHIP

Hugh D. R. Baker researched the impact of modernization on Chinese kinship dynamics. The Civil Code of the Republic of China was promulgated in 1931, and it made a huge impact upon and many changes to the Chinese traditional family system, which had been maintained since the last empire of China, Qing Dynasty. The Civil Code was strongly against the male-centered and big-family-oriented system.[39]

After several decades of the code, a new communist leader, Chairman Mao, took leadership. Chairman Mao continually led social

---

36. Flanagan, *Contemporary Urban Sociology*, 21.
37. Fischer, *Urban Experience*, 114.
38. Kim, "'Us' or 'Me'?," 91.
39. Baker, *Chinese Family and Kinship*, 179–80.

transformation that included furthering the family system. Baker said that there are two noticeable family issues that come from the impact of this new transformation: marriage law and abolition of the "family head system."[40]

During the Cultural Revolution, the government's demand for the abolition of the family head system leveled a serious attack on the family system. People were encouraged to publicly criticize their own family members and to report their family members to the government if they did not seem to follow the communist party's campaign. Since Chinese families once held their foundations on the filial piety tradition, this new push for political criticism against their family members was disastrous. This policy drastically weakened family and primary networks.

Later, in post-Chairman Mao China, the government began a new campaign in the early 1980s in which families were forced to have no more than one child. This one-child family system caused a lot of changes to kin dynamics and family networks.[41]

In the post-Chairman Mao era, Chinese minority families have continually experienced great changes. Jun Wen summarizes five big problems faced by Chinese minorities in a Chinese academic journal, *Ethno-National Studies*, along with analysis of the third and forth Chinese national population census in 1990 and 2000. These five problems are:

- Population growth gaps are increasing among minorities.
- A decreasing birth rate is causing an aging society.
- The education gap between average Chinese and minorities and their women is getting worse.
- The employment rate is low.
- High mobility enables western minorities to move to the eastern area. As a result, eastern well-developed urbanites are challenged by ethnic-religious issues.[42]

These challenges help to show that there are many changes in the kinship dynamics among the urban Hui.

---

40. Ibid., 183.
41. So and Walker, *Explaining Guanxi*, 140.
42. Wen, "*Ershishijijiushiniandaizhongguominzurenkoudebiandong Jianping*" (translation mine).

Martin King Whyte compares Chinese family systems before, between, and after 1949. He summarized three different trends among contemporary Chinese families: the tendency to form nuclear families, the decline in fertility, and the decreasing power of the aged.[43] This modernization trend naturally leads to changes in family size, extended family network density, and power holders in the family.

The traditional Chinese family had clear divisions between the work boundaries of men and women.[44] However, this traditional work concept had changed tremendously after the communist government's policy in 1950 and the post-Chairman Mao policy of 1978.[45] This female liberation policy enables Chinese women to have mobility, resources, and opportunity similar to that of the men.

William Jankowiak did his field research about family life in a communist society in Huhhot, a northern Inner Mongolia Chinese city. In his conclusion, he said the socialist transformation led to the reevaluation of kinship obligations, conjugal expectations, and parental duties.[46]

Whyte and his coworkers' observation said that filial obligation is still a strong value in the family, even after the Cultural Revolution. However, there are two forces that threaten the current social system that supports filial obligation traditions. The first one is that reforming the current markets will weaken all kinds of bureaucratic social benefits that the urban elderly are currently enjoying. Second, commercialization and the growing influence of global markets to China may weaken family ties. The Chinese family is facing challenges again from individualism and the global economic society.[47]

The Hui also have strong family units and filial piety traditions. In order to research this, my field research survey asked, "If you need advice from someone while making an important decision . . . with whom do you counsel?" (appendix A). This was to know whom they respect and who influences them the most. The answer was clear: 57 percent answered that their parents influenced them most. The next question asked whom the respondent would least likely inform of a shameful experience. The question was "If you did any shameful act (fail exam or business, religious

---

43. Whyte and Parish, *Urban Life in Contemporary China*, 191.
44. Mann, "Re-Drawing Boundaries," 15–28.
45. Entwisle, *Re-Drawing Boundaries*, 298–99.
46. Jankowiak, "Urban Chinese," 351.
47. Whyte, *China's Revolutions*, 85–111.

or ethical problem), which group would you be most afraid would find out? This question was also designed to learn who the real community leader is. Again, the answer was clear: 77 percent of respondents gave their parents as the answer. This data shows that the status of parents and filial piety are still strong in the Hui society.[48]

FRIENDS

In contrast to other elements in the primary unit, people form friendships by their own choices. Some people in Asian culture place a higher priority on friendship than on family. Friendship naturally builds peer pressure, and people feel shame and honor based on peer values. Asians often feel shame when one chooses personal and family priority over the bigger issues.

Regarding Hui friendship types, the questionnaire asked, "Among your 10 closest friends, how many of them are Muslims?" (appendix A). Amazingly, more than 70 percent of their friends are from different ethnic groups. This means that today's young urban Hui do not strictly limit their friendships within ethnic boundaries. This is because many Chinese meet closest friends during their school years and most schools are multiethnic, so the school system provides a great chance for building interethnic friendships. These friendships are a wonderful juncture to communicate the gospel to the Hui.[49]

Secondary Social Units

Compared to the primary unit, the secondary units are more extended relationships that go beyond kin and natural relationships.[50] As city size increases, the chances of community being bound together by personal ties are dropping rapidly.[51] For filling up this relational vacancy, urbanites seek and join social clubs or formal associations.[52]

---

48. Kim, "'Us' or 'Me'?," 92
49. Ibid.
50. Ibid., 91.
51. Fischer, *Urban Experience*, 115.
52. Ibid., 120.

Three Major Urban Components and Modernization Impact

Eames and Goode summarize three major components of the urban secondary social units: common residential territory (neighborhoods), common culture of origin (ethnic groups), and common roles in the division of labor (occupational status communities).[53]

First, neighborhoods form an urban secondary unit. Traditionally, people have regarded a neighborhood as a group of people who live close together; however, as urbanites have developed mobility and expanded activity zones, they begin to have neighbors and friends in different parts of the city. Though the network densities of residential neighbors have decreased, urbanites have more trans-local neighbors.

Second, ethnic groups form an urban secondary unit. Urban ethnic group members have the same origin. Eames summarizes several factors that hold urban ethnic group boundaries: ethnic structures and economic niches, political activity, cultural symbol (food traditions, institutions, language), religion, and institutional mechanism.[54]

Third, occupation forms an urban secondary unit. Sometimes, entire clans have the same type of occupation, for they introduce the job internally. Some ethnic groups dominate a niche. There are competitions and conflicts between ethnic groups to keep their superiority in the niche. For example, I observed this in the Hui food markets (mutton, beef, small bread, beef noodle restaurant, etc.). They also have a strong niche in truck labor in the city of Lanzhou, and several other niches in Xian, such as taxi driver, selling cloths, and beauty salons.

If those three components overlap on one individual, the leader of the components and the community would have a tremendous power over the person. Individuals would have very limited freedom within the activity zone.[55]

Those three components are generally overlapped in the Hui community. The Hui are born in the Hui community and raised within the extended family. As they grow into teenagers, they usually work in small work places that are run by other Muslims. Usually the owners are uncles, brothers, or fathers. Consequently, many of the Hui have overlapped those three components.

---

53. Eames and Goode, *Anthropology of the City*, 160; Kim, "'Us' or 'Me'?," 93.
54. Eames and Goode, *Anthropology of the City*, 186–96.
55. Ibid., 214.

However, instead of overlapping, the impact of modernization spreads those components. Mobility, information, new needs and abilities, higher education, and the media all encourage Hui individuals to build new networks and meaningful relationships even in the non-Muslim societies. Eames describes these phenomena: "In the urban industrial city or the city in developing nations, the three units show less overlap, and therefore barely share common boundaries."[56]

The Secondary Network in China and the Hui

Modernization and government policy have tremendously changed Chinese urbanites' secondary networks. Chairman Mao and his government forcefully led the Chinese to change their friendship into ideological comradeship.[57] The government asked people to contribute to the comradeship, which was a special second social network designed by the communist party. The general social atmosphere asked people to regard the primary network as negative and inferior in order to accomplish communist ideology. These government-driven and Chinese types of networks had two characteristics. First, neighbors and workers were in the same network and membership. Second, these government-led networks were quite dominant and gave little freedom of choice to individuals.[58]

Today, the Chinese—especially the Hui—are fast recovering their normal secondary relationships. Modernization gives more freedom of choice to young Muslims in their individual lives. A good example is in Gillette's book *Between Mecca and Beijing*. A new Hui bride decided to wear a Taiwan-made Western wedding dress in spite of Islamic leaders that criticized her choice because the dress style was not conservative and Islamic. The bride boldly chose what she wanted and her friends and other women in her primary networks indirectly supported her, but not openly.[59] Real Hui authorities that influence young Hui are changing from traditional ethno-religious community to their commercial and extended social networks.[60]

---

56. Ibid.; Kim, "'Us' or 'Me'?," 93.
57. Whyte and Parish, *Urban Life in Contemporary China*, 353–54.
58. Ibid., 354.
59. Gillette, *Between Mecca and Beijing*, 219.
60. Kim, "'Us' or 'Me'?," 92.

THE HUI NEW NETWORK MODELS

As the urban Hui experience modernization, their social networks also change. Their traditional primary and secondary networks have been influenced by filial piety traditions and a family-centered and community-centered mentality. Their primary networks seem not to have changed much, but the urban Hui are facing a big revolution in their secondary networks.[61]

The subculture theory better explains the concepts of Hui urbanism, social networks, and modernization impact. This section introduces the conceptualized identity of the urban Hui from an anthropological and sociological perspective. Then, it develops a synthesized subculture theory for the urban Hui.

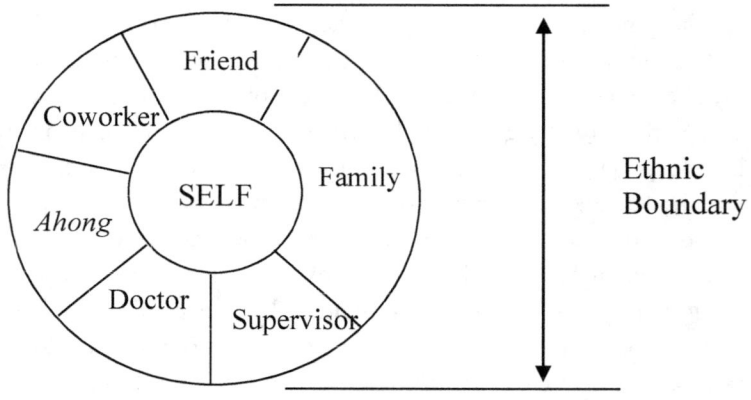

Conceptual Model of Traditional Secondary Networks

Traditional and Expanded Social Network of the Hui

Most of the Hui individual traditional network is limited to the inside of the ethnic network or community. The Hui have spent time within other Hui secondary networks, and few of them connect with outside networks. For example there are shoemakers inside and outside the Hui community, but Hui individuals usually go to their own shoemakers.

Figure 1 and figure 2 show a comparison between individual Hui traditional networks and networks expanded by the impact of urban

61. Ibid., 91.

modernization. Within the traditional model, the secondary networks of the individual are connected only within his or her ethnic boundary. The second diagram shows a new secondary network that expands beyond the ethnic boundary. Their connections and reachable zones are beyond the limitation of the community. The impact of modernization has allowed the Hui to expand their abilities, mobility, and social relationships. It enables the Hui to reach multiethnic and cross-ethnic networks. Some individuals can now enjoy new fashions, have friendships with non-Muslims, and work or study beyond their community.

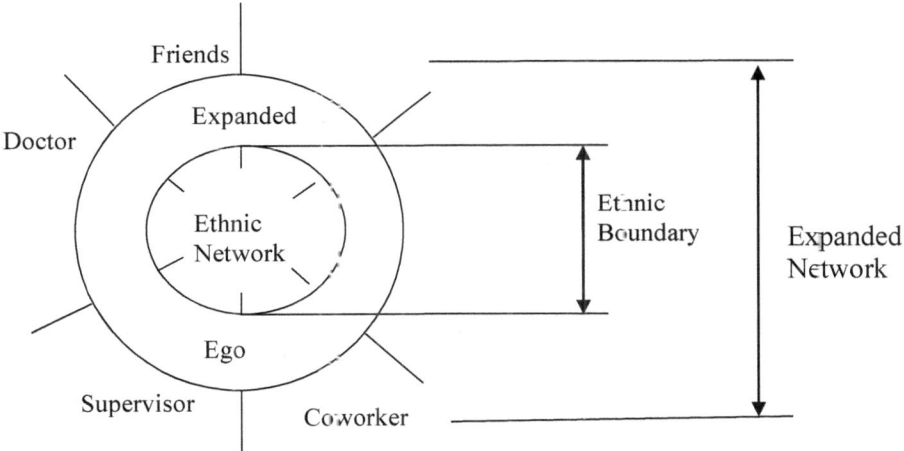

Conceptual Model of Expanded Secondary Networks beyond the Ethnic Boundary

Dispersing the Three Major Urban Components

Now, a Hui individual can choose from many different occupations. Eames and Goode introduced three major urban components: neighborhood, occupation, and ethnic group.[62] Figure 3 is a conceptual model of how those three components relate to a Hui individual. The first model shows that in the traditional Hui community the three components are widely overlapped. The second model in figure 4 shows how these three components are changed by the impact of modernization. Traditionally overlapped, the three components are now dispersed. Since some of the modern Hui in urban areas have diversified, their secondary networks

62. Eames and Goode, *Anthropology of the City*.

grow fast. As a result, the concept of neighbor refers to more than those in a shared location and includes those who have similar interests.

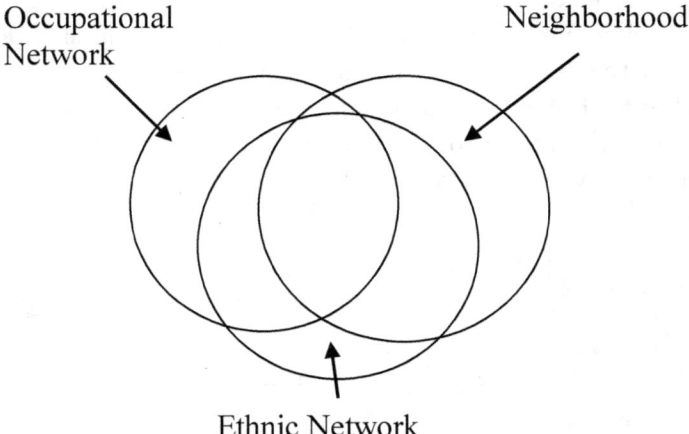

Three Major Urban Components in Traditional Community

Occupational networks are also very diversified and extended by the development of personal mobility and ability. For example, the person in the figure 4 has incomes from two jobs and studies at school. He or she has at least three kinds of activities—alumni association, Internet club, and parents and teachers' association—that give him or her many interactions within different networks. Those proximity groups and occupational networks go far beyond the Hui ethnic network.[63]

---

63. Kim, "'Us' or 'Me'?," 93.

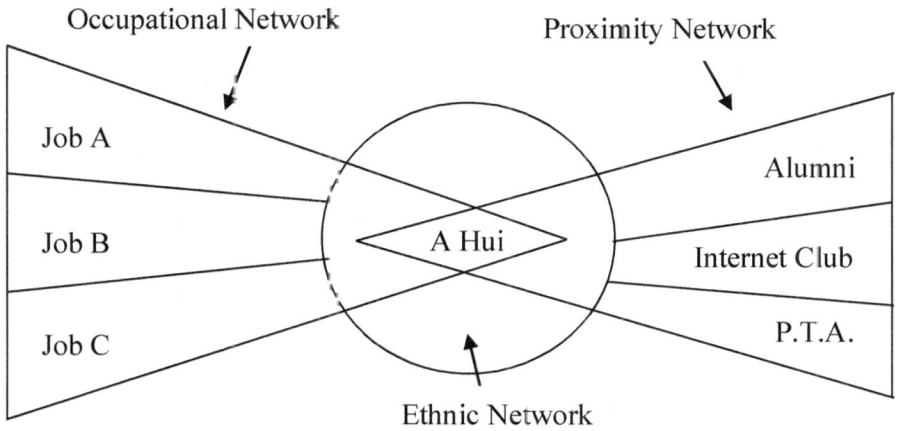

Changed Three Major Urban Components
in Modern Community

Hui Multi-ID, Multi Faces, and My Life Mentality[64]

Modernization society allows Hui individuals to connect with outside non-Hui networks. Depending on the person's ability and situation, the person can develop his or her secondary networks cross-ethnically and cross-religiously.

The number of urban Hui multi-ID (multi-identification) holders grows, which means that a people can identify themselves with more than one set of circumstances. Those people have the ability to selectively work and share their lives in multiple situations. Some Hui learn how to meet and act differently in different situations in order to act appropriately and increase benefits. In this pluralistic world, these multi-ID-holders develop several layers of worldview by experiencing multiple societies.

Where people can have "voluntary membership," they can easily have multi-ID because their relationships do not clearly limit their ethnic boundaries.[65] However, modernization and urbanization do not always require urbanites to have multi-ID. People may maintain traditional mono-ID if the ethnic relationship is clearly defined.

Multi-IDers are similar to people who have several different identification cards in one wallet. The person can decide which card to use

---

64. Ibid., 94.
65. Israeli, *Muslims in China*, 29, 120.

depending on the situation. This multi-ID concept naturally introduces a person's collective lifestyle in which he or she has several different lifestyles and selectively uses them. Because many individuals in the group have multiple networks, the individual can choose different networks when the person is not satisfied with the current group. When the individual thinks that one network is not helpful, the person may shift over to other networks. Modern network is characterized as being able to join easily and leave easily. Naturally, these modern secondary networks consist of quite weak ties, which means the relationship is shallow and functional rather than holistic.

This urban Hui collective lifestyle naturally enables the Hui to have multi-faces in relationships. Compared to those of the ruralites, urbanite networks are more separated, more professional; therefore, urban network members know very little about other members. For example, urban employees rarely know their coworkers' religions or children's names.[66]

Urbanites can have many different faces in each of their networks. The structural differentiation of cities offers individuals a relatively great number of social roles. Hannerz also makes this point.[67]

Among the Hui, the YEU-Hui group has a relatively strong tendency toward multi-ID. They have abundant social mobility, secondary networks, and a variety of common interests. As a result, the urban Hui have multiple communication channels through which to receive the gospel. The collective lifestyle may be helpful to mitigate community stress when a Hui decides to receive the gospel. Furthermore, since the multi-faces have more identities and connections they can hold several social identities at the same time.

Having multi-ID, collective lifestyle, and multi-faces gives Hui individuals the ability to achieve, experiment, and make decisions. Though subcultures still heavily influence their member's decisions, the most important and ultimate decision maker in the modern world is "I." The Hui used to make decisions by what "we" or "others" want, but now it is by what "I" want. This is a "my life" mentality, which is slowly forming in modern urbanites. Therefore, this mentality is getting more important than what "we and our community" prefer. Naturally, the community pressure that the Hui individual feels has lightened up because now "I"

---

66. Fischer, *Urban Experience*, 205.

67. Hannerz, *Exploring the City*, 232.

have more rights and abilities than before. As their community pressure lessens, the Hui will choose what they want. Hopefully, they will choose Jesus, who can give what they really want.[68]

SUMMARY

The study of urbanism lays out profound basal data for developing mission strategy to reach the urban Hui. For this study, three sociological theories are examined: determinism theory, composition theory, and subculture theory. Although two of them partially fit, the subculture theory is the most appropriate tool to identify the impact of modernization upon the urban Hui.

Viewing people groups in urban settings as a homogenous body does not seem proper; they should rather be considered groups in a mosaic. These urban subgroups selectively share influences that lead them to transformation, extinction, development, and continuation.

Because of their strong family-oriented and filial piety tradition, the Hui primary networks did not change much, but the secondary networks have changed. They extend new secondary networks beyond ethnic borders, and now share connections and common ground cross-culturally. Therefore, these secondary networks have become urban junctures of cross-cultural communication, and it offers effective opportunities for introducing the gospel. Christians need to develop modern urban junctures for the gospel and to be ready for effective modern mission strategy for the Hui.

When a Christian introduces the gospel at an urban juncture, knowing the receptor's cultural themes enables the delivery of a culturally appropriate message. This is another important strategy as Christians understand urbanism and the Hui in urban contexts. The next chapter will study these Hui cultural themes.

---

68. Kim, "'Us' or 'Me'?," 94.

5

YEU-Hui Identity

WE NOW TURN OUR attention to the group that is the focus of this dissertation: the YEU-Hui. YEU-Hui is, as mentioned above, an acronym for the phrase "young, educated, and urban Hui." It is necessary to identify those in this strategic group among the Hui who constitute an entry point for the gospel in that community.

The Hui has many social classes, and the whole people group is a mosaic of subculture groups. Each subgroup has a different level openness to change. There are two conditions for identifying the strategic group. First, they should have openness to new information. Second, the strategic group needs to have leadership and influence upon other social classes because this group will later become the source for spreading the gospel. This dissertation will prove why the YEU-Hui can be this strategic group.

THE YEU-HUI[1]

As its acronym means, there are three conditions for defining the YEU-Hui. First, the YEU-Hui are relatively young and limited to a generation who were born after the Cultural Revolution (1965–76). They belong to the post-Chairman Mao generation. This generation has lived with many large, significant, and rapid changes that have happened after Chairman Mao. They experienced Chairman Deng Xiaoping's *gaige kaifang* (改革开放), or "reformation and open door policies"; the Tiananmen Square tragedy on July 4, 1989; the 9/11 tragedies in 2001; the SARS (Severe Acute Respiratory Syndrome) outbreak in 2003; and events connected

---

1. Kim, "New Entrance Gate," 355–56.

with the 2008 Beijing Olympics. Hsiao-peng Lu sees that Chinese modernization began when this generation passed through such important social issues. Lu bestows the label postmodern on this generation based on the following criteria:

> Post-1989, post-Tiananmen, and "post-New Period" are all terms that cover the postmodern moment. Generally speaking, intellectual discourse about the "New Period" (ca. 1977–89) revolves around the issues of modernization, modernity, humanism, and reconstruction of a new subjectivity. The New Period came to an end in 1989 with the Tiananmen debacle, which is considered a watershed in contemporary Chinese cultural and intellectual history.[2]

The YEU-Hui generation has experienced a succession of rapid social changes in a manner not experienced by previous generations.

Second, YEU-Hui are educated, meaning that they have more than high school education. Traditionally, the Hui have educated their children in their mosques. Even adult Hui study the Qur'an in mosques. Andrew G. Findlay says the traditional Hui education is characterized by strong religious roots.

> Hwei-hwei youth are sent at a tender age to a school in the mosque to acquire knowledge of Arabic and Persian. Should he in time attain to a certain standard of efficiency in these studies, he is considered an honor to his family, and will most likely complete the course of a mullah.[3]

However, modernization has changed this traditional schooling pattern. Today, there are two types of public schools for the Hui: ethnic schools and general Chinese schools. Traditionally, the Hui prefer their ethnic schools because parents feel it is socially safe and culturally comfortable. However, with the influences of modernization, the number of Hui enrolling in formal school is growing because they feel that ethnic schools are of relatively poor quality and can only cover low grades of education. Hui students are two kinds: *minkaomin* (民考民) and *minkaohan* (民考汉). *Minkaomin* refers to minorities who study in minority education systems. *Minkaohan* refers to minorities who study in a majority-influenced school system. YEU-Hui are definitely *minkaohan* because the YEU-Hui are highly educated, and all of the

---

2. Lu, *China*, 11.
3. Andrew, *Crescent in North-West China*, 33–34.

high schools are run by the majority education system. Interestingly, the ratio of *minkaohan* is continually growing. These *minkaohan* represent a bicultural group, a collection of individuals who have been mostly exposed to modernization.

Third, the YEU-Hui are urbanites. Urban life provides the YEU-Hui with big changes and challenges. Urban life has become popular among the modern Hui and Chinese. During Chairman Mao's era, China was not zealous for urbanization because they believed that large cities could be easily contaminated by foreign imperialism and capitalism.[4] To prevent peasants from flocking to urban centers, the Chinese government used a household registration system (戶口) [*huko*] and state-owned work units (單位) [*danwei*]. Since these systems effectively controlled the residences, ruralites could not freely leave their designated areas without permission.[5]

Some Hui have traditionally resided in cities or have migrated into cities from outside locales. These traditional Hui have formed urban ghettoes in which the Hui maintain their ethnic traditions, socioeconomic activities, dietary rules, and religion.

With Chairman Deng's open door policy in 1978, mobility incredibly increased, and cities were filled with urban poor, the migrants from the rural regions.[6] The Hui also moved to the cities with "aspirations to find a 'city job.'"[7] The pattern of Hui migration usually followed a "kin-based migration" that was essentially a chain of relatives and friends.[8] Specifically, those in the first generation are the trailblazers. The second generation can then more easily function in the city to find formal education and jobs. From this second generation, the kinds of jobs are diversified though they are not quite high-level positions. Many of them are taxi drivers, tailors, small business owners, or other middle-class workers.

Many parts of urban life can guarantee anonymity or "facelessness."[9] Consequently, secularization can grow in at least three ways: increased nominal faith among Muslims, increased interaction with the Han, and increased compromised Muslim traditions.

4. Chen, *China Urban*, 5.
5. Ibid., 6–7.
6. Zhang, "Contesting Crime," c.
7. Hoffman, *Guiding College Graduates to Work*, 45.
8. Conn, "Urbanization and Its Implications," 69.
9. Hertz, *Face in the Crowd*, 274, 280.

MODERNIZATION AND THE YEU-HUI

Material and technical development, as well as abundance, are essential to Chinese modernization. Beginning in 1945, Chairman Mao became a unique leader in China, and urged his people to reach for economic development through several economic and political movements. Those movements were the Great Leap Forward, the Cultural Revolution, a Soviet-style planned economy, and an industry-manufacturing-centered economic system. While Chairman Deng Xioping became a leader in 1978, he campaigned for the four modernizations, which emphasized materials-centered modernization. The four specific areas of modernization were science and technology, agriculture, industry, and military affairs. In the early 1992, Chairman Deng visited southern Chinese cities and special economic zones in order to give full support to all-out economic liberalization and save a legacy he himself had inaugurated more than a decade earlier.[10]

In contrast to this government campaign of materialistic modernization, Hui Muslims are traditionally spiritual. As the Hui faced material-centered modernization, they dealt with many social repercussions, including anger, acceptance, and internal conflict between individuals and communities. Because of their new social circumstances that modernization provides, it has become easier to contact the YEU-Hui than the other Hui groups.

The YEU-Hui have also faced challenges from the impact of modernization. First, the newly formed labor market revolution challenges the YEU-Hui to change. Traditional Chinese job opportunity systems were assignment systems, but the new labor system became based on mutual choices between the laborers and the companies.[11] This new system leads the Hui toward individualism and competition. Ability becomes an important factor as they apply to companies.

Second, modernization increases generational and social conflicts in YEU-Hui society. The newly formed YEU-Hui secondary networks consist of quite different ethnicities, so many YEU-Hui work and interact with people of different ethnic groups in the workplace or in school. As a result, the different cultural zones cause them to act differently at home or away from home. Many YEU-Hui live in different valued spaces at different times: in the day or night, weekdays or weekend. Sometimes

---

10. Lu, *China*, 12.
11. Hoffman, *Guiding College Graduates*, 44–49.

they enter into interethnic marriages. These new trends and values create generational conflicts at home and in the community.

Third, the Hui style of consumerism is notably changing, as well. Quoting a Chinese statistics report, *Zhongguo Tongji Nianjian*, Deborah S. Davis says that Chinese "capital income doubled between 1978 and 1990. And between 1990 and 1994, it increased another 50 percent."[12] Higher incomes have naturally inaugurated a consumer revolution.[13]

Now, the market offers "a cultural product as well as a form of cultural production."[14] The Hui women are not an exception from this influence. Gillette says that "during the reform period, women, including young Hui women, and many other Chinese urbanites, had both the desire and the ability to follow such trends."[15]

Fourth, the media revolution has influenced the YEU-Hui, as well. Young Chinese and Hui are becoming familiar with the Internet, TV, DVDs, and other forms of telecommunication. This visual culture creates transnational interests since the "instantaneous introduction and airing of foreign TV programs" has become "a central feature of postmodern culture, global culture, [and the] global Chinese."[16] Even traditional and conservative Hui ghettoes and rural enclaves have become part of the global village through visual media, and among the Hui, the YEU-Hui are one of the most exposed groups to these media.

Hitching also summarizes four circumstances that have changed Muslim society: the school system, the media, the use of computers, and the ambient flow of culture.[17] Media are rapidly changing traditional values within the new school system, which often uses a Western cognitive framework.

Fifth, individualism and privatization have changed the YEU-Hui lifestyle in very powerful ways. Many Hui individuals live and work under the municipal system and modern business environment, rather than under the traditional community system. For instance, government planned urban redevelopments often scatter the Hui ghettoes, spreading the Hui all over the city to live in many Han neighborhoods. Naturally,

---

12. Davis, *Consumer Revolution*, 1–2.
13. Chen, *China Urban*, 10.
14. Ibid., 12.
15. Gillette, *Between Mecca and Beijing* 224.
16. Lu, *China*, 18, 102.
17. Hitching, *McDonalds, Minarets and Modernity*, 29–33.

Hui community social circles unravel, and they have more social interactions with Han neighbors. Consequently, the pressure to adhere to old, rigid rules has reduced.[18]

Sixth, the YEU-Hui are good at objective conversation. The YEU-Hui have been raised in modern school systems. In contrast to their parents, who were raised under traditional and subjective teachings, this YEU generation is relatively good at objective conversation with those of other ethnic groups. As Hitching emphasizes, the fact that these urban educated Muslims can have fact-based conversations with non-Muslims is the most powerful force for defining and redefining reality and could be the bridge to redefining their view of reality with reference to God and the meaning of existence.[19] This conversational ability can expand commonalities between the YEU-Hui and Christians and can facilitate reflection on the word of God without bias. However, cognitive education is not always helpful to evangelism. Nazih Ayubi explains that among the accused Jihad warriors, the "predominance of young militants" are "from the 20–30 year old age group," and "students represent the major category (around 44 percent in both lists)."[20] Muslims are exposed to new information, but this new trend will force the Muslims to decide between becoming more liberal or more conservative.

EARLY ADOPTERS AND INNOVATORS[21]

Everett M. Rogers categorizes five kinds of adopters of new information according to their timing: innovators, early adopters, early majority, late majority group adopters of innovation, and finally laggards.[22] Innovators and early adopters are strategic people for starting innovation. In a group, the first one to receive new information is the innovator.

As gatekeepers, the salient value of innovators is venturesomeness.[23] Rogers summarizes several prerequisites for innovators: financial resources, knowledge, and the ability to cope with uncertainty.[24]

---

18. Pillsbury, "Cohesion and Cleavage," 271.
19. Hitching, *McDonalds, Minarets and Modernity*, 54–55.
20. Ayubi, *Political Islam*, 162.
21. Kim, "New Entrance Gate," 355–56.
22. Rogers, *Diffusion of Innovations*, 281.
23. Ibid., 283.
24. Ibid.

These summarized prerequisites seem to fit the diffusion of new technologies and urban consumerism, but it also gives an idea how innovators lead in opening their ethnic group to new information. In the Hui situation, the innovators may geographically and socially be located far from the core of the ethnic group. Naturally they may have stronger relationships with different peoples. They may be the Hui in the United States or Singapore, or they may be the leaders of the IBM Beijing branch.

Early adopters identify much more with their own group than innovators do. They are geographically and socially part of the social group. Because of early adopters, other potential adopters can decrease their uncertainty about the new idea. Early adopters have similar characteristics to opinion leaders. They are no different from later adopters in age, have more years of formal education, are more likely to be literate, have a higher social status, have a greater degree of upward social mobility, and have larger-sized units (farms, schools, companies) than do later adopters.[25] Their personalities have greater empathy, rationality, and intelligence and they have more favorable attitudes to change or science. They are better able to cope with uncertainty, have a better ability to deal with abstractions and new ideas, are less dogmatic, and are less fatalistic than later adopters.[26] Their communication behavior differentiates from later adopters. Early adopters engage in more social participation, have highly interconnected interpersonal networks and change agents, have greater exposure to mass media and interpersonal communication channels, seek information about innovation, have knowledge of innovations, and have a higher degree of opinion leadership.[27]

YEU-Hui personalities and backgrounds seem to be quite similar to those in Rogers's characterization of the early adopters. Furthermore, compared to innovators, who have rare social participation, YEU-Hui social networks are quite overlapped with their traditional societies. At the same time, the YEU-Hui education level and China's rapidly forming middle class situation have lead the YEU-Hui group to influence the whole people group as opinion leaders. The field research will show the identification of the YEU-Hui and how quickly they adopt outside values and fashions.

---

25. Ibid., 288.
26. Ibid., 289–90.
27. Ibid., 290–91.

YEU-Hui Identity   61

FIELD RESEARCH PURPOSE AND GOALS

An initial field research was conducted to identify a possible entrance group (E-Group) for the gospel among the Hui. An E-Group is a sociological group that has the highest openness and receptivity to the gospel. The second purpose of this research was to identify relevant and available media and its program for the E-Group.

There were five goals for this research, and each goal has a number of information needs. The first goal was to identify the relative size of the Hui subgroups. The necessary information was their ethnic background, age, education level, urban background, and their dietary rules. The second goal was to identify a relevant social scale with which to address the degree of modernization, or change. The necessary information was what social scale effectively measures the degree of modernization and change among the Hui, and which crucial factors contributed to the social scale. The third goal was to identify the E-Group among the Hui. The necessary information was the background of this E-Group, as well as any potential Islamic fundamentalists in the E-Group. The fourth goal and its necessary information involved the kinds of media that the E-Group used. The fifth goal was learning about the E-Group's preferences for programs and media content. Necessary information included the preferences of program, media, felt-needs, and themes between both the E-Group and the YEU-Han.

SAMPLING PLAN AND DATA COLLECTION

This exploratory research data was gathered through direct visits using either questionnaire or oral questions. The main method used for data collection was a self-administered questionnaire, which offered undisguised, disguised, structured, and unstructured questions.

Researchers collected data from the Hui community, ghettoes, and campus Muslim restaurants through questionnaires and oral questions. They visited Islamic restaurants in four different universities, about seventeen Islamic restaurants in the Hui ghetto, and local markets. Complete anonymity of the respondent was maintained. To protect the respondents' privacy, no identification data was included on the pretest copy.

Ninety people answered the paper-based questions. Seventy-eight people answered about their dietary rules through oral questionnaire.

Sixty-four YEU-Han answered the comparison questionnaire. Therefore, 232 samples were used for tabulation.[28]

DEMOGRAPHIC DATA

Among the Hui who answered the paper-based and oral questions, the ratio of men to women was comparatively equal, which is shown in figure 5. Fifty-five percent were male, and 45 percent were female.

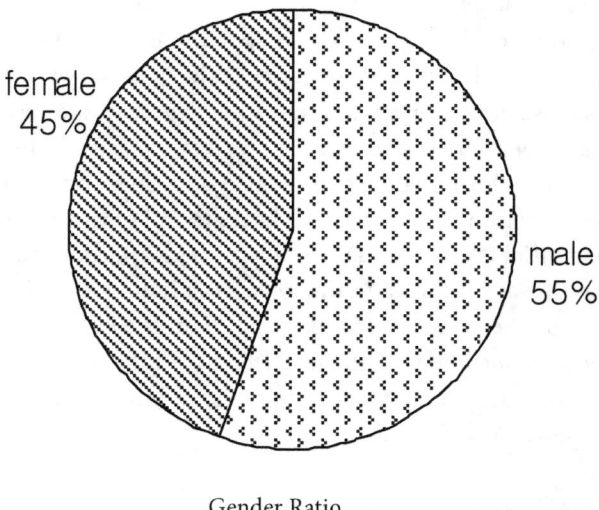

Gender Ratio

Figure 6 shows a breakdown of the respondents by age category. Ninety percent of those sampled were below thirty years of age. Since researchers intentionally visited campus restaurants and workplaces in the daytime, most of the respondents were naturally young, thereby screening most of the sample for this YEU precondition.

---

28. Kim, "New Entrance Gate," 357.

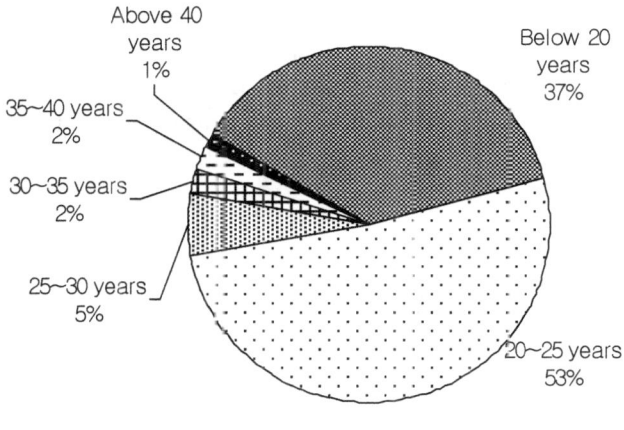

Age Categories

Figure 7 shows the period of time that respondents lived in urban areas. The urban residence periods seem relatively evenly distributed. About half of them (45%) had less than three years of urban residence. This means that they were not completely settled into urban life, probably preserving their original traditions and worldview patterns. At the same time, some of them might have made fast compromises within their new urban, pluralistic life patterns.

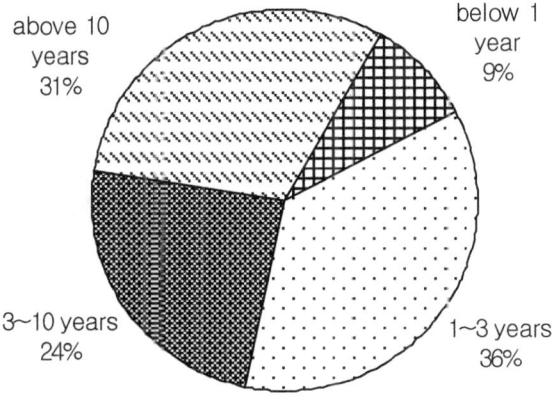

Urban Residence Periods

64   Part One: A Cultural Study of the Hui and YEU-Hui

Figure 8 shows the categorization of residence environment. Though there were various kinds of residence environments, the numbers residing at school dormitories (60%) and majority areas (16%) show that most of the respondents' houses were among the majority people. Seventy-six percent among the majority is quite natural, considering that the majority people dominate most of China's urban populations.

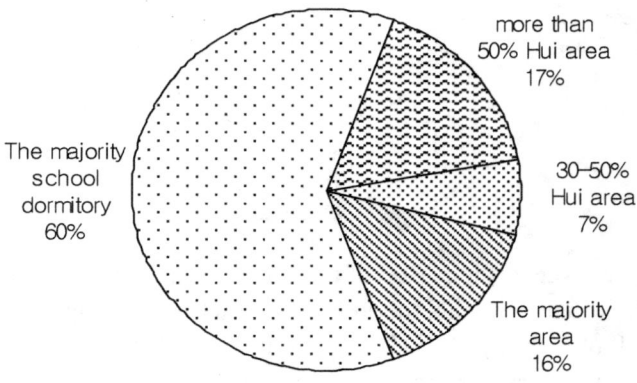

Residence Environments

Figure 9 shows the education level of the respondents. Eighty-eight percent have had more than a high school education. This is because researchers intentionally collected data mainly from various schools in order to screen most of the sample for the YEU precondition of "educated."

YEU-Hui Identity 65

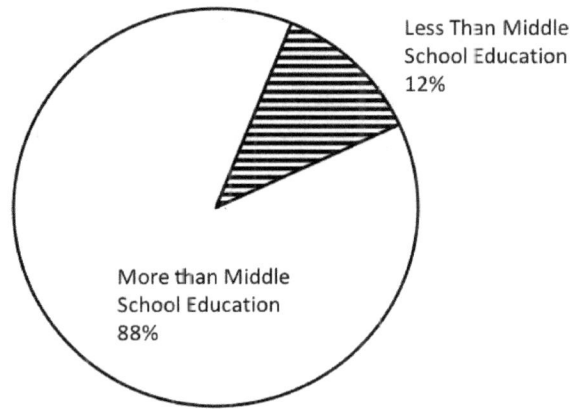

Schooliing Background

The Appropriate Scale for the Degree of YEU-Hui Openness

In order to have a relevant social tool that addresses the degree of modernization, it is necessary to develop a new scale. The scale needs to point to the individuals' degree of openness. It will also enable the strategist to categorize the YEU-Hui into several similar groups. Identifying the characteristics and background of the categorized group will then show which YEU-Hui are best to contact first for introducing the gospel.

Q-Scale

Q-Scale is an acronym for the *qingzhen* scale. *Qingzhen* [ching-jun] represents the Hui cultural symbols, and spirit. This Q-Scale represents the degree of individual Hui attitude about the taboos of eating pork. Eating pork is far more than an individual dietary habit; it is a distinctive ethnic behavioral pattern of the Hui. Therefore, this Q-Scale is based on a hypothesis that the Hui dietary habits influence their openness. The Q-Scale has five degree levels of personal conservativeness and openness regarding the dietary rule:

Q1 Eats pork anywhere

Q2 Eats at non-Hui restaurants, but does not eat pork

Q3 Eats mass-produced food (McDonald's or Coke) or goes to foreign restaurants

Q4 Eats only in *qingzhen* restaurants or in Hui houses

Q5 Eats only meat killed by *ahong* and that has the mark of *qingzhen*

For finding the contribution factor of Q-Scale and Q-Scale's appropriateness for measuring openness, conducting the following four kinds of analysis was crucial.

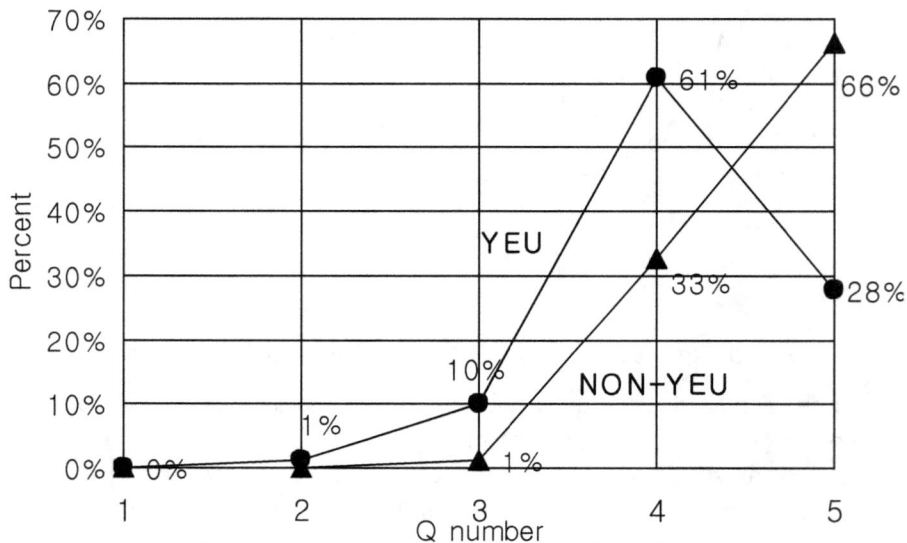

Q Number Comparisons between YEU and Non-YEU

The first analysis compares dietary habits between the YEU-Hui and Hui who are non-YEU. In contrast to expectations, figure 10 shows that both YEU-Hui and other Hui have quite strict rules about the taboo. Eighty-nine percent of the YEU and 99 percent of non-YEU answered Q4 and Q5. Therefore, dietary rules do not indicate differences between the Hui who are YEU and those who are not.

The second analysis of the Q-Scale test is a comparison between respondents' backgrounds and their Q-numbers. Figure 11 shows the correlation between the Q number and age category. The figure shows that there is not much relationship between the two. Regardless of age, most of the Hui are strict to the taboo.

YEU-Hui Identity   67

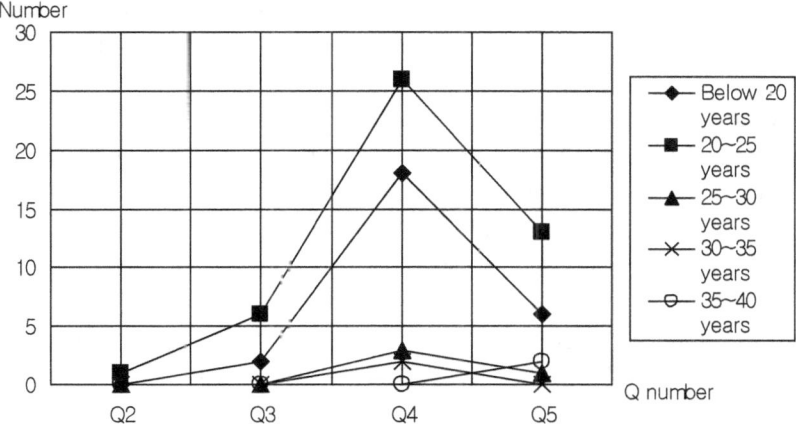

Relations between Q-Scale and Age

Third, figure 12 shows the correlation between the urban residence period and Q number. Low Q numbers, which show openness, grow as the residence period becomes longer. At first, there are only Q4 and Q5 in the zone below one year. Then Q3 appears at between one and three years of residence and increases in the zone between three and ten years. At above the ten years zone, the Q2 group begins to appear. This means that the longer they live in the city, the more they compromise their taboo. However, no one eats pork even if they live in city longer than ten years.

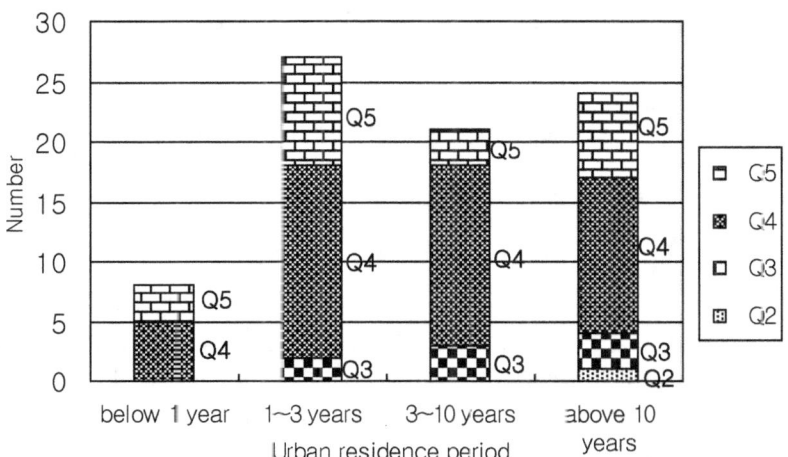

Relation Of Q-Scale to Urban Residence Period

Fourth, figure 13 shows correlation between the residence environment and the Q number. Though there is not a strong relationship between the Q-Scale and the residence environment, the Q2 and Q3 are found only in the two highly populated areas. This means that as they separate and live farther from their own ghetto, it is easier to compromise their tradition. Still, no matter where they live, no one eats pork.

No matter their background and situation, the degree of taboo against eating pork is almost the same for all Hui; however, the residence in the Han urban area period may change the Q number. The Q-Scale may help find the degree of urbanization, but is not an appropriate scale to trace and identify the E-Group, because most of the YEU-Hui dietary habits are Q4 and Q5. Therefore, Q-Scale is not a realistic tool to search for E-Group.

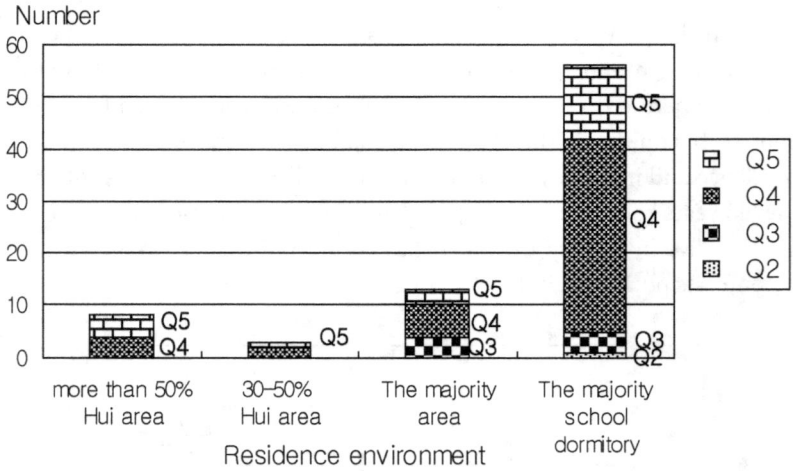

Relation of Q-Scale to Ethnic Residence Environment

M-Scale

The second tool to measure the YEU-Hui openness to modernization is the M-Scale (modernization scale). The questionnaire used Hitching's five modernization factors: urbanization, secularization, globalization and global horizontal generation, pluralization, and privatization. Each of the five factors has a maximum of ten points. Every respondent's grade comes from summing up the five factor's points.

YEU-Hui Identity 69

First, to learn the degree of urbanization, the questionnaire asked about their desire to live in an urban area and their plans to enroll their children in majority schools. Second, to learn the degree of secularization, it asked about their frequency of worship participation in a mosque. Third, to learn the degree of globalization, it asked how many hours they have contact with world news and how they feel about Western and Hong Kong fashions. Fourth, to learn the degree of religious pluralization, it asked how many of their close friends are Hui. Fifth, to learn the degree of privatization, it asked who influences their decision-making, and whom they would be afraid to tell if they did something ridiculous or shameful.

Figure 14 records the M-Scale results, which show the respondents' openness to modernization. Interestingly, most of the non-YEU have lower points, and none of them are in the high thirty-percentile group. This means that the YEU-Hui are concentrated in the higher M points zone. In contrast to the Q-Scale, the M-Scale is able to more clearly discern members of the YEU group.

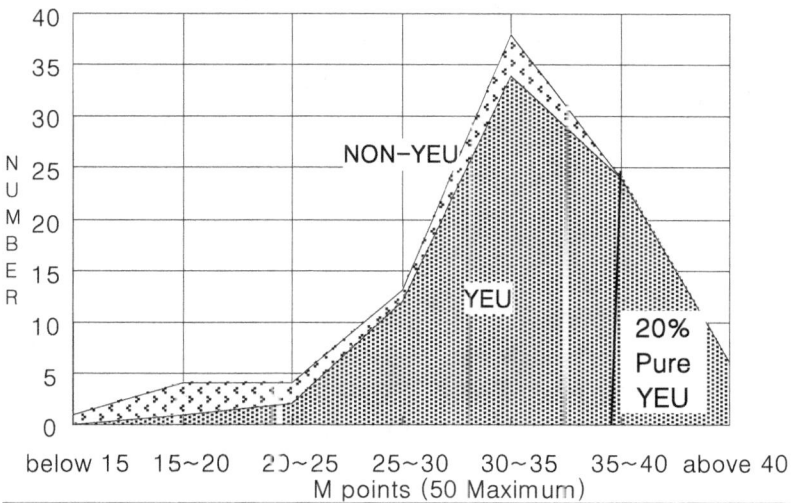

Classification of the YEU-Hui by M Number

MM-Scale

MM-Scale[29] is the third tool, which is more specifically designed to estimate the degree of openness to modernization. There are three steps in

29. "MM" stands for "more modernization."

scoring this tool: (1) extract the persons who scored in the high thirty percentile on the M-Scale; (2) analyze which factors more highly contribute to group members' high degree of openness; and (3) regrade all of the recipients, using only highly contributive factors.

The second stage is finding out which factors among the five are more contributed to form these thirty percent group members. For this, the Pearson Correlation Coefficient and Significance are used, which is defined in appendix C.

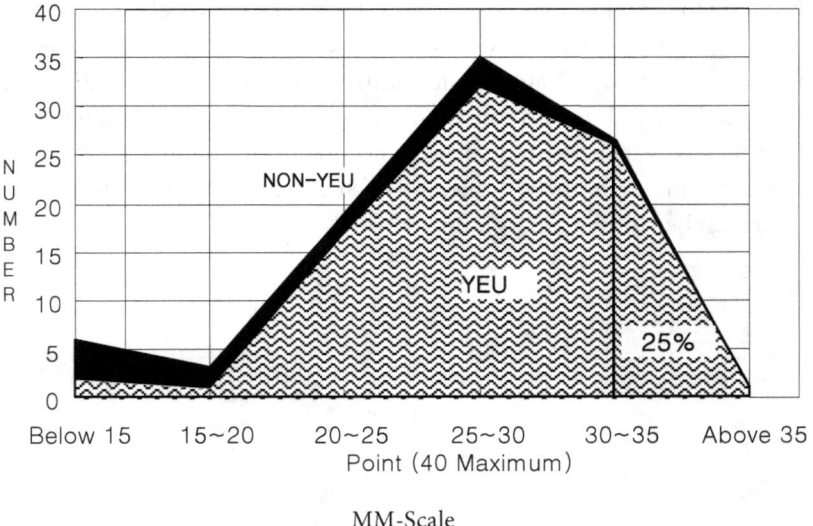

MM-Scale

Each of the five factors' null hypotheses is zero (0), which indicates a strong relationship between the factors and integrated points. It is necessary to compare the Pearson factors in order to analyze the details. Excepting the privatization factor (0.367), all four of the other Pearson values are higher than 0.52. This means that, overall, the privatization factor contributes relatively less to the scale that estimates peoples' openness to modernization.

Finally, by using four of the more highly contributive factors, all the recipients are rearranged on the MM-Scale. Again, each of factors has a ten-point maximum. Since the MM-Scale has only four factors, the maximum point available are forty. Figure 15 is a redrawing of the diagram using the MM-Scale.

Compared to the M-Scale, more non-YEUs are in the lower point zone of MM-Scale. Calculations show that there are non-YEU people in the upper twenty percent on the M-Scale, but not one non-YEU at twenty-five percent on the MM-Scale. Conclusively, the field data proves that the MM-Scale more effectively identifies and analyzes YEU.

In conclusion, the Q number can show limited aspects of Hui openness. It only shows the influence of their urban residence period upon their openness. The M-Scale is an effective tool for determining a group's openness, but it still lacks some influence factors. Finally, only the MM-Scale has highly contributive factors to show YEU openness to modernization. Therefore, this MM-Scale is the main tool used to identify E-Group.

Identifying the E-Group

E-Group is an acronym for the entire group. By using the MM-Scale, researchers will find out the group that is most open to the new information, and this is the E-Group. Regarding this E-Group as an entrance point for sharing the gospel is strategic. There are two types of research to do in order to identify the E-Group: categorizing E-Group by MM-Scale and extracting potential fundamentalists from the E-Group.

Identifying the E-Group and Non-E

Figure 16 is a conceptual diagram of an E-Group and its subcategorizations. By using the MM-Scale points, the sample is categorized into three parts: the high thirty, middle forty, then lowest thirty percentiles. Each group is named E1, E2, or Non-E, and they are all YEU-Hui. The diagram shows the YEU-Hui inside the whole Hui people.

72 Part One: A Cultural Study of the Hui and YEU-Hui

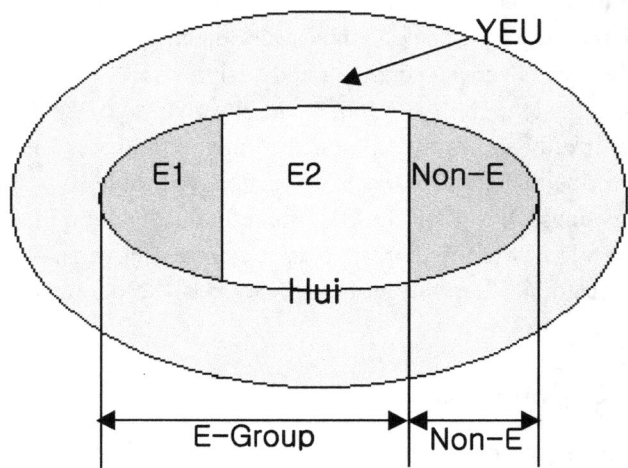

Identifying E-Group among the YEU-Hui

To characterize E1, E2, and Non-E groups, and identify their backgrounds, it is necessary to trace each group's demographic data. The data that characterizes their backgrounds include residence period, residence environment, school background, period of employment and education, mosque attendance, influence from Western and Hong Kong style, and proportion of Muslim friends. Appendix D shows the list of comparison tables by each of the E-subgroups.

Conclusively, E1 and E2 have similar backgrounds. The E1 group members have more than ten years of urban life, live in a majority residence area, and have fewer than forty percent Hui friends. They go to mosque only on special days, and have contact with Western media more than an hour a week.

The E2 group seems to be a transition group from Non-E to E1. They have between three and ten years of urban residence. Likewise, E1 has more openness to modernization than does E2 in most situations, like work periods, mosque attendance, influence by foreign fashion, and number of non-Muslim friends.

Islamic Conservatism and the E-Group

High openness to new information does not always mean openness to the gospel, but it often includes YEU-Muslims who are Islamic conservatives. If there were any potential Islamic conservatives in the E-Group, though their openness is similar, their receptivity to the gospel would be tremendously different than liberalists. In order to discern them, the questionnaire poses two questions regarding: (1) preference between benefits of modernization and religious purity and (2) feelings toward Western culture. Figure 17 shows the results, conceptualizing and segregating the conservatives among the YEU.

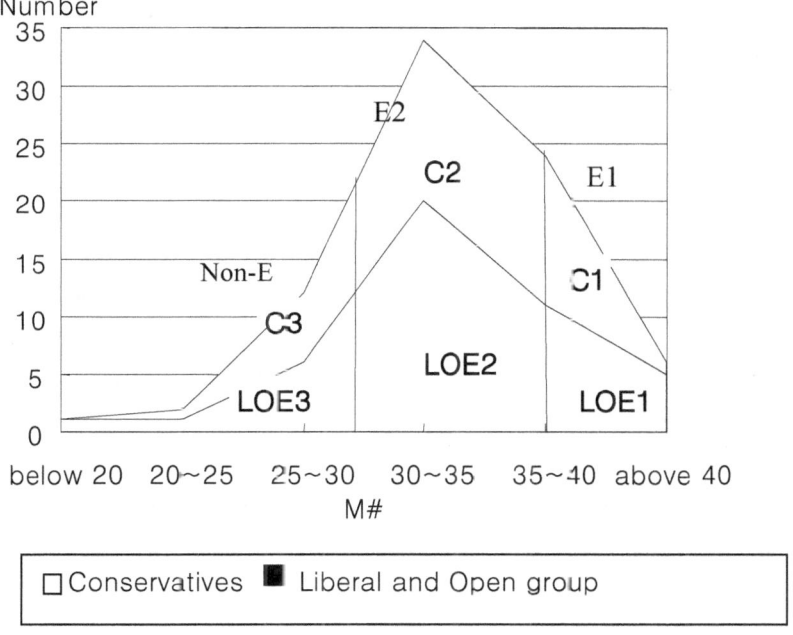

Conservative Groups in the MM-Scale

Figure 17 shows how much of the E-Group contains conservatives. In this case, C stands for conservative, and the C1, C2 and C3 correspond to their E-Group number. Roughly speaking, the results show that about half of those identified as from the E-Group can be identified as from the C-Group. Separating out this C-Group can leave a group of those who are more open to the gospel. This study names this group the LOE-Group, which means the liberal and open E-Group. Therefore, each E1, E2, and Non-E group contains a C1, C2, and C3 group, as well as an LOE1, LOE2, and LOE3 group.

The next question is: are those considered part of the C-groups really conservatives and not open to the gospel? Or are these just people who would like to be conservative? In other words, is it just an idea or do they really live their lives as conservatives? To answer this, the next question is asked about their practical lives and their real concerns as felt needs. The question asked them to prioritize their real interests and concerns in the following areas: money, status, honor, love, marriage and family, job, social service (contribution to the society), acceptance from others, revival of religion, ethnic revival, and revival of China. Each priority had a different weight in a statistics program that prioritized their real concerns. The result of their answers is table 1. Both the LOE-Group and the C-Group have similar concerns, generally related to money, honor, love, job, and relationships.

Table 1

Comparison of Real Concerns between Islamic Fundamental and Non-Fundamental Groups

Tendency's Concern	LOE-Group Weight	LOE-Group Percent	C-Group Weight	C-Group Percent
Money	18	20.0%	9	12.0%
Status, Honor	9	10.0%	7	9.3%
Love, Marriage/Family	24	26.7%	16	21.3%
Job, Social Meetings	9	10.0%	11	14.7%
Contribution to the Society (Service)	5	5.6%	5	6.7%
Acceptance from Others	9	10.0%	10	13.3%
Revival of Self-Ethnic-Religion	5	5.6%	6	8.0%
Power (Economy, Society)	4	4.4%	7	9.3%
Revival of China (Economy, Society)	7	7.8%	4	5.3%
Total	165	100 %	75	100.0%

The next part is about the differences in background between the C-Group and the LOE-Groups, including residence environment, proportion of Muslim friends, mosque attendance, and preference toward urbanization, child education, Western culture, and foreign fashion. Appendix E shows analytic comparison between the two groups' backgrounds. It shows that the two groups have very similar backgrounds, preferences, living situations, and information channels.

Surprisingly, the results of their concerns and background studies show that the C-group is not much more religious than the LOE-Group. In fact, the results are very similar. It seems that they are very different from the fundamentalists and conservatives in the Middle East who have received systemic education with the Qur'an and have religious faith. Therefore, this report will not divide the C-group from LOE-Group from this point forward. Though there might be conservatives in the E-Group, the C-group and LOE-Groups have similar openness to outside information and preferences. Therefore, it is will not be necessary to address these groups separately, unless we find significant new information about them.

E-Group's Media and Program Preference

The third research purpose dealt with favorite media themes among the YEU-Hui. The questionnaire asked what themes have widely influenced their lives and opened their hearts. This was an open question. Recipients first wrote the titles of the dramas, books, music, soap operas, and DVDs, and then they wrote the reasons why they liked them. Since it was an open question, researchers had to make categories in order to calculate the findings. The answers were of the following eight kinds:

- Romance: for both men and women
- Hobby: personal hobby
- Culture: culture of their own district or ethnic group
- National development: development of economy, social culture, rural district
- Family: realistic love among brothers and sisters, or parents and children.
- Experience: people's own experiences (e.g., people in rural areas)
- Religion: religion

Table 2

Favorite Themes of YEU-Han and E-Group

	E-Group		YEU-Han	
	N	Percent	N	Percent
Romance	13	13.8%	28	24.8%
Hobby	21	22.3%	28	24.8%
Culture	19	20.2%	10	8.8%
National Development	8	8.5%	6	5.3%
Family	6	6.4%	1	0.9%
Experience	17	18.1%	26	23.0%
Religion	4	4.3%	1	0.9%
Etc.	6	6.4%	13	11.5%
Total	94	100.0%	113	100%

There was a comparison done between the E-Group and the YEU-Han to find out if there was a difference in their favorite themes. Table 3 shows its result. Interestingly, the two groups had similar favorite themes. The three top favorite themes were hobbies, culture, and experiences. Surprisingly, religion was not one of the E-Group's favorite themes. This means that E-Group members' personal concern and interests are not very religious, but similar to other YEU-Hans. It seems that Christians and Christian media can use similar topics as they approach both the Han and the YEU-Hui.

The next comparison between the YEU-Han and E-Group is about felt needs and real concern. Table 1 and table 3, respectively, show the E-Group and YEU-Han's felt needs, and the underlined items identify the top four needs.

Table 3

YEU-Han's Real Concern

Needs	N	Percent
Money	23	12.9%
Status, Honor	12	6.7%
Love, Marriage, Family	45	25.3%
Job, Social Meetings	32	18.0%
Contribution to the Society (Service)	16	9.0%
Acceptance from Others	28	15.7%
Revival of self-ethnic-religion	0	0%
Power (Economy, Society)	7	3.9%
Revival of China (Economy, Society)	15	8.4%
Total	178	100.0%

Again, four of the top items are same for both groups. Those two tables show that those items are generally related to money, love, job, and relationship.

RESEARCH LIMITATION

While focusing on the YEU-group, the main data collection locations were ethnic restaurants. Some of the restaurants were in the universities. This was an intentional approach in order to meet with YEU-group members; therefore, most of the people in this sample group live in similar areas.

INTERPRETATION

Three scales have been developed for identifying the entrance group for reaching the Hui: Q-Scale, M-Scale, and MM-Scale. The MM-Scale is the most effective tool to measure the scale of modernization among the Hui people.

The MM-Scale more effectively identified a group that has more openness when compared to the general population of Hui people. The research has named this the E-Group. If God allows, the E-Group should be the first group approached for introducing the gospel among the whole Hui.

Gender and age difference is not a factor in being identified with the E-Group, but as the residence period becomes longer, people have more openness. Many of them move from Non-E to E2. After ten years in urban life, many of them arrive in E1, but the residence seems not to have much influence upon this movement.

In regard to the work and school period in urban areas, there are many cases of movement from Non-E to E2 within ten to fifteen years, and from E2 to E1 within fifteen to twenty years. The YEU-Hui are generally not religious: few of them go to mosque regularly. Contact with Western culture through media has a high influence upon their openness. Though the general tendency of those in the E-Group is to be highly influenced by the media, few Non-E are media-influenced. The proportion of Muslim friends is a good indicator of openness. Forty percent of the average E1's friends are Muslim, but the average Non-E has 80 percent.

By those data, the definitions of E1 and E2 are as following. The E1-group members reside more than three years in urban residences, have more than ten years of employment and education, receive more than one hour of media information a week, go to mosque only on special occasions, and have less than 40 percent of Muslim friends.

Meanwhile, E2-group members have between three and ten years of urban residence. This period seems to overlap with E2-group member's whole school period in the city. Also, it is enough time for E2 parents to raise and enroll their children in majority schools during this period. They have abundant opportunities to contact new information. Moreover, E-Group members have jobs in urban Han companies, and they have Han friends. By this contact with multiple cultures, social networks, and ethnicities, E-Group members may be used to receiving new information, and have objective thinking. Because of their long dietary habits, most of the YEU are strict about eating pork, but enjoy lightened community pressure in the urban context; few of them go to mosque. Though half of the E-Group members have potential to be Islamic conservatives, such a tendency seems not to come from religious zeal but ethnic spirit.

Though they are the Hui, the E-Group members have similar preferences and needs to the Han. In contrast to traditional contextualization theory, this means that, though they are different ethnically, modernization gives these two YEU groups many commonalities. Therefore the impact of modernization gives the YEU the most external new layer on their traditional worldview. Their traditional cultural, historical, and ethnic values can arise again at any time. Therefore, many E-Group members will be able to use the same materials already being used by YEU-Han Christians.

SUMMARY

Chinese modern history forms a new class among the Hui: the YEU-Hui, which is open to new information. To set mission strategy and find those in the entrance group of the gospel, a proper social scale is needed. By using the developed MM-Scale, the research found that, out of the YEU-Hui, the E-Group is the most sensitive to openness. The E-Group is, therefore, the entrance for sharing the gospel among the Hui. Therefore, among the YEU-Hui, it is strategic to contact people who have more than three years of urban life, live in majority residence areas, and have less than 40 percent of their close friends among the Hui.

By the grace of God, modernization partially offers a chance to introduce the gospel that has never been given to the YEU-Hui before. However, YEU-Hui traditionalism, which still exists underneath their external modernization, limits the messengers' influence. It means that discipline through Han materials at a lower stage might be possible, but as they go to deeper levels of Bible study, the development of more contextualized materials seems to be more desperately needed.

6

Biblical Teachings That Relate to YEU-Hui Cultural Themes

IT IS NECESSARY TO locate appropriate biblical messages for mission to the YEU-Hui, taking into consideration their backgrounds. These biblical messages must address their worldview and cultural themes, and they must be expressed in cultural ways, for the consideration of cultural messages, cultural themes, current situation, and biblical perspective are crucial factors.

The cultural theme of the Hui is power and pride. This theme is deeply rooted not only in the traditional Hui worldview but also in that of the YEU-Hui. YEU-Hui behaviors are influenced by at least two different worldview layers: traditional and modern values. The next chapters will deal with this YEU-Hui newly formed worldview that comes from the impact of modernization. A correct understanding of YEU-Hui traditional cultural themes helps in the formation of appropriate biblical messages. This chapter will identify appropriate messages for YEU-Hui who have this traditional theme: power and pride.

There are several kinds of contextualization tools. Among them, P. Hiebert's critical contextualization lays basal theoretical foundation regarding the YEU-Hui case by effectively facilitating both the Bible and the contexts in order to co-stimulate each other and produce proper message.[1] During the contextualization process, the communicator selects the biblical themes and terminologies that share meaning with the YEU-Hui cultural themes. Then, the selected biblical theme and terminologies offer new biblical meaning and perspectives to the YEU-Hui

---

1. Hiebert, "Cultural Differences," 21–29.

cultural theme. Finally, the message introduces new biblical meaning to the YEU-Hui and their old cultural themes.

BIBLICAL DEFINITION OF POWER AND PRIDE

Bible terminology often reflects a different meaning from similar vocabulary used in a different context. Therefore, it is important to select biblical terminology that has the closest meaning to those used by the Hui to communicate current power and pride themes. This is the first step in developing biblical messages for the Hui.

Pride-Related Terms in the Bible

Here are the semantic nuances of specific terms that are nearly synonymous with the concept of pride. The terms are pride, glory, boasting, and honor, with shame as an antonym.

Pride

The Zondervan Pictorial Encyclopedia of the Bible says that the root of the Hebrew word for pride means "to lift up" or "to be high."[2] The New Testament has a wide range of synonyms such as "empty display" or "swagger," "glorying" or "boasting," "haughtiness" and "arrogance."

The International Standard Bible Encyclopedia says that the Bible warns of the danger of pride but it also expresses some positive meanings behind the word, as well.[3]

Glory

Because the word "glory" encompasses a broad digest of meaning, and since we are discussing specific cultural themes among a people group, limiting its use to man or God-created things, and not to God himself, seems appropriate for the next study.

A closely related Greek term of modern glory is *doxa* (δοξα). *The Interpreter's Dictionary of the Bible* states, "No fewer than twenty-five Hebrew words are rendered by δοξα in the LXX."[4]

The Zondervan Pictorial Encyclopedia of the Bible says that among those Hebrew terms, *kabod* most frequently appears in the Old Testament.

2. Tenney, *Zondervan Pictorial Encyclopedia*, 849.
3. Bromiley, *International Standard Bible Encyclopedia*, 950.
4. Buttrick, *Interpreter's Dictionary*, 401.

The meaning of *kabod* includes "difficult," "weight," "heaviness," "worthiness," "reputation," and "honor."[5]

In the New Testament, glory usually comes from δοξα. Many uses of the word coincide with the Old Testament uses of *kabod*, meaning each of the following: the glory of the Lord;[6] Man's outward splendor;[7] Solomon in all his glory;[8] the kingdom of the world and the glory of the cities;[9] the glorious presence of Paul's converts.[10] The biblical writers also use δοξα to refer to the revelation of God in Christ.[11]

The Hebrew term *tiphǝ'ereth* is frequently used to express the idea of glory. The *Nelson Expository Dictionary of the Old Testament* presents the etymology of *tiphǝ'ereth*, explaining that it is a noun signifying glory, beauty, ornament, distinction, and pride. Overall, writers generally use this term to refer to the glory of God or humanity's divine honor.[12]

Honor

In the *Dictionary of New Testament Background*, Craig A. Evans and Stanley E. Porter define honor as "the public acknowledgment of a person's worth, granted on the basis of how fully that individual embodies qualities and behaviors valued by the group."[13] In *Merriam-Webster Online*, pride is "the quality or state of being proud: as (a) inordinate self-esteem; (b) a reasonable or justifiable self-respect; (c) delight or elation arising from some act, possession, or relationship."[14]

Evans and Porter labeled the two sources of honor as "ascribed honor" and "achieved honor." Ascribed honor is frequently beyond an individual's control—like kinship and family or state and politics. Achieved honor comes from piety, courage, reliability, success in competition, aggression, and envy.[15]

---

5. Tenney, *Pictorial Bible Dictionary*, 731.
6. 2 Cor 3:9.
7. Matt 6:29.
8. 1 Cor 11:15.
9. Rev 21:24.
10. 1 Thess 2:20.
11. Heb 1:3; John 1:14; 2:11; 2 Pet 1:16; Jas 2:1.
12. Unger and White, *Nelson's Expository Dictionary*, 151–52.
13. Evans and Porter, *Dictionary of New Testament Background*, 518.
14. *Merriam-Webster.com*, s.v., "pride."
15. *Dictionary of New Testament Background*, 518.

The etymology of the word honor is essentially related to glory, since it also comes from *kabod*. Evertt W. Huffard summarizes the six kinds of usability of *kabod* as righteousness of God, holiness of God, power of God, name of God, the faithfulness of God, and God as the source of *kabod*.[16]

The Greek translated *kabod* as *time* (τιμη), and the second volume of *The New International Dictionary of New Testament Theology* discusses the etymology of τιμη. In the Old Testament, the Hebrew term *kabod* (*time*) or *doxa* (also normally *time*) applies to human honor. Though *doxa* usually refers to God's honor, it appears in other situations: man's creation;[17] honor of office;[18] parents;[19] kings and the mighty;[20] to a teacher of the law;[21] and a man of honorable position;[22] or influence.[23]

In the New Testament, *time* generally represents the recognition of the dignity of an office or position in society: the authorities,[24] owners of slaves,[25] a wife,[26] the sexes in general.[27] "The τιμη of a person, state, or deity must be distinguished from that of another possession. Slaves had no *time*" and therefore, no apparent dignity.[28]

Boast

In Hebrew, the term nearest to meaning "boast" seems to be *halal*. According to *Nelson's Expository Dictionary of the Old Testament*, it means, "to praise, celebrate, glory, sing."[29] Boasting has both good and bad connotations in the Bible. Though there are several positive uses for the word

16. Huffard, "Thematic Dissonance," 216–25.
17. Ps 8:3–8.
18. Ps 139:17.
19. Exod 20:12.
20. Dan 2:37; Job 34:19 LXX.
21. Prov 12:21 LXX.
22. Gen 31:1; Isa 16:14 LXX; Job 29:20; 30:4, 8; 10:5 LXX.
23. Brown, *New International Dictionary*, 48–49.
24. Rom 13:7; 1 Pet 2:17.
25. 1 Tim 6:1.
26. 1 Pet 3:7.
27. 1 Thess 4:4.
28. Brown, *New International Dictionary*, 50.
29. Unger and White, *Nelson's Expository Dictionary*, 301.

boast, the New Testament usually uses it in the negative sense.[30] Biblical teachings that object to undue boasting reflecting arrogance, false pride, and self-righteousness can be found in Psalm 5:15; Proverbs 27:1; Romans 2:17, 23; 1 Corinthians 1:26–31; 4:6 ff.; 2 Corinthians 10:17ff; Ephesians 2:9; and James 3:14; 4:16.[31]

SHAME

The New International Dictionary of New Testament Theology introduces the root of shame. In LXX, the Hebrew term *bôš* is translated sixty-five times as *aischynō* in the Greek. In the Old Testament, *aischynō* refers primarily to the objective ruin of the individual evildoer or of the whole nation.[32] The Old Testament also uses *aischynō* in regard to sexual shame.[33]

In the New Testament, derivatives of *aischynō* appear only eleven times. In Philippians 3:19 and Revelation 3:18, *aischynē* is used in a sexual sense. *Aischros* signifies disgracefulness but is found in the New Testament chiefly in the phrase *aischron estin*, meaning "it is a disgrace."[34] *Aischrologia* means "foul talk,"[35] and *aischrokerdēs* denotes "greedy for base gain."[36] These words are found listed in catalogs of sins.[37]

Power-Related Terms in the Bible

Power is the second Hui cultural theme. The related terms found in dictionaries and encyclopedias are "power and authority."

In *The Dictionary of Jesus and the Gospels*, authority is the right to affect control over objects, individuals, or events. While human authority may be delegated, God's authority arises from himself alone. Power, meanwhile, is the ability to bring about what one desires.[38] Citing other authors, Louise Joy Lawrence also explores several similar terms defining power, authority, influence, and prestige.[39]

30. 1 Cor 1:12; 3:21; 2 Thess 1:4; Jas 4:16.
31. Bromiley, *International Standard Bible Encyclopedia*, 528.
32. Ps 69:4; 6:10; 35:26; 40:15; Isa 1:29; 20:5; Jer 2:26.
33. Ezek 16:36; 23:10, 18, Gen 2:25. Brown, *New International Dictionary*, 562.
34. 1 Cor 11:6; 14:35; Eph 5:12.
35. 1 Cor 3:8.
36. 1 Tim 3:8; Titus 1:7.
37. Brown, *New International Dictionary*, 562–64.
38. Green et al., *Dictionary of Jesus and the Gospels*, 50.
39. Lawrence, *Ethnography of the Gospel of Matthew*; Bourque and Warren,

Power

Regarding power, *Nelson's Expository Dictionary of the Old Testament* explains that *Kōach* in the Old Testament usually means "strength, power, force, and/or ability." The root is uncertain in Hebrew, but the verb forms in Arabic are *wakaha*, "batter down," and *kwh*, "defeat." The Bible uses *Kōach* 123 times. *Kōach* is a poetic word that is used most frequently in poetic and prophetic literature. The basic meaning of *kōach* is an ability to do something. In some cases, *koach* refers to property,[40] wealth,[41] or when God demonstrated his strength to Israel.[42]

The Anchor Bible Dictionary defines the power concept in the New Testament as *dynamis, ischus* and *kratos*.[43] L. J. Lawrence explained δυ–ναμις denotes supernatural divine power or deeds, and εξουσια, denotes authority, right and power.[44]

Authority

In the Bible, authority is virtually synonymous with the Greek *exousia* (εξουσια). *The International Standard Bible Encyclopedia* defines the meaning of *exousia* as (1) "to be free, unimpeded," and (2) "to have a right or permission," which may include moral as well as legal rights.[45]

According to the second volume of *The New International Dictionary of New Testament Theology*, *exousia* (εξουσια) denotes unrestricted freedom of action power, authority, or right of action. In contrast to *dynamis*, where any potential strength is based on inherent physical, spiritual, or natural powers, and is exhibited in spontaneous action, powerful deeds and natural phenomena, *exousia* denotes the power that may be displayed in legal, political, social, or moral affairs. It often means (a) official power, (b) despotic, (c) the office appropriate for specific authority, or (d) office-holders and the "authorities."[46]

"Women of the Andes"; Weber et al., *Theory of Social and Economic Organization*; Goldthorpe and Hope, *Social Grading of Occupations*.

40. Ezek 2:69.
41. Ibid.
42. Ps 29:4; Exod 15:6; 32:11; Num 14:13; Isa 50:2; Ps 111:16; Deut 8:17–18. Unger and White, *Nelson's Expository Dictionary*, 299–300.
43. Freedman et al., *Anchor Bible Dictionary*, 444.
44. Lawrence, *Ethnography of the Gospel of Matthew*, 117, 18.
45. Bromiley, *International Standard Bible Encyclopedia*, 365.
46. Brown, *New International Dictionary*, 606–7.

In the New Testament, *exousia* appears 108 times. It is used in a secular sense, meaning the power to give orders.[47] In a concrete sense, it also means jurisdiction[48] and officials or authorities.[49]

Similar Concepts of Power and Pride

Terminology research helps the scholar compare the terms power and pride with the same terms used in the Bible. Then, finally it allows scholars to learn which terms have the closest meanings to the same terms used today by the YEU-Hui. The Bible broadly uses terms in the pride etymological family. Related terms may denote negative situations such as "arrogance" or "spiritual blindness." The terms referring to "glory" seem more neutral. It seems that both of the Hebrew terms *kabod* and *tiphə'ereth* share a similar denotation of the term pride, which is familiar in the Hui context. Though there are some exceptions, *kabod*—translated into Greek as *time* (τιμη) and *doxa* (δοξα)—is usually used to refer to the glory of God. Since *time* generally denotes dignity, as associated with an office or position in society, it more aligns with the meaning of the Hui concept of "pride."

According to Colin Brown's summary, between the two power terms, *exousia* (εξουσια) is closer to the Hui concept of power than is *dunamis* (δυναμις).[50] This is because the Hui concept of power denotes more tangible aspects found in the legal, political, and social arenas. The YEU-Hui search for power revolves around the political arena. Therefore, the YEU-Hui seek power to ensure survival and ethnic identity.

POWER AND PRIDE FOR MARGINAL GROUPS IN THE BIBLE

How did Jesus see marginal groups? There were many kinds of marginal groups around Jesus, whether geographically, socially, or religiously marginalized. The Hui is a marginalized people group in China. Therefore, understanding how Jesus identified and treated the marginalized groups will give us an idea of how to develop a biblical message for the Hui.

---

47. Matt 8:9; Luke 19:17; 20:20.
48. Luke 23:7.
49. Luke 12:11; Titus 3:1. Brown, *New International Dictionary*, 608.
50. Ibid.

Marginal People in the Book of Matthew

Observing marginal people in the Gospel of Matthew is a good place to study how Jesus comforted and cared about those living at the margins of society. Matthew himself was from a marginal people in Jewish society because he was a tax collector working for the Roman government.

According to the Gospel of Matthew, Jesus himself was a marginal group member of that society, as well. Even when he was born, there was no place for his family to stay except in a manger. Jesus' public life was marginalized, as well. From this social position, Jesus naturally called disciples who had similar backgrounds. Jung Young Lee says, "The people Jesus called to be his disciples were marginal people."[51]

In the eponymous gospel, Matthew compares people who lived in Jerusalem with those from Galilee. According to Paul Hertig, Galilee was not the center of Israel. Jerusalem Jews looked down on the people in Galilee.[52]

Matthew developed a theme for Galilee by contrasting it with Jerusalem. Jerusalem was the center of religion, society, and politics. In Galilee, Jesus saw a new possibility of ministry and identified himself with the marginalized. Hertig summarizes:

> The Galilee theme portrays Jesus as a marginalized man among a marginalized community of disciples who nevertheless take up privileged roles as change agents in society. The very people whom the world rejects, Jesus accepts as his very own. We discover that Jesus as Messiah is at the center, but chooses to move from the center to the margins and back again as a strategy for social transformation.[53]

As a result, these same marginal and oppressed people became the center of a new revolution, the revolution of Jesus.

Marginal People in the Book of John

Robert J. Karris researched Jesus' concern regarding the marginalized in the Gospel of John, first detecting the dimensions of a category of "Jesus and the marginalized" in the gospel.[54]

---

51. Lee, *Marginality*, 86.
52. Hertig, "Messiah at the Margins," 130.
53. Ibid., 8–9.
54. Karris, *Jesus and the Marginalized*, 11–12.

In the Gospel of John, the disciple describes that Jesus and the Johannine community cared for the marginal group from the first to the end. As a result, many followers of Jesus were from this oppressed segment of society. Jesus ministered to the people of the land, healing the physically incapacitated and relieving the oppression of the geopolitically marginalized.

Sometimes, this marginal people can heighten sensitivity to the Holy Spirit and the truth more than central groups. Marginal people are ready to open their hearts to the genuine Word of God. Karris summarizes the plight of marginal people who followed Jesus and became heroes and heroines in doing so. They are strengthened in their dedication to Jesus by the example of Mary. Their missionary endeavors find encouragement in the Samaritan woman and Mary of Magdala. Their patience with the marginal groups may yet bear fruit as the story of Nicodemus illustrates. The story of the man who was born blind shows that the Father of Jesus will never cast out the person who believes in Jesus. Sharpened by the Johannine polemic against the Jewish synagogue and religious leaders, these stories proclaim that the religious leaders are far from God, and the marginalized are near.[55]

ISSUES OF BIBLICAL MESSAGES ABOUT POWER AND PRIDE IN MUSLIM CONTEXT

There are several general and broad cultural issues that the messenger of the Bible needs to bear in mind while forming culturally appropriate messages for Muslim societies. When introducing the gospel with the Muslims, Christians need to consider that the concept of the cross, the gospel, honor, and shame are good examples, and it's necessary to know how to make culturally appropriate messages of those themes. Considering these issues as a frame of reference is crucial as messenger prepares messages.[56]

The Honor of the Cross in the Muslim Context

In his dissertation, Huffard pointed out that Muslims can easily misunderstand the symbolism of the Western Greco-Roman cross message because the two cultures approach it from a different frame of

---

55. Ibid., 106–7.
56. Kraft, *Communication Theory for Christian Witness*, 15.

understanding. Huffard compares the frame of understanding inherent in each culture; then, refines the cultural themes to shape an acceptable message for the Islamic world that maintains the Western message. To do this, Huffard introduces a "paradigm of thematic dissonance" as illustrated in figure 18.

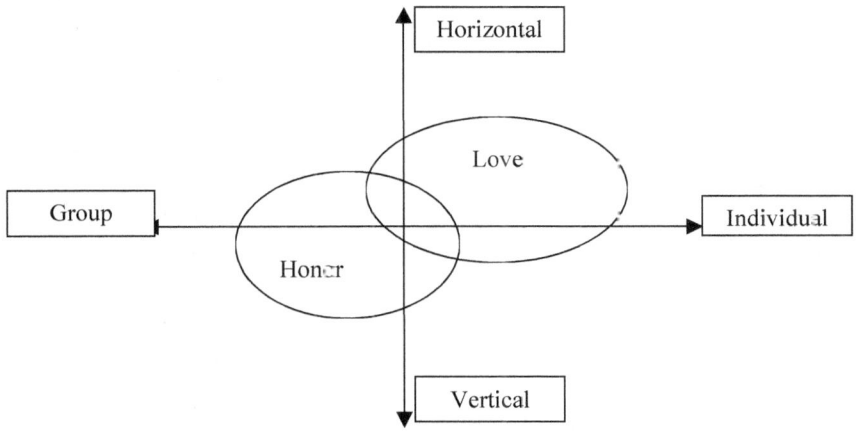

A Paradigm of Thematic Dissonance[57]

According to Huffard's diagram, Westerners live in a society structured on individuality and horizontal relationships; whereas Arab society emphasizes the group and vertical relationships. The greater the emphasis on individuality and horizontal relationships, the more appealing the concept of love would be in the gospel message. Conversely, the greater the social emphasis on group and vertical relationships, the more honor would be valued.[58] Therefore, these two cultural zones will derive a very different understanding of the cross depending on the emphasis asserted in the message on either love or honor.

The message that emphasizes love and sacrifice, therefore, may not be effectively appealing in the Islamic context. Rather, Huffard explains that the honorific message of the cross would be more appealing in an Islamic context.[59]

57. Huffard, "Thematic Dissonance," 71.
58. Ibid., 69–80.
59. Ibid., 279.

It is important to propose here that Huffard's theory is worth applying to the Hui situation, since the Hui emphasize the group over the individual and a strong vertical relational hierarchy is in place. It is important to consider at least two factors. First, the message should be a "theocentric message on the honor of God," more so than anthropocentric. Likewise, "the cultural influence reflected in the goal of the catechism as personal enjoyment of God rather than a desire for service, loyalty, or faithful relationship" should be clearly conveyed.[60] Second, the honorific paradigm is a better kerygma in evangelism directed toward Muslims than is the sacrificial paradigm.

Therefore, the message shared with the YEU-Hui people needs to describe Jesus as the ultimate example of the faithful one, wholly submitted to God in his obedience to suffer on the cross. There is no greater model of submission than Jesus. Moreover, God's honor was established at the cross by the loyalty of Christ to him and his will.

If this picture of faithful obedience is contrasted with the loving intimacy with a personal God, the theology of honor allows several different viewpoints about Jesus' ministry and the YEU-Hui response. The new view sees salvation as a process of building honor to establish loyalty to the family of God. Therefore, the cross washed away our shameful sin and recovered our honor. Accordingly, baptism becomes the symbol of a committed loyalty to God through a new birth into the family of God.

Honor and Shame in Muslim Enclaves

According to Roland Muller, today's Western world is a guilt-based culture, while from North Africa to Far East Asia are strongly preoccupied with honor in a shame-based culture.[61] In other words, these cultures share a heightened concern for saving face. Interestingly, most of Islamic cultures are situated in this cultural zone of honor and shame.

Many Western missionaries stationed in Islamic countries incorrectly try to explain and prove the validity of the Bible by arguing with Muslims through polemical logic. Of course, if the Westerner proves the point, a Muslim on some level loses and shame inevitably surfaces, creating reflexive hostility to Westerners and Christianity.

For more effectively reaching the people who are from the honor- and shame-based culture, the delivery of the Christian message needs

60. Ibid., 281–82.
61. Muller, *Honor and Shame*, 18.

to be reframed. Therefore, Muller says, it is rather the cultural and community side that holds its followers in an iron grip.[62]

Notably, understanding how Muslims process the concept of honor will open entry points. Muller suggests that one of the ways is through honorable acts, specifically honorable acts that include honoring elders, showing hospitality, and giving gifts to a meaningful person. Muslims are generally proud when they have advanced education, marriage, money, heritage, wisdom, charisma, physical strength, alliance, bravery, and royalty.[63] In this respect, Muller makes significant observations relevant to this study, despite his research context being specifically Middle Eastern. The significance of his research touches upon the character of his Middle Eastern research group, and much like them, the Hui are part of a strongly relational-based culture that is highly sensitive to honor versus shame.

Biblical Themes Relevant for Shame-Based Culture

Then, how might the gospel message be presented to a culture sensitive to shame? Muller introduces the redemptive messages that relate to five basic doctrines: repentance, sacrifice, redemption, propitiation, and reconciliation. Accordingly, Muller summarizes repentance, sacrifice, redemption, propitiation, and reconciliation as several types of messages appropriate for cultures strongly rooted in relational issues of honor and shame.[64]

SEVEN MESSAGES AS BRIDGES OF COMMUNICATION

God has led the Hui culture throughout their history. God gave wonderful cultural themes to the Hui and the themes are expressed by their cultural symbols, signs, and social structures. However, since they do not have the divine word, their cultural themes have been distorted and developed by their own will. Now, God wants to recover the Hui, and give them godly and genuine power and pride.

Here are the seven messages that will suggest basal ideas as the culturally appropriate message to the YEU-Hui. The seven messages will be a bridge of communication for the gospel. The messages will introduce Jesus to the YEU-Hui and can give them undistorted power and pride.

---

62. Ibid., 12.
63. Ibid.
64. Ibid., 102–3

Message 1: The Message of Jesus to the Marginal Group

What is the message of marginal groups in Matthew and John to the YEU-Hui? It is the message of hope, pride, and power for the hopeless, the weak, the ignored, and the mistreated![65] Jesus wants to help marginalized people who seek power and pride. Like Jesus has chosen a few visionaries among the marginal group, he also has hope and vision for the Hui today.[66] Jesus knows that the Hui hunger for God just as the Galileans did.[67] People from the fringes of society can share a passion for seeking God that the majority often does not have.

The Hui are wanderers in China. They live in China, but their hearts are not in China. As Jonathan N. Lipman titled his book *Familiar Strangers*, the Hui are insecure and restless wanderers in China.[68]

Jesus came to the YEU-Hui to give them peaceful hearts—something that the world could not give. Finally Jesus wants to provide the Hui their roots.

> Abide in me as I abide in you. Just as the branch cannot bear fruit by itself unless it abides in the vine, neither can you unless you abide in me. I am the vine, you are the branches. Those who abide in me and I in them bear much fruit, because apart from me you can do nothing.[69]

Jesus remembers the gruesome, sad history of the Hui, and knows that they need a more stable cultural identity. Therefore, he respects and loves the YEU-Hui. Jesus is not only mighty enough to give them power to survive and prosper among the majority, but he also wants to lift them up among the nations in much the same way he lifted Galileans from oppression.[70] This is what the YEU-Hui truly want and need: pride and power. Islam cannot give this deep, true meaning of power and pride; only the Bible can.

---

65. Matt 5:3; 11:19.
66. Matt 10:1–4.
67. Matt 4:25.
68. Lipman, *Familiar Strangers*.
69. John 15:4–5.
70. Matt 4:15–16.

Message 2: Power and Pride and a Lack of Introspection

The Hui traditionally have lived in a Muslim community, and the societies were quite introspective, which means quite immaterial and spiritual. As the Hui test modernization, many of them have new desires. Many young, urban Hui seek social elevation. They often shift their concerns from spiritual issues to material things.

L. J. Lawrence's book proved how anti-introspective people in the New Testament failed when dealing with the issues of power and pride.[71] They compromised the things that should not be compromised in order to retain power and pride.

To retain power and position, King Herod failed to be introspective in Matthew 2:1–23. As he knew that the Magi were looking for the king of the Jews, Matthew says that King Herod's heart was "frightened."[72] Then, King Herod concealed his fear and concern, and secretly obtained information from the Magi. After calling the Magi, he killed Bethlehem's children, all to retain his power and position.[73]

Second, Herod, the tetrarch, at the request of Herodias's daughter also failed to be introspective.[74] He had to choose between keeping his promise to Herodias and protecting John. He did not want to be considered a liar in front of people, so finally he gave Herodias the head of John.

Third, Pilate was a governor, who identified himself through his political position. Unfortunately, Pilate became a prisoner of his own position. Apparently, he believed he was a person of high status. Yet, ironically, he was controlled by those he was supposed to rule. In contrast to Pilate, Jesus was free from the bondage of power and position. Jesus did not even explain who he was to Pilate in Matthew 27:11–26. Because of his lack of introspection, Pilate impotently handed over Jesus to the people. His inner voice begging for position and power was too loud for him to hear his conscience. Finally, by public display—hand washing—he tried to defend his own reputation.[75] Though Pilate was so close to Jesus' message, he could not come to Jesus as his savior.

In contrast to those politicians, Jesus was transparent, and was not concerned with position and power, given his message. First of all, in

71. Lawrence, *Ethnography of the Gospel of Matthew*.
72. Matt 2:3.
73. Matt 2.
74. Matt 14:1–12.
75. Matt 27:24.

front of Pilate, Jesus did not declare himself the Son of God, nor try to reveal the power of God.[76]

What is the message for the YEU-Hui? Individuals who strongly seek power and position can easily lose their introspection. Though Herod and Pilate were near to Jesus and listened to him, they were too focused on seeking power to listen to Jesus. In the case of many Chinese minorities, the YEU-Hui, in particular, seek social elevation to penetrate the Chinese mainstream. However, they need to learn that real joy does not come from an elevated status or materialism but from Jesus.

Message 3: True Honor (in Sermon on the Mount)

In the Sermon on the Mount, Jesus introduced a new understanding of honor to the Jewish and Greco-Roman audiences.[77] Jerome H. Neyrey (1998) divided this text into three parts. The first part is Matthew 5:3–12. In this part, Jesus changes the meaning of honor. Neyrey emphasizes that genuine honor and shame do not always come from public approval. Furthermore, some things that the general public may think shameful (e.g., poverty, mourning, meekness, hunger and thirst, mercy, purity, persecution, or exile) can be honorable. The verse says that for anyone afflicted by these problems, theirs is the kingdom of heaven; they will be comforted, given an earthly inheritance, filled, shown mercy; they will see God and be called the children of God. Truly honorable people can deny worldly personal wealth, honor, recognition, a stable background, and the expectation that basic desires will be satisfied by the world. Among those who instead seek heavenly rewards, Jesus honors his followers who have been shamed for his sake.

The verses in Matthew 5:21–48 represents the second part. According to the text, the way of acquiring honor was completely contrary to the ideas found in the Greco-Roman and Jewish cultures of the day. Jesus mentioned several acceptable ways for males to gain honor. Yet, Jesus used antithetical ideas to explain real honor. He would be prohibited from seeking honor by physical assault, sexual conquest of women, or lying.[78]

Finally, Matthew 6:1–18 expresses Jesus' revolutionary concept of how to show honor in relationships. He wants us to abandon the

---

76. L. J. Lawrence summarizes this attitude of Jesus in the Gospel of Matthew, in *Ethnography of the Gospel of Matthew*, 129.

77. Matt 5:3—6:18.

78. Neyrey, *Honor and Shame*, 211.

male-dominated public space where people generally think honor could be found. Instead, honor can be found in secret. By mentioning Philo, an urban elite (30 BCE–45 CE), Neyrey says that this male public space represented a kind of "open-air life," "market-places," and "council-halls."[79] By contrast, female space is linked with the house or household world. In the male public places, people can get public honor from other people. Yet, Jesus challenges false honor by commanding not to blow a trumpet, or to love to stand in the synagogues and the streets, or to create the appearance of fasting, because those hypocrites who do have lost their heavenly reward. Jesus claims that true honor comes by "giving alms, praying to our heavenly Father, and fasting in secret."[80] He further warns his followers that they may literally lose family, respect, and honor, as well as suffer under strong community pressure.[81]

Jesus' reformation of honor involves seeking the honor of God, and rejecting public honor (through physical, verbal, and sexual aggression). Therefore, in many cases, Jesus asks people to relinquish shame in seeking his honor.

Then, how does this message relate to the Hui? The message declares what is true religion to the YEU-Hui. True religion is not derived from religious hypocrisy or found in public approval from society. Since their religious activity is community-based, the YEU-Hui can find satisfaction when they sincerely follow religious and community activities. However, the Gospel of Matthew says God wants the YEU-Hui to truly thirst for him and that eternal honor will come only when they encounter God. The inherent antithesis in the text tells the YEU-Hui that Jesus is the source of true religion and promotes a thirst for God. Therefore, the YEU-Hui can find true honor if they follow him. However, Jesus warns the YEU-Hui that the community and people's admirers often miss the correct path to the true honor of God.

Message 4: The Heart of the Father
(The Story of the Prodigal Son)

In the Gospel of Luke 15:11–32, there are three persons in this story: a father, his prodigal son, and his elder brother. Kenneth Ewing Bailey

---

79. Ibid., 213–14.
80. Matt 6:1–5.
81. Neyrey, *Honor and Shame*, 227–28.

introduces abundant evidence of oriental life and poetic lifestyle that are the background of this parable.

In the story, the second son made two big mistakes in asking his father to give him his inheritance before the father's passing away.[82] First, the request for his inheritance before the father's death, itself, should not have happened in that culture. "This request in village society can mean only one thing: The younger son is impatient for his father's death. The division of the father's wealth would naturally come only after the father dies."[83]

The son's selling of his wealth was the second mistake. Typically, the son had to manage and work on the farm for his father's honor, but the son in the story sold out his right, and spent it. The prodigal's action creates two bigger problems: division of inheritance and an implication of father's early dying.[84]

The father represents the heart of God in this story. When he was asked to redeem his wealth for the second son, the father did not punish him like other fathers, but granted the second son's request with an unexpected act of love.[85]

The Middle Eastern culture would not normally welcome the return home of the prodigal son. However, the father welcomed the son unconditionally, and even protected his son from the hostile community. "The father is fully aware of how his son will be treated, if and when he returns in humiliation to the village community he rejected."[86] By waiting for his son at the edge of the village, the father took the initiative from the villager to criticize. "The father makes the reconciliation public at the edge of the village." Thus, "his son enters the village under the protective care of the father's acceptance."[87] The father opened a celebration with the community, which Bailey estimates to be rather sizable.[88] To protect the son, the father announced his return and thereby protected him from humiliation—saving his face.

---

82. Luke 15:12.
83. Bailey, *The Cross and the Prodigal*, 30.
84. Ibid., 266.
85. Ibid., 268.
86. Ibid., 298.
87. Ibid., 299.
88. Ibid., 308.

Generally, the older son was expected to be a reconciler, but in this case he did not do so. He refused to enter the banquet. The older son clashed with his father's intentions. In Asian culture, when family members clash on ideas, they must calmly follow the father's lead. Therefore, the eldest son's public refusal of the father's invitation was a great insult to the family.

Jesus used this parable to talk to the Pharisees and scribes in Luke 15:2–3. In the story, Jesus introduces the two sons. Both of them break the father's heart. Allowing the second son his wealth is not just a money issue, but it is a face issue, as well. The father's relatives and community humiliate him because the father allows his younger son's request. The father, through his love, finally chooses the shame of humiliation to honor his son. True love can overcome the fear of shame as the Bible says.

> There is no fear in love, but perfect love casts out fear; for fear has to do with punishment, and whoever fears has not reached perfection in love.[89]
>
> Above all, maintain constant love for one another, for love covers a multitude of sins.[90]
>
> Love is patient; love is kind; love is not envious or boastful or arrogant.[91]

This is a very important message for the YEU-Hui for several reasons. First, honor bestowed by the community may differ from honor originating from God. While Muslims and Christians may seek honor and righteousness through religious activity and law, God the father is comforting and caring for the YEU-Hui on a very personal level. It is not due to their righteousness, but to God's unconditional love for them. The father's heart is wider and deeper than the YEU-Hui imagination. Likewise, God accepts people with love before he judges others for their religious activities. Jesus told this parable to Pharisees and the teachers of the law because he wanted them to understand the unconditional love of the Father.[92] The YEU-Hui also need this message, because they also need to know this unconditional love. The YEU-Hui need to know God who accepts them without any religious condition.

89. 1 John 4:18.
90. 1 Pet 4:8.
91. 1 Cor 13: 4.
92. Luke 15:1.

Message 5: Jesus' Honor and Shame in Hebrews

The book of Hebrews has many terms that express honor and shame. The text emphasizes that Christians need to deny the social value of honor, but keep the new value of honor and shame. David A. DeSilva's work provided the basal idea for this section.

The book of Hebrews introduces Jesus and the epic heroes of the faith as examples of "despised shame."[93] Jesus endured the cross, despising shame, and sat down at the right hand of God. The book of Hebrews introduces several examples of those like Abraham and Moses, who "have chosen what was of less esteem in the world's eyes in their pursuit of the reward promised by God."[94] Hebrews introduces an ironic evaluation, which challenges the world's system of honor and values with some examples of those who suffered society's disgrace in the form of physical abuse and censure.[95]

Then why does the book of Hebrews ask us to accept the shame and rejection by the dominant culture? It is for the "something greater," which God has prepared for them.[96] The author of the book of Hebrews adds the promise of future reward and honor which are attainable only by the person of πιστιζ, which in Hebrews combines "faith" in the reality and beneficence of God as well as commitment to persevere in answer to God's call.[97] The true shame and honor dichotomy for Christians comes when they heavily rely on Jesus and his values but devalue their fit into the dominant culture.

Then, what is the honor and reward of followers of Jesus? It is being a "partner with Christ," first. That means "believers can expect to have a share in the honor and dignity which Jesus as Son has attained," and "'as partners in a heavenly calling' (μετοχοι), share in the inheritance with the children of God."[98] Second it is "purification, sanctification, and forgiveness of sins."[99] Third, "the believers' access to God himself is a high privilege. It is an honor which they enjoy through the work of Christ"

---

93. DeSilva, *Despising Shame*, 5.
94. Ibid.
95. Heb 11:36–38.
96. Heb 11:39–40.
97. DeSilva, *Despising Shame*, 152, 206–7.
98. Heb 3:14; Matt 19:28; John 17:22; Heb 1:2; 1:14; 6:17; 9:15.
99. Heb 7:11–10:18. DeSilva, *Despising Shame*, 152, 292.

in Hebrews 4:16; 10:19; 13:10.[100] Finally, it is "God's declaration of association with them, by which He commits to them a share in the honor and commits to preserve their honor as an extension of God's dignity" in Hebrews 1:16.[101] DeSilva names this as honorable disgrace.[102]

The concept of "despising shame" and "honorable disgrace" is a big challenge to some Hui who have been challenged to follow Jesus. When the Hui convert to Christianity, great pressure from their community is anticipated. The converts will suffer shame and threats from their community. Hebrews frequently refers to an inheritance as the goal to reach for at the end. When there is persecution, Hebrews guarantees that there is true reward and honor awaiting the Hui seekers. First, it is "often described in general terms as the inheritance of salvation, and "what was promised.""[103] Second, the honorable prize that the Hui need to seek is access to God in the heavenly sanctuary. This is the place where "Christ went as a forerunner on their behalf (Heb 6:19-20). As they also run their race, looking ahead to the pioneer (Heb 12:1-2), they can look forward to attaining the prize of entrance into this Sanctuary."[104] Finally, though the reward is not clearly described in the book of Hebrews, it was Moses who "considered abuse suffered for Christ to be greater wealth than the treasures of Egypt, for He was looking ahead to the reward."[105] God never forgets his reward to the YEU-Hui who obey Christ. Furthermore, Jesus promised the reward and encourages the YEU-Hui, "Do not, therefore, abandon that confidence of yours; it brings a great reward."[106]

Message 6: Jesus Washes Away Our Shame

The good news is that God wants to rescue YEU-Hui from shame and give them honor. For it states in Scripture, "See, I am laying in Zion a stone, a cornerstone chosen and precious; and whoever believes in him will not

---

100. Ibid.
101. Ibid.
102. Ibid., 301.
103. Ibid., 305.
104. Ibid., 306.
105. Heb 11:26
106. Heb 6:10; 10:35.

be put to shame."[107] Many ideas of this section come from Muller's book *Honor and Shame*.[108]

God Moves Us from Being Defiled to Being Cleansed

The YEU-Hui wash parts of their body before they participate in worship. They believe that Muslims can move from defilement to cleansing before God. By washing, people get honor and can enter the worship place. The Bible also introduces similar cleansing rituals. Aaron and his sons were to wash their hands and feet to enter the tent of meeting or the altar in Exodus 30. In Leviticus 13–14, by the instigation of the priest, God provides a way of cleansing to the lepers who were in a tremendous position of shame. In the New Testament, there are many examples of cleansing: the cleansing of the lepers, the defiled Gentile woman, and the Jewish woman who bled for twelve years.[109]

The Bible describes that YEU-Hui can be cleansed by the blood of Jesus Christ who washed away any of our sin on the cross. The ultimate avenue for divine cleansing is Christ's work on the cross to remove our sin once and for all.

> For if the blood of goats and bulls, with the sprinkling of the ashes of a heifer, sanctifies those who have been defiled so that their flesh is purified, how much more will the blood of Christ, who through the eternal Spirit offered himself without blemish to God, purify our conscience from dead works to worship the living God![110]

From Naked to Clothed

When Adam and Eve sinned in Genesis 3, they lost their eternal life, and immediately knew that they were naked. Much like they longed to be clothed, we groan to be clothed with proper and eternal clothing. "For in this tent we groan, longing to be clothed with our heavenly dwelling."[111] Isaiah also describes the great joy of being thusly clothed:

---

107. 1 Pet 2:6.
108. Muller, *Honor and Shame*.
109. Luke 5:12–14; Matt 15:21–28; Mark 5:25–35.
110. Heb 9:14–15.
111. 2 Cor 5:2.

Biblical Teachings That Relate to YEU-Hui Cultural Themes 101

> I will greatly rejoice in the LORD, my whole being shall exult in my God; for he has clothed me with the garments of salvation, he has covered me with the robe of righteousness, as a bridegroom decks himself with a garland, and as a bride adorns herself with her jewels.[112]

As the prodigal son returned to his home and his father robed him first, Jesus clothes the YEU-Hui to cover their shame, and died on the cross.[113] When Jesus was on the cross, he bore all the shame and nakedness to recover YEU-Hui honor. The most wonderful story of honor is prominent in the final chapters of the Bible: starting out naked and ashamed in Genesis, but clothed through God's grace provided by Christ, and finally coming forth in our wedding garments at the marriage supper of the Lamb.[114]

As they have persecution, the YEU-Hui need to know what the real and ultimate shame will be at the marriage supper of the Lamb. The current and earthly shame will be washed away and compensated by God.

What can these messages mean to the Hui? First, God moves the Hui from being defiled to being cleansed. Now, we can find the real meaning of *qingzhen* (clean and truth) in the Bible. God cleanses the Hui by his truth. God is concerned about the Hui, and he wants them to be lifted out of shame to honor. Second, God covers the YEU-Hui shame with spiritual clothing. When Jesus was naked on the cross, he covered the YEU-Hui shame. This is real power and pride. Hui sought the *qingzhen* for thousands of years from their ethnic and Islamic identity, but God wants to give them a new power and pride through a divine *qingzhen*. Jesus and the gospel are a divine *qingzhen*. The Hui can find this divine "cleansing and truth" in this gospel.

Message 7: Power Made Perfect in Weakness

Much like other groups, the Hui also seek power for survival, achievement, and spirituality. Then, how does the Bible tell about these Hui needs? Paul gives us some insight through his testimony.

> Therefore, to keep me from being too elated, a thorn was given me in the flesh, a messenger of Satan to torment me, to keep

---

112. Isa 61:10.
113. Luke 15:22.
114. Muller, *Honor and Shame*, 62.

> me from being too elated. Three times I appealed to the Lord about this, that it would leave me, but he said to me, "My grace is sufficient for you, for power is made perfect in weakness." So, I will boast all the more gladly of my weaknesses, so that the power of Christ may dwell in me. Therefore I am content with weaknesses, insults, hardships, persecutions, and calamities for the sake of Christ; for whenever I am weak, then I am strong.[115]

Paul paradoxically said that he would boast all the more gladly of his weaknesses so that the power of Christ may dwell in him. After God denied Paul's prayer request, Paul understood the reality of powerlessness.

Actually, Paul had a splendid background of which he could reasonably boast. In the former part of the text, Paul said, "Since many boast according to human standards, I will also boast."[116] Then, whatever anyone dares to boast of, he also dares to boast about his Jewish lineage, hardships and dangers as a true servant of Christ.[117] However, Paul suddenly proclaimed his weakness.[118] Colin Kruse says about Paul's weakness that "this does not mean he enjoys weaknesses as such; what he delights in is the power of Christ that rests upon him in these weaknesses."[119] This message directly challenges the Greco-Roman or Jewish concept of power and weakness.[120]

Paul thought that Jesus in us is like treasure in a clay jar, and, as Gerald F. Hawthorne, Ralph P. Martin, Daniel G. Reid point out, Paul attributes his ability to the "grace" of God, that is, the power of God working in him and through him.[121]

By this, Paul came to know that God's real concern was not answering Paul's prayer, but God led him to know that miracles and real power come when God appears through our weakness.[122] The theology of weakness as power finds its roots in the central teaching regarding the cross of Christ.[123]

---

115. 2 Cor 12:7–10.

116. 2 Cor 11:18.

117. 2 Cor 11:21–27.

118. 2 Cor 12:7–10.

119. Kruse, *Second Epistle*, 207.

120. Frederick Houk Borsch compares those cultures, in *Power in Weakness*, 117.

121. 2 Cor 4:7; 1 Cor 12:9; Eph 3:7. Hawthorne et al., *Dictionary of Paul*, 724.

122. Bromiley, *International Standard Bible Encyclopedia*, 928.

123. Humble, "Power as a Cultural Theme," 290.

What is the message to the Hui? Compared to the majority, the Hui are relatively weak, and this naturally motivates the YEU-Hui to seek power here on earth. However, the Bible can teach them that the power that comes from physical, economic, and political manipulation is not real. This message can show the Hui that the cross has stronger power than they are seeking. The cross is the origin of the power that can truly empower the YEU-Hui. The text says that when the Hui are weak, God is close to them, and there is reason for God to allow them to be weak. Weakness is not a curse, but a channel through which God may empower the Hui if they come to Jesus.

SUMMARY

Jesus was in a marginal group and lived among them. Jesus also knows the gruesome and heartbreaking history of the Hui. That although the Hui have lived in China more than a thousand years, they are still familiar strangers to the Chinese majority.

The Hui cultural theme is power and pride, and the representative cultural symbol of this power and pride is *qingzhen*. The *qingzhen* character means "purity and truth," and it symbolizes the Hui ethnic superiority and unity. The Bible introduces new and divine meaning to the *qingzhen*. For a new view of *qingzhen*, seven messages were built as a bridge for communicating the gospel. The Bible also has messages about these themes, but it will give divine and ultimate *qingzhen*. Seven messages that are introduced in this chapter seem to be a bridge for communicating the gospel. The following are abstracts of these seven messages.

Jesus is not only mighty enough to give the YEU-Hui power and prosperity to survive among the majority, but he also wants to lift the Hui up among the nations as he raised the Galileans from their plight. This is what the Hui truly want and need: a means to realize pride and power.

The Hui need to know God who has a father's heart. The father's heart is wider and deeper than the Hui imagination. God accepts the YEU-Hui with love before he judges them religiously. The Hui need to know God, who can receive them unconditionally into his kingdom. Jesus wants to save the YEU-Hui from shame and recovers their honor as the father recovered his second son.

Jesus' antithesis in the Sermon on the Mount (message 3), and the book of Hebrews' call to despising shame, and honorable disgrace (message 5) tells the Hui to learn true honor. The Hui should know that fearing persecution from their community could turn into absolute reward from God. Therefore, if the YEU-Hui are persecuted for following Jesus, they should expect true honor on the day of judgment. Christ assumed the YEU-Hui shame on the cross, and prepares to give real *qingzhen* to the Hui.

The Hui need to know the divine paradox. The weak Chinese minority is not weak in Christ. As he experienced God's power through weakness, Paul says that God will divinely reveal his power through the Hui weakness. God has a plan for the Hui and wants them to be strong by the power of God. Jesus saved his people and empowers them by the power of God, and he will do the same for the Hui.

The seven cultural messages become an important part of church planting among the YEU-Hui. By including this cultural message, church planting will be a more integrated and complex contextual process.

7

Necessity of a Contextual Church among the YEU-Hui

A CULTURALLY APPROPRIATE CHURCH is necessary for effective communication of the gospel. In order to design an appropriate church for the YEU-Hui, it's necessary to integrate appropriate sociocultural understanding, background study, and cultural themes. A contextualization process will guide this integration process, which will produce a culturally appropriate church for the Hui. This design for culturally appropriate churches will provide basal data for receptor-oriented communication strategy.

PRECEDENT THEORIES TO CONTEXTUALIZATION

In order to form contextualization theories, it is necessary to study and integrate precedent studies in theological approach, missiological approach, and biblical approach. In addition to this, having a theoretical understanding of the indigenous and nonofficial church in the Chinese context will lay a foundation for the contextualization process.

Theological Foundations

What is contextualization? What is the difference between contextualization theology and traditional theology? Traditional theology places emphasis upon what the text says, and people see their problems primarily through their own scriptural perspective. This view may preserve the authority of the Scripture, but through this, Christians have limited understandings of their very world because they see the context through their understanding of the Bible, and their viewpoint of the Bible is also limited by their perspective. As a result, the word has only one direction of communication with the world; there is no dialogue. In this perspective, Christians cannot try to rediscover the word from their cultural situation. Through this one-way conversation, theologians have caused unbalanced communication between people's needs and the teachings of the Bible. As a result, this theology has become isolated from the people's context.

Contextualization theory, however, is a dialogue between the people's needs and biblical themes. Therefore, contextualized theology is the dynamic reflection carried out by the particular church upon its own life in light of the Word of God and historic Christian truth.[1] The contextualization process tries to bind faith and life. It combines God and our lives. Harvie M. Conn emphasized this point:

> Contextual theology merges the two questions of proclamation and presence into one: "doing the will of God" (Mt. 6:10; 7:21) in "doing the truth" (1 Jn. 1:6). Doctrine and Christian living, faith and life, "orthodoxy" and "orthopraxis" cannot be separated, held in balance, or even considered apart from each other.[2]

Kraft describes God, who seeks to employ appropriate sociocultural vehicles to reach those receptors, as reaching people in a way that shows us an example of what it means to be a contextualizer.[3]

Incarnation is a core spirit of contextualization. Disclosure of God himself—his humble attitude when he communicated with people as a human being—is an example of incarnation. Jesus chose to be "within the frame of reference of human beings, so that, in spite of the tremendous risk involved, he might earn the respect of and, therefore, the right to be listened to by human beings."[4] Therefore, Gilliland said, "The Word which became flesh dwells among us. . . . Contextual theology will open up the way for communication of the gospel in ways that allow the hearer to understand and accept."[5]

There are several kinds of contextualization models. Stephen B. Beavans introduces five different models of contextualization theology:

1. Gilliland, *World Among Us*, 12–13.
2. Conn, *Eternal World and Changing Worlds*, 232.
3. Kraft, *Contextualizing Communication*, 135.
4. Kraft, "Incarnation," 212.
5. Gilliland, *World Among Us*, 3.

anthropological, transcendental, praxis, synthetic, and translation.⁶ Beavans characterized and categorized each of the five models by how they put different weight on either the cultural situation or the Scripture. Some models put their emphasis on the Scripture, so they see and analyze their situation from view of Scripture. Others put their emphasis on the situation, viewing and analyzing Scripture from the view of situation.

According to P. Hiebert, when facing a new culture, missionaries sometimes "reject most of the old beliefs and customs as 'pagan,'" in contrast to a missionary who "opens the doors to syncretism of all kinds." Finally they "will mix with their new found faith and produce various forms of neopaganism."⁷ To avoid these two extremes, he introduced "critical contextualization."⁸

P. Hiebert, R. Daniel Shaw, and Tite Tienou introduced the four steps of "critical contextualization," as a process: phenomenological analysis, ontological reflection, critical evaluation, and missiological transformation.⁹ This model enables Christian messages to be internalized within a Muslim context. Clayton Parnell Cloer explains critical contextualization.

> Whereas colonialism disguised the Gospel in a Western costume and syncretism diluted the Gospel with cultural accommodation, critical contextualization reveals the pure Gospel message in the forms of the host culture. Critical contextualization benefits the hearers.¹⁰

According to Gilliland, P. Hiebert's critical contextualization neither denies nor indiscriminately accepts original forms or culture. Rather, it analyzes and critiques old forms, symbols, and rituals by gathering information from the original culture, extracting the meaning of the form, comparing biblical definitions, reviewing biblical contexts of specific events, and evaluating the old forms in light of biblical teaching. Finally, critical contextualization can create a new contextualized Christian practice, embracing change and renewal.¹¹ In particular, P. Hiebert

---

6. Beavans, *Models of Contextual Theology*, 27.
7. Hiebert, "Cultural Differences," 381–82.
8. Hiebert, "Critical Contextualization," 111.
9. Hiebert et al., *Understanding Folk Religion*, 22.
10. Cloer, "Samuel Zwemer," 150.
11. Gilliland, "Doing Theology in Context," 37.

emphasizes that missionaries should exercise a heightened sensitivity to cultural forms and meaning.[12]

This critical contextualization becomes a basal tool in developing church-planting strategy for the Hui. Chapter 6 already used this tool to identify Hui cultural themes.

Syncretism and Contextualization

Syncretism makes the culture or situation a master of the gospel. Syncretism "involves an accommodation of content, a synthesis of beliefs, and an amalgamation of world views."[13] Conn introduces three areas in the hermeneutical process where syncretism can exist: in exegesis, in perception, and in communication with the receptor. "The sender may refuse to adapt God's meanings to new cultural forms." Or, "the receptor may be overly dependent on their culture thus may not able to 'hear' the message."[14] James F. Engel describes that cultural syncretism can "integrate the biblical message and cultural norms in such a way that the two become almost indistinguishable. The message then becomes so contaminated that its truth is obscured."[15]

Dynamic Equivalence in Churchness

The dynamic equivalence model introduces how to remove the messenger's situation from messenger, and then redress the message with the new situational form. Regarding dynamic equivalence in churchness, Kraft said that "the cultural forms through which these meanings are expressed are to be as appropriate to today's cultures as were those of biblical peoples to their cultures. Christians should function in today's contexts."[16]

Church also needs to change its form when the gospel is transferring to another cultural zone. Every church in different cultures and times need to have their own appropriate cultural forms as a vehicle of transmitting God's word without changing its meaning. As John Parratt said, "The Gospel has never existed, and can never exist, in abstraction outside a particular and specific context."[17]

12. Hiebert, "Form and Meaning," 109.
13. Nida, *Message and Mission*, 131.
14. Conn, *Eternal World and Changing Worlds*, 189.
15. Engel, *Contemporary Christian Communication*, 25.
16. Kraft, "Dynamic Equivalence Churches," 115.
17. Parratt, *Guide to Doing Theology*, 35, 19.

Some churches may claim to be indigenous, having achieved the three-self goals, "yet not be contextual, while it is hard to conceive of a fully contextual church that is not at the same time autonomous in these three areas."[18]

In some cases, a three-self church will merely let the local leaders maintain their churches with foreign ways. Kraft said that the three-self does not ensure indigenous. The cultural structures are operated and the meanings attached to them both by the church itself and by the surrounding community.[19]

In addition to the three-self criteria, P. Hiebert and E. H. Meneses have suggested the need for a self-theologizing procedure by locals. He said of local Christian leaders that "their theology is shaped more by their culture than by Scripture. They often see better than we where our theologies are more a product of western culture than of biblical teaching."[20]

The dynamic equivalence of churchness seeks to let the local church have the original church dynamics of the Bible. Kraft explains,

> In each case the pattern developed in response to the felt needs of the members of the culture and subculture in which the particular local church operated.[21]

The dynamic equivalence of churchness addresses cultural themes and the situation of church, then reorganizes the church systems and structures in culturally appropriate ways, just as the New Testament church did.

Biblical Foundations of Contextualization

The Bible shows many cases of contextualization. In many cases, Jesus did not communicate with people from where he was, but instead he incarnated himself into each situation. He used different manners to communicate with different people. Jesus and Paul both diversified their form of the gospel in every case. Phil Parshall introduces the examples in the gospels:

> In the Bible we observe a wide array of approaches to people. . . . A basic principle was to start where the person was in his own

18. Gilliland, *Pauline Theology*, 212.
19. Kraft, *Christianity in Culture*, 320.
20. Hiebert and Meneses, *Incarnational Ministry*, 164.
21. Kraft, *Christianity in Culture*, 323.

orientation to life. . . . In each case, Jesus was meeting people on their own unique level. The needs of the receptor group were uppermost at all times in His thinking.

Christ embraced a strategy that was contextually related, in initial witness, to felt needs. The receptor's attention was captured by a message that quickly entered into his worldview.[22]

Cultural issues were debated as far back as the early church. In the book of Acts, one issue was that some Jewish Christians asked Gentiles to follow the Moses' law, which caused leaders and apostles to hold the council at Jerusalem.[23] By the conclusion of the Jerusalem council, both the Jewish believers and Gentiles could discern culturally appropriate forms in different churches and "were glad for its encouraging message."[24]

The cultural issues are often a matter of cultural form and its meaning. The church in Corinth had debate about food that had been sacrificed to idols. Here, Paul did not say whether the meat itself was clean or not, but people's spiritual strength could decide whether to eat meat or not.[25] Paul was more concerned with the situation than with the form of the action of eating food itself. Parshall points out five distinct contextual roles in which Paul grappled with serious and complex contextual issues as he crossed the great barrier that separated the Jewish and Gentile worlds.[26] These are "servant role," "Jewish role," "proselyte role," "Gentile role," and "weak role."[27] Paul chose these roles depending on the situation for "the sake of the gospel that I may share in its blessings."[28]

When the gospel is spread cross-culturally, cultural issues are always being raised. The Bible respects culture and the receptor's situation, and yet its message form needs to be transferred while preserving the meaning.

According to contextualization theory, when church planters design the future YEU-Hui church, the internal dynamics of the new church need to be biblical, but in a form that is culturally natural for the YEU-Hui. Therefore, understanding the real essence of the church in the Bible

---

22. Parshall, "Contextualized Approach," 19–20.
23. Acts 15:2, 5, 9.
24. Acts 15:31.
25. 1 Cor 8:10–12.
26. 1 Cor 9:19–23.
27. Parshall, "Contextualized Approach," 24–25.
28. 1 Cor 9:23.

is essential. David Watson's summary of Christ's glorious picture of the purpose of God's church on earth in John 17 seems to be the essence of church. Those essences are the glory of God, the word of God, the joy of God, and unity under the love of God.[29] He also introduces four different ways the word *ekklesia* is used in the New Testament. These are as a universal church, a particular local church, an actual assembly of believers gathered anywhere, a small house church, and the regular meeting place for a small group of believers in any one town or city.[30] The future YEU-Hui church needs to have these four essences of *ekklesia*.

The terms in Acts 2:46–47 also show us the core issues of the New Testament church. These are "day by day," "one mind," "in the temple," "house to house," "meals together with gladness and sincerity of heart," "praising God," "having favor with people," and "growth." All of these terminologies represent crucial and core strategies within the church.

Missiological Foundation of Contextualization

Approaching contextualization from a missiological view is also important. There are several missiological factors that need to be considered as Christians plant churches among Muslims. Two of these issues must be considered in regard to contextualization: Muslim community pressure and commonness between the two religions.

First, one big missiological issue in a traditional Muslim society involves Muslim community pressure that comes from adopting a new faith along with the changing community concepts in modern society.

In traditional Muslim society, everyone is a member of his or her community, and at the same time, all the community gives community and peer pressure to individual. Saving face is more than an individual problem in cultures that are centered upon honor and shame, like many Muslim communities. Since "wherever [Muslims] go, they represent their families and tribes," an individual's decision is not limited to himself or herself.[31] When a Muslim decides to convert to Christianity, it means betraying their people, and family. Shaw describes shame in a face-to-face society: "Accordingly, an activity is bad because the individual is caught, thereby disrupting group harmony.... The individual involved is shamed

---

29. Watson, *I Believe in the Church*, 39.
30. Ibid., 66.
31. Muller, *Honor and Shame*, 48.

because of this disharmony (the *result* of the action) not because of the action itself."[32]

Therefore, unless the community network looses their density of relationship, the personal stress of the convert and shame of the family still exists. In modern society, though the YEU-Hui primary network—kin and family—is still the same, their secondary networks are rapidly changing and expanding. Therefore, rather than being concerned with traditional community pressure, the YEU-Hui are becoming more concerned with how they are seen by their friends, company, or social organizations. Family still puts a lot of pressure on Hui individuals as well. This is their new modern community pressure.

Second, the reuse of commonness between Christianity and Islam as Muslims convert is another issue. One of the ongoing theological debates is how much the new Christian believers of Muslim background can adapt or reuse their Islamic forms in exercising their new faith. Woodberry demonstrated the theoretical basis of "re-using common pillars," and found that there is commonness, so that MBBs can continue to use their Muslim worship forms even after beginning to follow Jesus. He suggested reusing five common pillars: confession of faith (*shahada*), ritual prayer (*salat*), almsgiving (*zakat*), fasting (*sawm*), and pilgrimage (*hajj*). Woodberry said that the MBB can reuse those rituals because those "'pillars of Islam' have for the most part been used before by Jews and Christians and with some adjustments, are being used again."[33]

Later, Woodberry and Shah Ali developed a contextualized church-planting strategy in a South Asian Muslim society. Woodberry and Ali described it as Christian faith in Muslim dress.[34]

John and Anna Travis summarized the several factors that "impact individual Muslim contexts at the ground level, determining in part the ways in which Muslim background believers (MBBs) in Jesus follow Christ."[35] Those factors are political, social, demographical, historical, cultural. Added to these, several more factors are closely linked to this impact. Those are aspirations and future directions in which Muslims of a particular ethnic group, ethnic realities like whether they are multiethnic or monocultural, socioreligious variance, interaction that the people have

---

32. Shaw, *Transculturation*, 100.
33. Woodberry, *Muslim and Christians*, 306–7.
34. Woodberry and Ali, "South Asia," 680–82.
35. Travis, "Factors Affecting the Identity," 196.

with those called Christians in the past, and finally, on the individual level, what has the experience of Islam meant to a particular Muslim?[36]

In *Evangelical Missions Quarterly* (*EMQ*), John Travis introduces six levels of contextualization for Muslim evangelism, labeled C1 through C6. Those using level C1 do not change their church tradition and language for approaching Muslims. Level C2 is the same as C1, but uses the Muslims' language. Level C3 is contextualized, Christ-centered communities using insider language and religiously neutral insider cultural forms. Level C4 is contextualized Christ-centered communities using insider language and biblically permissible cultural and Islamic forms. Level C5 is Christ-centered communities of Messianic Muslims, who have accepted Jesus as Lord. They are still legally and socially bonded to the community of Islam, but participation in corporate Islamic worship varies from person to person. Level C6 goes further. It is Christ-centered communities of secret, underground believers.[37]

Parshall criticized the C5 for being "on very shaky theological and missiological ground" regarding it "as high syncretism . . . regardless of motivation."[38] As a response to this, both Gilliland and Travis said we should not decide in haste, but we need to put much missiological effort into seeking the path and trust the Holy Spirit to guide these Muslim converts.[39] Finally, Ralph D. Winter recalled the fact that Christianity also spent a long history forming sound doctrine as current Christians regard natural doctrine, so Christians should "not hastily judge the level of faith of Muslim seekers."[40]

Later, Travis and Travis reported about 86 percent of cross-cultural workers' ministry falls into the C3–C5.[41] Travis and Travis continually prove this and want to identify the C5 MBB as a part of the believers of Christ.

---

36. Ibid., 197–99.
37. Travis, "C1 and C6 Spectrum," 407–8.
38. Parshall, "Danger!," 404–10.
39. Gilliland, "Context Is Critical," 411–15; Travis, "Must All Muslims Leave."
40. Winter, "Going Far Enough," 667.
41. Travis, "Factors Affecting the Identity," 195–96.

Part One: A Cultural Study of the Hui and YEU-Hui

Planting Nonofficial and Indigenous Churches among the Chinese Muslims

In order to create a church-planting design among the YEU-Hui, there are at least two areas that need to be studied: church-planting situations in China, and theories of indigenous church planting. Studying those two areas is important for two reasons. First, understanding Chinese church growth among the Han is important. Both of these people groups are under the same government, and the Han indigenous and nonofficial churches have grown quite successfully during the last several decades. Second, in order for the YEU-Hui to be self-sustaining and prosperous, it's necessary to understand indigenous theory for the future church. This combination of two studies will suggest a new design of planting nonofficial indigenous churches among the YEU-Hui.

First, in order to develop an effective strategy for planting nonofficial churches among the YEU-Hui, it is worth studying the characteristics of the Chinese church under the Chinese government. The goal of the Cultural Revolution (1966–76) "was elimination of the 'Four Olds': old ideology, old customs, old habits, old cultures."[42] The government led people to eliminate all kinds of religion. In 1951, the Chinese government decided that the Three-Self Patriotic Movement (TSPM) church was the only Christian religious organization allowed. Therefore, the government views house churches as politically illegal groups. However, the house church group is much bigger than the TSPM. Patrick Johnston and Jason Mandryk in Operation World summarize that there are about sixty-nine million Christians in China. Among them, there are 8.1 million Catholics, 17 million members of TSPM, and 44.1 million other unofficial Protestants. This means that the total of all unofficial church members—so-called house church or underground church members—is about 2.6 times the members of TSPM.[43] Since, underground church seems to have quite a political flavor, this research will express it as a house church.

House churches in China have quite similar dynamics to churches in the books of Acts (2:42–47). Carl Lawrence and David Wang summarized six characteristics of the Chinese house church that had a basis in the New Testament: learnable church (2:42), praying church (2:42),

---

42. Adeney, *China*, 247.
43. Johnstone et al., *Operation World*, China section.

miracle church (2:43), praising church (2:47), accepted church (2:47), and mission-minded church (8:4).[44]

In order to understand these better, it's necessary to know the theology of Chinese house churches. William A. Dyrness has characterized it as a theology of suffering. In Chinese churches, these sufferings, especially from persecution, still exist, even today.[45] Dyrness said that "suffering, then, becomes a key theme in their testimonies and singing, and leads them to strongly identify with the sufferings of Christ."[46] According to David Aikman, people think recent persecution "is because of China's Olympic Games in 2008 and they want to be sure they control everything very tightly in their country."[47]

Chinese church grows mainly by the members' natural networks and relationships. New members come to church through the influence of their friends and family members. The meeting locations and times are not always fixed. No matter when and where they meet, they have fellowship. Their meeting programs are quite flexible. Their community activity is not limited to the worship meeting, but includes all kinds of fellowship. For example, Christians often introduce job opportunities to other Christians, or visit and spend time with others. In my observation, when there was a SARS (Severe Acute Respiratory Syndrome) outbreak in 2003, students could not leave their school, and had to remain in dormitories for two months. They had their meetings without spiritual support from outside. They got together in their dormitories or yards, visited weak believers, and helped to wash other members' clothes, believing that those were Christian activities. In these days, in my observation, Chinese Christians rapidly reshaped their programs in modern directions, like G-12, Church Planting Movement, Charismatic movement, and intercessory prayer meetings.

Though Chinese house churches are not official, and the government regards them as illegal groups, the church has similar characteristics to the church in the book of Acts. Chinese Christians have built their church on the theology of suffering under persecution and historical disasters.

---

44. Lawrence and Wang, *Coming Influence of China*, 31–53.
45. Dyrness, *Invitation to Cross-Cultural Theology*, 52.
46. Ibid.
47. Aikman, "Reason Is Christianity," 5.

Second, understanding indigenous church planting is important for designing YEU-Hui churches. Indigenous church is a group of believers who live out their life, including their socialized Christian activity, in the patterns of the local society, and for whom any transformation of that society comes out of their felt needs under the guidance of the Holy Spirit and the Scriptures.[48]

Melvin Hodges observes that the New Testament church was indigenous. Indigenization has the three-self factors: self-propagating, self-governing, and self-supporting.[49]

Charles Brock added two more selfs as he characterized indigenous church as having five selfs: self-governing, self-supporting, self-teaching, self-expressing, and self-propagating.[50] Of the indigenous church, Brock described that "people must be met where they are in the native context of things."[51] Applying the command to "let each man abide in that calling wherein he was called" to the mission field,[52] John L. Nevius also emphasized that "Christianity should not disturb the social relations of its adherents, but requires them to be content with their lot, and to illustrate the Gospel in the spheres of life in which they are called."[53] In order to plant indigenous churches, Tom A. Steffen emphasizes that mission agencies should have a phase-out strategy.[54]

The indigenous movement is not driven by expatriates, but rather by local leaders who are led by the Holy Spirit. Roland Allen summarizes two of the Apostle Paul's principles for indigenous church planting: "(1) that he was a preacher of Gospel, not of law, and (2) that he must retire from his converts to give place for Christ. The spirit in which he was able to do this was the spirit of faith."[55] Allen concluded that the indigenous church movement allowed us to go back to the Bible to revive the spontaneous expansion of church. He said that spontaneous expansion means the "unexhorted and unorganized activity of individual

---

48. Smalley, "Cultural Implications," 55.
49. Hodges, *Indigenous Church*, 12.
50. Brock, *Indigenous Church Planting*, 90–95.
51. *Principles and Practice*, 95.
52. 1 Cor 7:20.
53. Nevius, *Planting and Development*, 19.
54. Steffen, *Passing the Baton*, 20.
55. Allen, *Missionary Methods*, 148.

members of the Church explaining to others the Gospel which they have found for themselves."[56]

Donald A. McGavran's homogeneous unit principle also supports this need of planting indigenous church. "People like to become Christians without crossing racial, linguistic, or class barriers," then he insisted that "the conversion should occur within a minimum of social dislocation."[57] McGavran's idea of "a people movement" lays a profound theoretical basis for indigenous church planting. He said,

> A people movement results from the joint decision of a number of individuals all from the same people group, which enables them to become Christians without social dislocation, while remaining in full contact with their non-Christian relatives thus enabling other segments of that people group, across years, after suitable instruction, to come to similar decisions and from Christian churches made up exclusively of members of that people.[58]

R. D. Winter and Bruce A. Koch said that "the church does not readily grow within people where relevant churches do not exist."[59] Without being an indigenous church, local church continually depends on foreign support and cannot expect to naturally grow.

Based upon this theoretical framework of indigenous church planting, Daniel Sinclair introduced the seven steps of pioneer church-planting phases:

Phase 1: Forming, preparing, and launching the team

Phase 2: Learning the language and culture

Phase 3: Preaching the gospel to groups and individuals

Phase 4: Discipling believers and working toward gathering

Phase 5: Developing the body of believers

Phase 6: Empowering and installing leaders; Beginnings of reproduction

Phase 7: Reproduction and movement.[60]

56. *Spontaneous Expansion* 7.
57. Wagner, *Understanding Church Growth*, x.
58. Ibid., 223.
59. Winter et al., *Perspectives*, 510.
60. Sinclair, *Vision of the Possible*, 56–57.

Sinclair explains the practical purposes for these seven steps as an indigenous church-planting resource.[61]

CURRENT SITUATION OF YEU-HUI CHURCH PLANTING

Before designing a contextual church, reviewing the current situation and checking the resources of the YEU-Hui mission can help Christians to address where to begin their next mission. Mission to the Hui is at quite an early stage, but the strategists can make a good start if they learn exactly what their particular ministry situations are.

Current Situations of Ministry Teams

To protect the related people and for other security reasons, the church-planting teams will be referred to as A, B, C, and D. Data was collected from them through interviews. Members in teams A and B are from Western backgrounds, and C is an international team. Team D is an Asian team. Team A is comprised of three couples and three singles, and team B has two couples. Team C has been divided and multiplied into new teams, so the records in the following section are not current. In contrast with those from other teams, team D members do not live together in one city; some live in China and some live outside of China. Team D's ministry is quite focused on community development in rural areas.

Several Ministry Cases

The ministries of these four teams can be categorized in four areas: initial-stage evangelism and community development, facilitation, direct evangelism, and mobilizing the Han churches.

Team A and D put all their effort into initial-stage ministry. Those activities include medical ministry, digging wells, and tent-making. Some of the team A members work as facilitators or catalysts. For example, they distribute the *Jesus Film* or translate Hui ministry materials. Some workers are in ministry as strategic coordinators, and they network and share resources with other workers who are working with the Hui.

Team B and C are in direct contact with the Hui and are introducing the gospel, but slowly. There are two types of direct evangelism to the Hui. First, workers create ministry opportunities for the YEU-Hui through campus ministry. Though there are few success stories at this

---

61. Ibid., 56.

point, the fruit of this ministry will have a huge influence. Another type is friendship evangelism.

Many house church groups send their workers out for church planting. These workers are called *yiminxuanjiao* (移民宣教) [eeminsuanjiao], which means "immigrant missionaries."[62] Though their numbers are few, some of these local evangelists have a burden for the Hui. In particular, the "Back to Jerusalem Movement" received the spotlight and became very effective among Chinese and expatriate Christians. Leaders of this movement have stated, "We believe the very least we should do is give a tithe of these leaders to foreign missions. That is how we first arrived at the figure of 100,000."[63] This movement encourages many Chinese to have a vision for spreading renewal from China to the West and to Jerusalem.

Reviews of Current Church-Planting Efforts

Upon reviewing the current efforts of indigenous church planting and contextualization among the YEU-Hui, four significant points were discovered.

First, church planters need to consider cultural appropriateness. In many cases, Western or Chinese materials are directly applied in missions to the Hui without contextualization. Very few materials have been developed for Chinese Muslims, and local leaders and expatriates introduce the gospel without contextualization. Sherwood Lingenfelter says that as a result of this, expatriates bring some tools and methods that may be "thoroughly contaminated by their culture."[64]

Second, a healthy and indigenous mission movement among the Chinese house church network is needed for successful, long-term missions mobilization. Recently, some of Chinese churches have had a vision for reaching Muslims. In reality, many Christians' vision for missions is strongly influenced by foreigners. However, this mission movement also needs to be indigenous.

Third, the initial stage of evangelism is an important component to Hui ministry. Having a holistic approach is quite important. For instance,

---

62. Despite this interpretation, *yiminxuanjiao* does not always mean missionaries who go abroad. It quite rather means evangelists who left their hometown or home church for ministry. Sometimes church leaders who frequently visit and do itinerary ministry are called *yiminxuanjiao*.

63. Hattaway, *Operation China*, 116.

64. Lingenfelter, *Transforming Culture* 12.

community development can be a wonderful ministry in this holistic approach. Sadly, many workers ignore this initial ministry stage, and jump into direct ministry, but the results are quite poor.

Finally, there is a strong need for developing contextualized tools, like books, programs, and methods. Current tools are mainly translated from overseas.

CRITERIA FOR YEU-HUI CONTEXTUALIZED CHURCH

Having completed theoretical studies and reviews related to the current situation, now it is time to find the criteria for contextual church planting among the YEU-Hui. There are two ideas that are quite innovative and have outstanding suggestions for contextualization theory among traditional Muslims: (1) Woodberry and Ali's idea of "Muslim dressed Christian faith," and (2) Parshall's idea of "the Christian *umma*."[65] These ideas prepare a theoretical basis for MBBs to continue using Muslim rituals and lifestyle along with Christian meaning. By having influence from Woodberry and Ali's and Parshall's idea, the author suggested six new forms of the Hui that will touch their needs.[66] Those forms are togetherness, networking, ceremonies, brother and sisterhood, to be a social model, power-oriented Christianity.

However, these theories—Muslim-dressed Christian faith, or the Christian *umma*—do not seem to always be applicable to YEU groups. Even though they have Muslim background, many YEU-Hui people's lifestyles are quite far from the traditional religious rituals. They rarely go to mosque and scarcely participate in religious and community activities. This means that a new approach of contextualization is needed, and the new approach needs to better emphasize their social relationships and lifestyle in modern society.

The process of contextualization needs to begin where the people are familiar. Therefore, identifying the current YEU-Hui situation is important for church planting. The process of first contact for evangelism to the YEU-Hui is quite similar to the YEU-Han dynamics. As it was proved in the field research, the impact of modernization gives the YEU-Hui much commonality with the majority YEU-Han group. The YEU-Hui are similar to the YEU-Han at least in their preference

---

65. Woodberry and Ali, "South Asia," 680–82; Woodberry, *Muslims and Christians*, 306–7; Parshall, *Beyond the Mosque*, 219.

66. Kim, "New Entrance Gate," 83–85.

and needs. Therefore researching how the YEU-Han group receives the gospel is a good starting point for introducing the gospel to the YEU-Hui. From my observations and experiences, many young and urban Han Christian groups use printed materials that are directly translated from Western discipleship training and evangelism materials. One interesting point about Chinese Christians is that they are quite relationship-centered, and the relationship is quite holistic. The human factor and relationships are more primary channels for communicating the gospel than are the media. Most Christians have received the gospel from people who they already knew. When they get together, leaders not only care for members' spiritual needs, but also care for all kinds of other needs. They encourage helping each other do school homework together, going out for picnics, introducing job opportunities, and visiting parents' houses during the vacation.

Second, though their initial situation as they receive the gospel is similar, the YEU-Hui church-planting and discipleship process seems to be quite different from that of the YEU-Han. As the converted YEU-Hui grow spiritually, the community needs to reach deeper levels within the new Christian lives; therefore, fellowship needs to consider their traditional cultural themes: power and pride. At the same time, there are many issues that a small new YEU-Hui Christian group can deal with. In an urban situation, by emphasizing the YEU-Hui person's needs to belong, to be accepted, to be proud, and to be honored, the new church will touch upon the Hui traditional theme of seeking power and pride. The new healthy Christian in YEU-Hui fellowship needs to deal with those newly-raised cultural issues.

Since *qingzhen* represents the center of their traditional spirit, the new YEU-Hui community of believers needs to touch and develop a biblical *qingzhen* concept. Because *qingzhen* means purity and truth, under this new biblical *qingzhen* spirit, people will seek purity in the Lord and enjoy the truth of God. The following design contains suggestions for the YEU-Hui church with consideration of contextual theories.

New Identity of MBB

The Muslim background believer (MBB) identity is most broadly and profoundly characterized as being a follower of Jesus. Here are several identities that new MBBs need to know about who they are.

First, MBB status and position is dramatically changed from "a person who submits" to a son and daughter of the Almighty. The meaning of a Muslim is "one who submits or obeys" and "the implication is one who submits to God and obeys."[67] The Bible says that we are children and heirs of God.[68] At the same time, the MBBs are those who are reconciled with God and are his ambassadors.[69]

Second, followers of Jesus need to obey what he said to his disciples. Jesus said that each follower "must deny himself and take up is cross daily and follow me."[70] Therefore, a follower is one who has totally volunteered a spiritual allegiance to a relationship with God.

Third, a follower of Jesus needs to be salt and light in community.[71] The new believers should not to be extracted from their origins. As it is written, "So, brethren, in whatever state each was called, there let him remain with God."[72] John D. C. Anderson says, "Why should not the converted Muslim reach his fellow-Muslims in the same way, i.e. by not repudiating the 'state in which he was called'?"[73] Through the MBB being salt and light, other community members may praise the Father.

H-H Ratio and Contextual Worship Style

The YEU-Hui group is not culturally static, nor homogeneous, but it has many subculture groups. Each Hui subgroup has a different degree of adaptation toward the majority Han culture. The Chinese call this adaptation as *Han hua*, which means Hanization. Since each degree of Hanization is different, each subgroup in the YEU-Hui has different responses to outside culture. In order to identify the degree of Hanization among the Hui, a newly conceptualized terminology needs to be defined. This new definition is called H-H ratio, and it is an acronym for the Hui to Han ratio. The H-H ratio is a scale from 1 through 10, and represents the degree to which Hui individuals or groups adapt to the Han culture. Low points on this scale mean that the person has very low Hui identity, and vise versa.

67. Braswell, *Islam*, 301.
68. Rom 8:16–17.
69. 2 Cor 5:18–20.
70. Luke 9:23.
71. Matt 5:13–16.
72. 1 Cor 7:24.
73. Anderson, "Missionary Approach to Islam," 296.

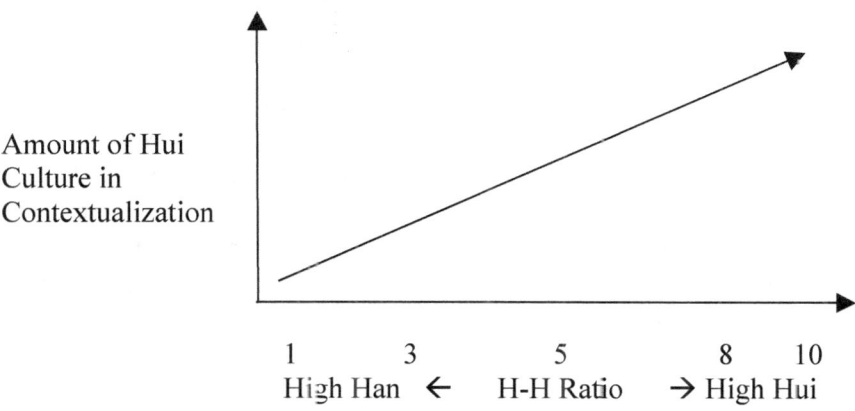

H-H Ratio vs. Contextualization Scale

Groups with different H-H ratios need a different degree of Han factors in the process of their contextualization. Figure 19 shows this concept. The vertical axis is the degree to which they require Han culture in their contextualization. Therefore, a group that is marked low on the H-H ratio scale needs more consideration of Han traditional culture in the contextualization process, and vice versa.

No matter how much of a degree a group requires cultural consideration, all the meetings should have at least three objectives in their worship: focus directed toward the living God, edifying the body of Christ, and dependence on the presence of the Holy Spirit.[74] Here are several areas that need to be considered in contextualizing YEU-Hui meetings.

Prayer and Praise

If it is possible, YEU-Hui pray five times a day, participate in a contextualized *shahada* (confession of faith), or reuse *salat* (ritual prayer). However, since, the YEU-Hui are quite modernized urbanites, and their religious activities are not quite active, considering this traditional religious ritual in their contextualization process does not seem to be appropriate. They may prefer a more freestyle prayer rather than a traditional religious style. This can be accomplished in cell groups or in one-to-one discipleship time. This freestyle prayer may not be appropriate in the formal worship time.

---

74. Watson, *I Believe in the Church*, 197–98.

Praise and song need to be contextualized to YEU-Hui. Chinese Sufism typically has chanting during worship. Interestingly, Hui music does not seem well developed. However in my observation, in a multi-ethnic Christian meeting, most MBB YEU-Hui enjoy Western-style and Han Chinese gospel music. Therefore, it seems better to develop Bible-based chanting. Having Chinese and Western gospel songs in a YEU-Hui meeting seems to be proper. As their fellowship grows and training goes deeper, the development of new worship songs is recommended. The development of Chinese Christian fashioned, minor key songs or Bible verses with Muslim chanting style is suggested.

Evangelism

The process of conversion from Islam to Christianity needs to be as simple as a Muslim confessing his or her faith. The Bible simply says, "Confess with your mouth Jesus is Lord and believe in your heart that God raised him from the dead, and you will be saved."[75]

As in other Han churches, the YEU-Hui may hear about Jesus from a person who they know already. As a result, the YEU-Hui church network may overlap with their social network. Because of this, the church may have members who came from similar occupations or families. In this situation, *oikos*, or personal network evangelism, seems to be effective.

McGavran's theory of "a people movement" seems to work among the YEU-Hui just as in an Asian church. People generally accept Christianity because their friends or father believes. A father's conversion has a serious influence upon the conversion of family members.[76]

Urban junctures and virtual spaces, like coffee shops, universities, cell phone shops, Western fast food restaurants, and virtual communities are modern places where non-Hui Christians can freely meet the YEU-Hui. Job training and English lessons can meet the needs of the YEU-Hui since personal ability is of great concern to young people.

The Word of God

Having a practical Bible study is recommended for the development of YEU-Hui spiritual growth. The Bible study topics need to be easy to

---

75. Rom 10:9.
76. Wagner, *Understanding Church Growth*, 223.

apply and must aim for change in the member's lifestyle. For example, conflict management, how to love your enemy or neighbor, how to demonstrate filial duty, how to love one's spouse and children, how to listen to the voice of God, how to be salt and light within a Muslim family, ethical issues regarding engagement and marriage, and business are all good themes to study.

The style of teaching can depend on a more pictorial, parabolic approach to the gospel rather than on a European conceptual approach. Martin Goldsmith summarizes the three pragmatic advantages of the style Jesus used for teaching: (1) it does not cause anger, opposition, and rejection; (2) parabolic preaching suits traditional storytelling cultures; (3) parabolic preaching is ideal for teaching fundamental religious ideas, which are at the foundation of the gospel.[77] Additionally, a comparison study of the Bible and the Qur'an may not be a good way to equip leadership since, unlike those in Middle Eastern contexts, very few Hui can read the Qur'an.

Power and pride can be a crucial theme in their message, since this cultural theme touches upon their felt needs. Seven messages seem to form a basal message that relates to their cultural theme as a marginal group in China. Additionally, the power of Holy Spirit in their message also touches their culture.

A Model of Han Church-Based Hui Church Planting

Here is the criteria and procedure for planting a YEU-Hui church. In this procedural model, a multiethnic church is a nest of the new YEU-Hui church. In the following detailed procedures, circles represent the Hui, and squares represent the Han.

First, expatriate and Chinese Christians form a task team to plant a YEU-Hui church. The team needs to be familiar with the YEU-Hui, and must include several seekers, meaning nonbelieving Muslims. The Han members should be quite mature.

---

77. Goldsmith, "Parabolic Preaching," 219–20.

Step 1: Organize a cell with Hui and mature Han

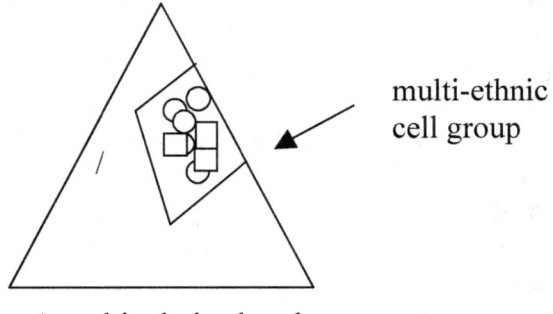

multi-ethnic cell group

A multi ethnic church

Step 1: Process of Launching Hui Church
from a Multiethnic Church Model

Second, the task team launches a multiethnic cell group of both Hui and Han; the first members should be the task team.

Step 2: Forming a half-self-governed cell

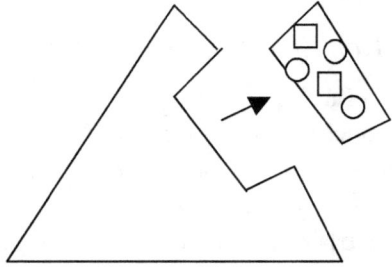

Step 2: Process of Launching Hui Church
from a Multiethnic Church Model

Third, the cell group continually focuses on evangelizing the Hui. The evangelization team members may consist of church leaders, several Hui believers, and several who have the gift of evangelism. The Hui take the initiative in the new cell, and the Han members slowly go back to their mother church.

Step 3: Forming a highly Hui concentrated cell church

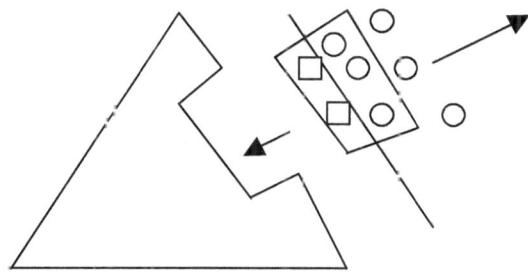

Step 3: Process of Launching Hui Church
from a Multiethnic Church Model

Fourth, the cell group is an incubator for a new YEU-Hui church. The mother church is ready to start the same process a second time. The new contextualized MBB cell multiplies into different forms.

Step 4: Multiplication

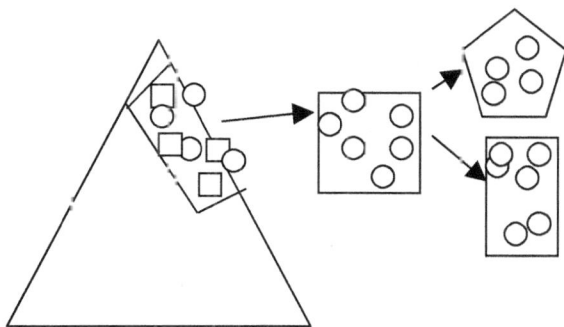

Step 4: Process of Launching Hui Church
from a Multiethnic Church Model

Fifth, the cell group multiplies, and as it grows, church leaders slowly return to their original churches. The mother churches become facilitators, continuing to support the cell groups. Different cell groups have different worship styles. Each cell becomes independent, but begins to network with other cells and churches.

Step 5: Forming the YEU-Hui church by networking

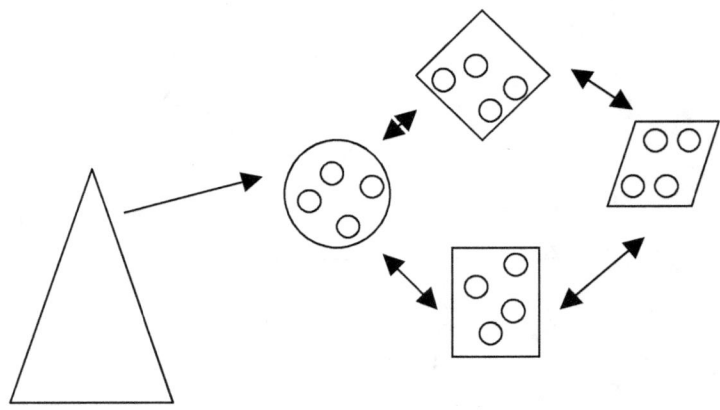

Step 5: Process of Launching Hui Church
from a Multiethnic Church Model

Contextualized Social Practices

Though many young urban Hui do not go to mosque very often, they still participate in special religious and community activities as a social practice. Chinese Muslims have three major social practices: *Kuerbangjie* (古尔邦際), or *zaishengjie* (宰牲祭); Ramadan, also known as *Fengzhai* (封斋); and *Kaizhaijie* (开斋祭). In all of these social practices, community members get together and celebrate or fast. It is very difficult for a new MBB not to participate in community activities. Rather than extract the MBB from community activity, the fellowship needs to develop its own culturally appropriate Christian community traditions.

Kuerbangjie means the day of sacrifice; it is similar to Easter or Passover. The Hui people sacrifice a lamb or cow during *Kuerbangjie* to remember God's request to Abraham to sacrifice his son Ishmael. Rather than recognizing Isaac, Ishmael, or Abraham, the Hui can instead celebrate Jesus who died for us as a lamb.

In *Kaizhaijie*, the final date of Ramadan, the YEU-Hui can partake in the Lord's Supper and love feast as a community activity. *Kaizhaijie* seems to connect well with the Lord's Supper because it is celebrated "to look back and to remember with thanksgiving, God's mercy on his people when he delivered them from the bondage of sin through the once-for-all death of his own Son."[78]

Every Hui has several ceremonies in his or her life cycle. Therefore, an MBB meeting can celebrate a contextualized life cycle, as well. According to collected data from an interview with a Hui friend, Mr. Ma, there are significant events to be celebrated annually in each community. Parents invite *ahong* to celebrate the gift of a new baby, whose religious name is given thirty days after birth. This is called *qijingming* (起经名). On the fourth day of the fourth month of the baby's fourth birthday, the parents invite *ahong* and let the child recite a few verses from the Qur'an. This celebration is called *yingxue* (迎学). At the age of twelve, parents invite *ahong* and circumcise their son; they call this *geli* (割礼). The fourth ceremonies are engagement and wedding. The Hui recognize these four ceremonies as the four big ceremonies in a person's life; this is called *xidananxingyishi* (四大男忄生儀式).

The funeral is definitely a religious and community ceremony. Extended family, neighbors, and friends get together for the funeral. Based on the meaning of the traditions, the new YEU-Hui MBB communities need to develop these ceremonies as well.

Church System

Church growth by cell group proliferation is recommended to maintain growth rate and to ensure security.[79] It is not good to carelessly open a large worship meeting to just anybody; it is safer to invite a limited number of people. However, cell groups are generally more tailored to nonbelievers who are friends of members. For security reasons, one cell's information should not carelessly be transferred between cells.

Which day between Friday and Sunday is the best day for holding a worship meeting? The Bible never mentions an exact day for worship. Most YEU-Hui are employed in modern jobs and work Monday through Friday. Therefore, leadership might consider a flexible choice between Saturday and Sunday.

What is an appropriate leadership style? Muslims respect *imam* and *ahong*. In order to answer this question, another question is raised. What kinds of people do the YEU-Hui respect these days? From my

---

78. Watson, *I Believe in the Church*, 239.

79. Security issues are treated with greater urgency in Chinese and Muslim contexts.

observations, the YEU-Hui generally respect people who are respected by other YEU-Han, no matter their ethnic origins. This means they have similar standards of respect. Asians expect their leaders to have a fatherhood leadership style—protective, brave, and strong. Parshall suggests four conditions to define a leadership style among the MBB: a man of the word of God; who feels a pastoral responsibility; who exhibits holiness, love, and righteousness; and who financially manifests a lifestyle similar to that of the local *imam*.[80] *Additionally, the modern young Chinese seem to prefer a big brother type of leadership as well.*

The New Church within the Community

As it grows, the church can impact the urban community. Like any other churches, Jesus expects the YEU-Hui church to be as salt and light in their community.[81] Since modern community consists of networks more than geographical neighborhoods, church members need to be an example, be respected, and be praised by their network members.

The new MBB church among the YEU-Hui need not limit its activities as a religious zone. They need to build stronger Christian networks not only within the church, but also in their very business area and where they live. Like Muslim business networks, the new YEU-Hui churches should not only be concerned about the religious side, but it is also recommended to think about practical and financial benefit by forming Christian business networks. Developing mutually beneficial financial relationships within the Hui ethnic group has been a long-held Hui society tradition. Through this, the Hui have protected themselves and have maintained power and pride. Additionally, the global *umma* spirit also connects the Hui and other foreign Muslims and facilitates their international business.

Through Christian brotherhood, church members can help YEU-Hui believers in business, just like it is done in the mosque, which is not only a religious place, but also the social and business center. The YEU-Hui church can facilitate international business lines among Christians.

---

80. Parshall, *Muslim Evangelism*, 182.
81. Matt 5:13–16.

SUMMARY

Theoretical studies and empirical data clearly support that the Hui need their own type of church. This new type of church needs to be indigenous, contextual, and dynamically equivalent to the church in the New Testament.

Reviewing cultural and contextual issues necessary for strategy development is important. The future YEU-Hui church needs to be more modern than are other MBB churches. Therefore, rather than reusing Islamic formal traditions, it is practical to address the YEU-Hui cultural situation and begin a contextualization process from where the YEU-Hui currently are. Because of the impact of modernization, the YEU-Hui have at least two layers in their worldview: traditional and modern. That means the mission strategy to the YEU-Hui needs to have at least two steps as a process of contextualization. The early approach steps can be similar to the YEU-Han approach, but as the YEU-Hui individuals need deeper levels of discipleship, more consideration of traditional culture is necessary.

Part Two

Communication Principle and Strategy

8

Communication Principles

IN ORDER TO COMMUNICATE his message, God gave the church an apostolic commission for the world.[1] Therefore, one calling of church is to spread the gospel into the world to expand the kingdom of God by being salt and light. The church obeys this commission through communicating the gospel, so the church needs to know how to communicate. Christian and non-Christian scholars have developed communication principles since ancient times. By studying those principles, Christians can improve their communication skills and be able to set up a more effective mission strategy to reach the YEU-Hui.

The role of the church in the world is a reciprocal relationship according to Robert Webber, quoting Paul's epistle as a root of the role of church.[2] The church needs to take responsibility and obey the commandment of God by redemptive communication with the world. Viggo Søgaard identified this biblical foundation of the commission to communicate the gospel:

> This commission to communicate permeates all aspects of Christian ministry, and it is a primary driving force for commitment and dedication We find that it is not "just" the so-called Great Commission, but this "communication for a purpose" seems always present in Scripture. God communicated himself to the prophets and then commissioned them to be his communicators to others. . . . Today those who have experienced

---

1. Acts 1:8; Matt 28.
2. Webber, *God Still Speaks*, 187.

his revelation are called to be his ambassadors, representing and communicating him in the world (2 Co. 5:20).[3]

Christians received this commission of communication from Jesus. At the end of his ministry, Jesus said, "As the Father has sent me, so I send you."[4] Jesus expects Christians to communicate with the world as he did.

Then, how can Christians obey this commission of communication? For this, Webber suggests two things. Christians need to communicate the exact image of the biblical Jesus, and Christians need to directly introduce Jesus to this contemporary world. Regarding these two tasks, Webber stated,

> In sum, we may conclude that the Scriptures supply us with the data we want to communicate, and the current perspective supplies us with the context through which this data must be filtered. But the goal is not the communication of mere data; we want the hearers of the gospel to experience the living God and His saving action in Jesus Christ.[5]

The YEU-Hui have both Chinese and Muslim backgrounds, but this alone cannot fully explain who they are. Any kind of communication method that is successful within the Muslim or Chinese worlds cannot guarantee success in communicating the gospel to the YEU-Hui. In order to obey the commission, the gospel should also be carefully communicated to the contemporary YEU-Hui, so it's necessary to develop communication principles that are appropriate to the YEU-Hui. This developed communication theory can lay theoretical bases for mission strategies to the YEU-Hui.

LESSONS FROM THE BIBLE

What is the best model of Christian communication? God created the entire universe and is also the source of all wisdom,[6] "for the Lord is the God of knowledge."[7] Therefore, the Bible shows the best model of communication.

---

3. Søgaard, "Applying Christian Communication," 63.
4. John 20:21.
5. Webber, *God Still Speaks*, 34.
6. Job 11:6.
7. 1 Sam 2:3.

God as a Communicator

The Bible offers several profound communication models, demonstrating God's desire to communicate with human beings. The Bible introduces God, the creator, who desires that the whole universe know him, and continually exposes himself to human beings: "For since the creation of the world God's invisible qualities—his eternal power and divine nature—have been clearly seen, being understood from what has been made, so that men are without excuse."[8]

Julian Sundersingh introduced three origins of communication in the Bible. First, the triune God initiated the first dialogues in history.[9] Sundersingh said, "The Bible clearly speaks of the intimate communion that exists between the persons of the Godhead."[10] Second, one can see the origins of communication present when the triune God created the world.[11] Sundersingh said, "God of the Bible communicates not only within himself, but also in and through his creation."[12]

God has used many creative ways to communicate with people: direct communication through human language, punishment, miracles, the words and actions of prophets, enemy attacks, protection, songs and psalms, written messages, people's testimonies, and so on. Therefore, Christian communication is not limited to just several kinds of messages, but the "Christian religion itself is a religion of communication."[13] Hendrik Kraemer described God as a communicator:

> The God of the Bible is a God who speaks. One of the well-known, outstanding characteristics of the Bible is the great recurrence of the expression: the word of God coming to man. The word is the symbol par excellence that stands in human intercourse for communication. The meaning of this constantly recurring speaking of God is not only that he is the Lord, who commands and thereby creates, but also that God wants personal relationship and invites to personal relationship as the fulfillment of human existence.[14]

---

8. 1 Sam 2:3.
9. Gen 1:26; Matt 17:5; John 16:14, 28.
10. Sundersingh, "Toward a Media-Based Translation," 66.
11. Ps 19:1; Rom 1:20.
12. Sundersingh, "Toward a Media-Based Translation," 67.
13. Søgaard, "Applying Christian Communication," xiv.
14. Kraemer, *Communication of the Christian Faith*, 15.

Jesus' incarnation is the core instance of God's communication. God sent his own son, Jesus Christ, to his people. Though he was the Son of God, Jesus gave up all of his prestige. He was born in Jewish culture of the first century, lived with human society, and learned the Jewish language, laws, and social principles. After he humbly received baptism, he began to preach his Father's message and performed miracles. Webber said the incarnation was the best model of communication in the Bible: "Jesus' identification with us bears a significant implication for communication. It is this: The incarnation is the perfect model of communication."[15]

Webber further extended his application of the model of the incarnation, and claimed that Christian communication should be incarnated as well.

> God communicates through incarnation. In the incarnation God set forth the ultimate standard of communication. If we would reach others as God reached us, we must be willing to identify with the very life, the social context, and the needs of those with whom we communicate.[16]

The model of incarnation teaches Christian communicators a precious principle. Messengers need to deliver their messages for the listener's understanding, not for the speaker's own satisfaction. In doing so, messenger needs to consider the listener's situation. Kraft theoretically identified the incarnation further as being connected with a humble attitude and a serving nature in order to earn the respect of listeners.[17]

Kraft also explains that Jesus likewise set an example for us, by establishing credibility among humankind.

> Jesus established his credibility as a human being among human beings. This is one aspect of God's communicational activity that was hard to establish before God came as a man.[18]

This incarnational attitude is not excused in Christian media. In his dissertation, Knud Jorgensen theoretically developed and applied this incarnation to Christian media. He contended that Christian media and programming should be incarnational in order to effectively communicate the gospel.

---

15. Webber, *God Still Speaks*, 101.
16. Ibid., 204.
17. Ibid.
18. *Communication Theory for Christian Witness*, 18.

Christian media communication is to model God's incarnational way of communicating by relating to actual history and culture and to the questions of the audience in a dialogic fashion, respecting the basic communication principles of a common frame of reference, credibility, specificity and self-discovery. It must aim at cultural relevancy and contextual dialogue, must focus on the entire human being, and present God in the midst of human and public life.[19]

Both before his crucifixion and after his resurrection, Jesus gave his message to the disciples in incarnate ways. He lived as an example, quoted the Old Testament, offered explanations through parables, and showed signs and wonders. From the early church history until even today, when Jesus communicates with us, he chooses the best method for our understanding. He carefully considers appropriate culture, languages, sound effects, colors, emotions, and tools to effectively communicate with us. This is God's wonderful, gracious, and unique communication method. Eugene A. Nida describes God's uniqueness:

> Uniquely in Christianity, God does not merely communicate concepts about Himself (as in Islam). He communicates Himself, in the person of His Son, in whom the World becomes flesh. In our faith it is God who takes the initiative in communication, and through the Incarnation, both by word and by life, communicates to men.[20]

God's way of communication in the Bible was receptor-oriented. God did not use the so-called language of heaven. God may use specific dialects to communicate with rural people and may speak in the standard language to urban citizens. In Jesus' parables, he used example of seed and field for those with agricultural backgrounds, nets and fish for fishermen, and wine and skin for those who were familiar with them. Kraft defines God's receptor-oriented communication:

> To do this he (a) develops high credibility with his receptors, (b) demonstrates, not just speaks, his messages, (c) deals with specific people and issues, (d) leads his receptors to discovery, and (e) trusts those who respond to do the right thing with his messages.[21]

---

19. Jorgensen, "Role and Function of the Media," i.
20. Nida, *Message and Mission*, 22.
21. Kraft, *Communication Theory for Christian Witness*, 18.

God still communicates with the YEU-Hui today; God was always there with them and has led their long history. For example, He saw how the YEU-Hui group has formed as they experienced large, rapid social changes after Chairman Mao. Jesus still wants to communicate with the YEU-Hui today. Jesus, who testified through the incarnation, is commending today's church to send an incarnational message to YEU-Hui through incarnational media.

God Wants Us to Communicate Effectively

In the meaning of "As the Father has sent me, so I send you," there is not only the commission of evangelism but also the commission of efficiency, because Jesus communicated effectively.[22] For this, Engel emphasizes that the church not only has God's message but the church itself is also a medium. This means that if the church is unhealthy, its message also becomes unhealthy and ineffective.

> Viewing the church as both medium and message has powerful implications. At the very least, it is obvious that a church not exemplifying the Kingdom is moribund and ineffective in the whole cause of world evangelization. Indeed, it is the author's conviction that insurance of the health and biblical fidelity of the church must precede evangelistic strategies.[23]

With these principles, Christian communicators can develop effective communication skills. Just as Jesus, who was sent by God, we need to speak effectively.[24]

COMMUNICATION PROCESS

An inadequately defined communication process may cause a communication breakdown or misunderstanding between speakers and listeners. An understanding of the communication process has been developed throughout thousands of years, and every development helps us understand human nature and communication elements that need to be considered. A well-defined communication process enables Christians to introduce the gospel, being careful not to cause misunderstandings.

---

22. John 20:21.

23. Engel, *Contemporary Christian Communication*, 31.

24. Kraft has suggested these seven guidelines for the church in order to conduct effective communication. Kraft, *Communication Theory*, 150.

Communication Defined

Since ancient times, scholars have wanted to define communication.[25] D. Smith researched the original meaning of the word communication, and emphasized the importance of commonness in communication.[26] The root word is *communis*, and from that came many related words, including common, commune, community, communism, communion, and communication.[27]

All of these terms include the meaning of involvement and relationship among the people. Through the communication process people create commonness. D. Smith said that communication was the activity of "creating understanding."[28]

Rudolph F. Verderber further developed Smith's definition of communication, saying that communication is a "transactional process of creating meaning."[29] Then he said that

> by transactional, we mean that the persons communicating are mutually responsible for what occurs. Communication is transactional whether the communication involves two people in conversation, a group discussion, or a public speech.[30]

Kraft described communication by using a theory of gaps and bridges. He conceptualized the two communicators as two ends and the communication as a bridge that connects the two ends.[31]

Finally, it is difficult to arrive at a single definition of communication. Søgaard prefers not to overlook the process of communication. Because of the factor of time, he argues that communication cannot be finished in one event. He says communication is a lifelong process.

> Communication is both process and event. That communication, like all of life, is a process that is foundational to our understanding of communication. It is, furthermore, a consecutive, interrelated number of communication processes, some of short-term duration, others involving years, which are going on

---

25. David J. Hesselgrave explained how communication and speech technique was important to ancient speakers, in *Communicating Christ Cross-Culturally*, 24.
26. Smith, *Creating Understanding*, 24.
27. Ibid.
28. Ibid., 20–21.
29. Verderber, *Communicate!*, 4.
30. Ibid.
31. Kraft, *Communication Theory*, 3.

at the same time. But this process consists of individual segments or events that in themselves may not overtly relate to a process.[32]

Communication cannot be described and defined as a one-time event but as a process of creating understanding and increasing commonness through multiple instances of sending and replying to messages, both verbal and nonverbal. Generally, speakers cannot achieve receptor-oriented communication through either one-time or one-way communication.

Communication Processes and Types

In ancient times, Aristotle introduced three elements of communication reference: the speaker, the speech, and the audience.[33] From his idea, scholars developed "the action or sender model" of communication. Jorgensen says that "this type of communication clearly implies a one-way action by which the communicator aims at changing the audience by means of information transmission."[34] This model describes communication as when the speaker's meaning penetrates the audience's situation and arrives to the audience's heart. This model is similar to medicine that arrives in the muscles through a syringe needle.

Hesselgrave developed this model in which he conceptualized the source and the respondent. The message is transferred between them through a system of encoding and decoding. He advances the traditional model by adding the factors of noise, context, feedback, and content.[35]

Jorgensen introduces and categorizes interaction models. An interaction model is rather reciprocal, having mutual exchange of conjoint influences. He characterizes this model with four points: "communication is a process; communication is circular; response is central to communication; communication is complex."[36] In their book *The Process and Effects of Mass Communication*, Wilbur Lang Schramm and Donald F. Roberts said that the three most important aspects of communication are the communicator, the message, and the receiver. Though their model seems similar to Aristotle's, they disagree with the idea of "shooting a

---

32. Søgaard, *Media in Church and Mission* 30–31.
33. Hesselgrave, *Communicating Christ Cross-Culturally*, 29.
34. Jorgensen, "Role and Function of the Media," 20.
35. Hesselgrave, *Communicating Christ Cross-Culturally*, 37.
36. Jorgensen, "Role and Function of the Media," 29–31.

magic bullet into a receiver"[37] because they don't think the receiver passively receives the sender's message in a mechanical and magical process. Rather, they emphasize that the effect of communication depends on both the communicator and the receiver.

Schramm introduced a useful process model that was schematized.[38] In the model, there are encoding, interpretive, and decoding functions in both the speaker and receiver. The first stage is the encoding process in the speaker's mind, as the speaker develops and sends some meaning as a message. Once the receiver senses the message, the receiver reinterprets it by his or her own interpreting system and then understands it.

David K. Berlo diversified the elements of communication. He introduced the six vital ingredients of communication as: the communication source, the encoder, the message, the channel, the decoder, and the communication receiver.[39]

Engel clearly defined the important concept of feedback: the receptor's understanding of a sender's message and channel modes causes it.[40] From Hesselgrave to Osgood, Schramm, and Engel, this concept of feedback became an important factor of the receptor-oriented principle. The speaker can be more receptor-oriented after sensing the receptor's feedback.

Verderber's summary of the elements of communication is similar. They are context (physical, historical, psychological, and cultural), participants, messages (meaning, symbols, encoding, and decoding, form or organization), channels, noise (external, internal, and semantic), and feedback.[41]

Daniel P. Kelly combined several components of communication in one model, which is comprised of the speaker, the receptor, grids or filters, the message, the channel, noise, feedback, and context. He emphasizes that commonness between the speaker and listener—which he called "life-experiences in common"—gives them motivation for communication.[42]

---

37. Schramm and Roberts, *The Process and the Effects*, 16.
38. Schramm, *The Process and the Effects*, 8.
39. Berlo, *Process of Communication*, 32.
40. Engel, *Contemporary Christian Communication*, 39.
41. Verderber, *Communicate!*, 5–10.
42 Kelly, "Receptor Oriented Communication," 24.

Søgaard developed his own communication model, which includes most of the preceding scholars' concepts and elements.[43] Figure 25 is a conceptual diagram of Søgaard's model. He introduced eleven elements of which the communicator must be aware: source/sender, receiver, context of audience, research to get the information, selection of content, channel, reception, message, monitoring and evaluation, response and research, and noise. Søgaard added numbers to each of elements.

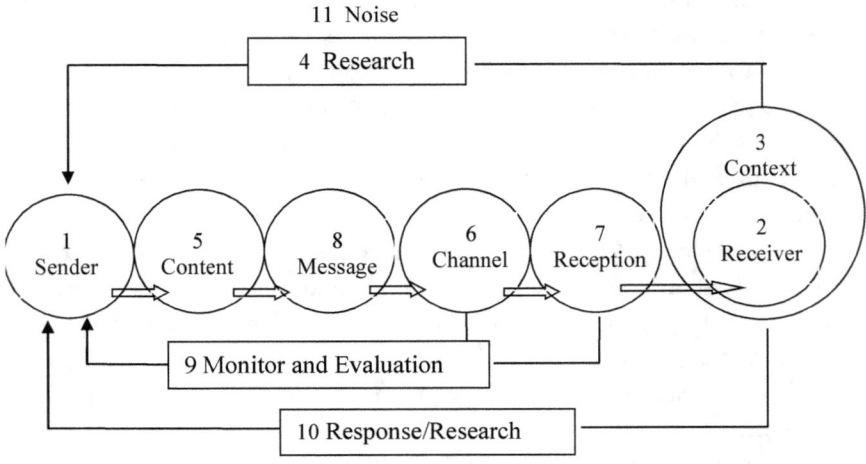

Søgaard's Communication Model[44]

In Søgaard's model, in order for the message to be effectively received, the sender must understand and research the receiver's context, then select the proper content and channels. During the communication process, the sender continually monitors and evaluates the channel, reception, and receiver's response. Finally, Søgaard says that "noise affects all aspects of the communication process."[45]

Since Søgaard's model integrates most of the communication elements, it seems proper to apply it to communicating the gospel to YEU-Hui. As the cross-cultural missionary (sender: 1) introduces the gospel to the YEU-Hui (receiver: 2), the sender needs to know the YEU-Hui context (3), which includes their worldview and the impact of modernization, as well as the individual or group's special situation, preferences,

---

43. Søgaard, *Media in Church and Mission* 51.
44. Ibid.
45. Ibid.

and needs. Knowing YEU-Hui cultural themes can also help the sender use proper content (5). There could be many channels (6) used. Understanding how to touch upon their felt needs, personal relationships, and historical-social situation can affect the reception (7). The proper channel decides the proper type of message (8). In the YEU-Hui situation, printed media and vocal messages are the primary message form. At the same time the usability of audio-visual–based personal media, especially computer and online media, are dramatically increased. Except for those working in huge NGO projects, monitoring and evaluation (9), plus response research (10) are quite difficult because of the political situation. However, since current ministries are quite small groups, most of the feedback can be achieved through personal interviews or small-scale questionnaire methods. Finally, noise (11) is a huge factor in communicating the gospel to the YEU-Hui. One of the biggest noises is that the YEU-Hui have historically formed misunderstandings about the gospel. Second, both governmental regulations and Hui ethnic society do not allow freedom for Christian evangelism and meetings. These days, modern Chinese society has created new desires that make young urbanites very busy, further reducing their concern for the gospel. This is another noise in communicating the gospel with the YEU-Hui.

As communication proceeds, senders and receptors can create commonality, which shapes the meaning created between senders and receptors. This meaning is not static; it changes at every step of communication. Bonnie McDaniel Johnson explains this process of building and changing that involved different attentions, different interprets, different judges. In other words, different communication factors create different meaning.

Communication is a continuous process.[46] It builds up meaning even before communicators begin conversation and continually changes and develops the meaning.

RECEPTOR-ORIENTED COMMUNICATION

If Christian speakers know that every person listens with a different heart and from a unique situation, they realize that they need to research their audience just as Jesus did. The speaker's serving nature and understanding of the receptor will bring the listeners to have a clearer understanding of the speaker's mind. This is the basic nature and principle of

46. Johnson, *Instructor's Manual*, 62.

receptor-oriented communication. In order to design a mission strategy for the YEU-Hui, it is important to study these theories along with a biblical foundation.

What Is Receptor-Oriented Communication?

Kraft said that receptor-oriented communication is "to put oneself to whatever inconvenience necessary to assure that the receptors understand."[47] In contrast to communicator-oriented communication, receptor-oriented communication tries to ensure that receptors have "a clear understanding of our message."[48] To this end, the communicator needs to be both situationally and culturally receptor-oriented because the receptor will judge "what has been communicated" and whether it has been done with "accuracy and correctness."[49]

For effective receptor-oriented communication, communicators should identify the receptor's frame of reference, which includes "the culture, language, life situation, social class, or similar all-embracing setting or context within which one operates."[50] The communicators need to carefully employ the cultural forms of communication, which are to convey the message. Kraft stated that the receptor-oriented communicator is "careful to bend every effort to meet his receptors where they are."[51] Therefore, such a communicator "will choose topics that relate directly to the felt needs of the receptors," and "he will choose methods of presentation that are appealing to them," then finally "he will use language that is maximally intelligible to them."[52]

With regard to receptor-oriented communication, Mogens Stensbaek Mogensen summarized six effective conditions:

1. Effective communication is a personal interaction between the communicator and the receptor.

2. Effective communication presupposes a thorough knowledge of the receptor by the communicator.

---

47. Kraft, *Communication Theory*, 15.
48. Box, "Communicating Christianity," 141.
49. Kraft, *Christianity in Culture*, 148.
50. *Communication Theory*, 15.
51. *Communicating the Gospel*, 7.
52. Ibid.

3. Effective communication requires that the communicator has a clear goal for the communication of his or her message.
4. The selection of channels for the communication of the message is critical for the receptor's perception of the message.
5. Effective communication is not just an event, but a process or a series of events.
6. Effective communication takes into account the context, which influences all aspects of the communication process.[53]

Feedback provides "a greater chance of the Source-meaning and Receptor-meaning coming to a closer approximation of each other."[54] Feedback is "the information that a source gets back from a receiver in order to judge the effect of his message, or the degree to which the receiver understands the source's meaning for the message which he is sharing."[55] Without feedback, "we could never exchange ideas, test new theories, or even learn about each other."[56] In cross-cultural conversation, without feedback, achieving the transfer of accurate meaning is more difficult "if the Source is endeavoring to introduce new ideas that call for major changes on the part of the Receptor."[57] Communication is not one-way traffic, but rather a dialogue that produces continual feedback. Through this multiple feedback conversation, communicators can approach receptor-oriented communication.

God's Example of Receptor-Oriented Communication

The Bible is filled with examples of receptor-oriented communication. God showed an example of receptor-oriented attitude in his communication. Kraft says,

> God's strategy is that *God is receptor-oriented, seeking to reach his receptors by entering their frame of reference* and by participating in their life, in order to be maximally intelligible to them.[58]

---

53. Mogensen, "Contextual Communication," 10–14.
54. Box, "Communicating Christianity," 138.
55. Kincaid and Schramm, *Fundamental Human Communication*, 106.
56. Burgoon and Ruffner, *Human Communication*, 84.
57. Box, "Communicating Christianity," 138.
58. Kraft, *Communication Theory*, 16.

In addition to this, Kraft has continually described that the nature of God's communication is humble, and it is expressed with receptor-orientation.

> Instead of asserting his right to require us to operate within his context, though, he designated our frame of reference, our familiar turf, as that within which the communication would take place. He, therefore, has had to do all the adjusting, allowing us to be the ones on familiar ground. It is an indication of his love, acceptance, and respect for us and a mark of his receptor-orientation that he has chosen our frame of reference rather than demanding that we use his.[59]

It is very easy for people to become communicator-oriented; however, the Bible introduces two bases for Christian speakers to be receptor-oriented. First, Christian messengers need to have a posture of service. The Bible says, "If anyone wants to be first, he must be the very last, and the servant of all."[60] Second, God showed us his receptor-oriented posture when he communicated with people.[61] In the book of Mark it is said, "Above all, He was not source oriented. He always had the receptor in mind. The call for repentance/change was repeated numerous times by John the Baptist, Paul, and Jesus Christ Himself."[62] As God communicated receptor-orientedly, having receptors in mind is biblical.

Audience Sovereignty

There is a crucial reason that speakers need to be receptor-oriented. It is because the audience is subjective and has sovereignty in receptivity. Sometimes, two people have two different understandings as they hear the same message. This often happens, not only because of the speaker, but also because audiences are subjective and are from different situations and backgrounds. The audience understands the speakers' message through self-selection, self-interpretation, or bias and social opinion. Because the audience receptivity is actively subjective, the efficiency and selectivity depends heavily on the audience. This means that the audience

---

59. Ibid.
60. Mark 9:35.
61. Kraft, *Christianity in Culture*, 170.
62. Kelly, "Receptor Oriented Communication," 11.

possesses some sovereignty over the message. Thus, human information processing is highly selective.[63]

So, in order for the audience to clearly understand the speaker's meaning, the speaker needs to know the receptor's interpretation process. To stimulate the audiences' senses, information must have some amount of impact, and if the impact is big enough, the audience will react to the information.

People use their selectivity when they listen. Most people hate to change! They feel pain when they have to change. "People resist change in strongly held beliefs and attitudes and do so through selective information processing."[64]

Therefore, when people listen, they try to select less painful information first thereby limiting the amount of pain in change. Engel said that receptors use three kinds of selection as they receive information: selective exposure, selective attention, and selective reception.[65] Through this selectivity, the audience's sovereignty controls their receptivity.

Similar to interpersonal communication, audiences have their sovereignty in mass communication, as well. Schramm and Roberts distribute audience responses on the continuum from the least active to very active. Mass communication audiences are generally less active than those participating in individual conversations.[66]

Though there are differences of involvement, the audiences of mass communication are very active and are decision-makers regarding the effect of communication. They actively listen, watch, select, and decide to receive the information. They continually analyze and respond to the information. Again, this fact verifies that Aristotle's bullet theory is improper to describe communication. Audiences are always reinterpreting the message with their own viewpoints and contexts. They exchange their opinions with other audience members and then develop new ideas through conversation.

Since the audiences are sovereign in the effect of communication, the need for receptor-oriented communication is more important. Studying their background and situation, as well as determining proper media and channels may increase the receptivity. In Hui society, the

---

63. Engel, *Contemporary Christian Communication*, 47.
64. Ibid., 52.
65. Ibid.
66. Schramm and Roberts, *The Process and the Effects*, 191–92.

gospel may not be understood well if the speaker does not carefully design the message, taking YEU-Hui background into consideration. Considering these factors will contribute to the design of a mission strategy for the YEU-Hui.

SUMMARY AND REFLECTION

The study of communication theory offers profound knowledge for developing mission strategy. Proper communication principles for mission strategy need to be biblical and strategic, and they should consider all the elements that contribute to the process of communication. Considering all of those factors, effective communication is receptor-oriented. The speaker who is receptor-oriented takes the receptor's frame of reference into consideration. This effectively decreases barriers within the audience members, who have sovereignty in message reception.

God wants Christians to communicate the gospel with the YEU-Hui, so cross-cultural missionaries need to be YEU-Hui oriented. For this reason, Christian communicators need to understand their culture, context, and situation. It is necessary to develop effective channels and media that will deliver the proper message.

Studying this Christian communication theory leads readers to have new questions. With regard to having proper messages, cultural studies, and trust building with the YEU-Hui, which we studied earlier, the problem of which media and channels to use in the message transfer becomes important. The next chapter will review different kinds of media that may be effective for Christians in witnessing to the YEU-Hui.

9

Media and Signals

As discussed in the previous chapters, receptor-orientation also requires using the right media and communication channels. In China's urban situation, where the YEU-Hui live, the importance of understanding the media is more and more important for Christian activity, and media has become important in the lives of the YEU-Hui. This chapter focuses on the third objective of this research: to identify the relevant communication channels. A general study of media and mass communication theory will lay the theoretical foundation. In order to set up a mission strategy, it is necessary to describe several kinds of media preferred by the YEU-Hui.

SIGNALS

Human beings communicate through their senses and a variety of signals, which become vehicles for messages. People not only use verbal signals, but also facial expressions, body language, color, smell, and so on. Each of these signals contributes to the communication process and effect. For example, although a messenger's message content is elegant and gentle, the listener may be embarrassed by the speaker's facial expressions or body language.

The use of signal systems is very different in each culture since each culture expresses the same meaning in different ways. The same signal may therefore have different meanings in different cultures, which is a challenge to Christian cross-cultural workers. Their message could be distorted in a different context, or they might misunderstand the nationals' message.

These common communication signals are categorized into twelve different kinds: verbal, written, numeric, pictorial, artifactual, audio, kinesic, optical, tactile, spatial, temporal, olfactory.[1]

The manner of our communication is not limited only to verbal communication. Nida introduces paralinguistic, extralinguistic, gestures, space, and noise as conversation factors.[2] However, people usually use only several of the twelve signals at a given time. Jesus expressed himself not only through words, but also through such forms as storms, signs and wonders, dying on the cross, living harmoniously with others, and eating with others. Likewise, Christians need to study how many signals they can utilize in their service and programs. Cross-cultural workers, especially, need to learn about and be familiar with local signal systems. This learning posture can reduce many mistakes.

MEDIA

The audiences and their uses of media are quite varied. For example, some individuals may enjoy using an MP3 player as personal media in a private place, or they may read newspapers.[3] Two people may have a private dialogue using their cell phones while an announcer's voice broadcasts to billions of people at the same time. Media changes the characteristics of communication and the perception of the receptors.

Søgaard categorized media into three areas by their characteristics: personal media, group media, and mass media. He defined personal media as that which is "used by a single person. Print becomes a personal medium when a person decides to read and use it."[4] Group media in his definition includes items "that are used to enhance or stimulate interaction with or among a group of people."[5] A cassette tape is a good example of this category. Mass media may "aim at communicating with multiple audiences at the same time. A given audience may be small; in fact, it may consist of just one person, and the receptor may not necessarily understand or feel a 'mass' situation."[6]

---

1. Smith, *Creating Understanding*, 146.
2. Nida, *Signs, Sense, Translation*, 2–11.
3. MP3 is a popular abbreviation for MPEG-Audio-Layer-3 formatted digital files.
4. Søgaard, *Media in Church and Mission* 39.
5. Ibid., 40.
6. Ibid.

Since ancient times, people have used oral communication and signals to communicate with each other: fire, flags, scratching on cave walls, pictures, etc. Today we use electric and digital media for communication, which has challenged many scholars to research the media. An outstanding scholar who leads the field of media philosophy is Marshall McLuhan. He categorized human communication methods in his book *Understanding Media: The Extensions of Man* and compares the impact of media influence on human society.[7] According to McLuhan, human beings traditionally founded their society and expressed their ideas as content through oral communication. After Gutenberg, however, printed materials became popular, and the oral communication society faced detribalization by literacy. Compared to the oral society, the literate society became uniform and continuous and sequential. The literate society asked people to move into a typographic society.[8]

McLuhan said that as media changes, society is asked to change their system in order to fit the media. If the society is successful in changing its system, the country becomes outstanding and leads other societies. McLuhan emphasized that, just as Europe used the fruit of Gutenberg, modern countries need to change again with the use of electronic media. Today, electronic media is strong enough to change the traditional Gutenberg culture. He warned the Gutenberg culture and called for change: "The electric technology is within the gates, and we are numb, deaf, blind, and mute about its encounter with the Gutenberg technology, on and through which the American way of life was formed."[9]

Furthermore, McLuhan foresaw that the impact of today's electric media like TV and radio would have a stronger influence than written media's impact had on the oral communication society.[10]

Traditionally, communication scholars thought about message and media separately, viewing media simply as a vehicle that carries the message. They viewed media as making changes in the message's scale, pace, and pattern, but eventually expanding to transmit the same, unchanged content. While that may have been true for periods of print or typography, things changed as electronic media appeared.

---

7. McLuhan, *Understanding Media*.
8. Ibid., 30–32.
9. Ibid., 32.
10. Ibid., 31.

McLuhan emphasized that it is impossible to separate the media and message in electronic media; rather, the medium itself is the message. Therefore, McLuhan tried to describe the media rather than define it. Since the medium is a message, people needed to see it as an extended body of human beings. For example, the voices and faces of actors come to a viewer's room through TV, rather than one simply watching it. It is important for audiences to know that the carrier of communication—oral voice, books, TV, etc.—influences the message, the effect of mass media, and the receiver more than before. Therefore, McLuhan said that, though most of the program content is interchangeable, the effects of each media, or carrier, are not exchangeable. This means that the carrier may have a greater impact than does the content.[11] McLuhan's point alerts Christian strategists to consider the fact that not only media content, but also the media itself, affects the receptors' receptivities.

MASS COMMUNICATION AND INTERPERSONAL COMMUNICATION

Today, people are surrounded by mass media. Charles R. Wright explained the distinctiveness of mass communication as compared to interpersonal communication in three areas.[12] First the nature of the audience is relatively large, heterogeneous, and anonymous. Second, the nature of the communication experience is different. Mass communication can be characterized as public, rapid, and transient. It is an organized communication that is produced by an extensive division of labor and a lot of expense. Third, the nature of the communicator is different.

Schramm and Roberts pointed out four distinctions between mass media and interpersonal communication. First, in contrast to interpersonal communication, mass communication is led and managed by big organizations that decide upon the information process with complex procedures. Second, mass media can send a large amount of information to many places at the same or at different times. Copy, print, and electric machines enable this multiplication ability. Third, choosing content is more difficult in mass media than in interpersonal communication, where the relationship is direct and feedback is usually immediate.

---

11. Ibid., 28.

12. Wright, *Mass Communication*, 6–9.

Finally, social demands and social controls on mass media are louder and stronger than on the individual.[13]

There are, however, similarities between interpersonal communication and the mass media process. Like interpersonal communication, the media encodes and decodes the meaning by electronic, digital, or print methods. Media changes human lives, affects worldview, and increases the mutual relationship. These mass and interpersonal communications have more similarities than differences in their hurdles, like attention, acceptance, interpretation, and disposition. They also have both sender and receiver dynamics.[14]

A strong point of mass communication should be its multiplying and expanding; however, this quantitative expansion does not guarantee its quality. A lot of messages are "unavoidably dropped," for mass media is not like interpersonal relationships that require "demanding involvement." So "such hidden characteristics diminish the impact of the Christian message in mass media."[15]

In a developing country, leaders often want to use mass media for the purpose of changing and leading their people. Most world leaders seem aware of the power of mass media. Schramm discusses the role of mass communication as being fivefold: It can (1) serve as watchman in a learning and education role, (2) widen horizons by helping more people understand the world, (3) focus public attention toward who is important, who is dangerous, or what is interesting, (4) raise aspirations for a better life, and (5) thus create a climate for development.[16]

Developing countries have much potential but unexpected obstacles when it comes to change. As a result, people may sometimes criticize or stand against the government and its change leadership. Often people in developing countries are divided into many sects by geography and ethnicity, and in many cases are generally against each other. Many of them are very conservative and resistant to change. Since leaders use mass communication for change, there can be conflicts between the government and traditions in developing countries.

Since China is currently a developing country, and the Hui have been barely connected with the outside world for a long time, it is very

---

13. Schramm and Roberts, *The Process and the Effects*, 30–31.
14. Ibid.
15. Smith, *Creating Understanding*, 179.
16. Schramm, *Mass Media and National Development*, 127–31.

important to understand the characteristics of mass media in developing countries in order to plan to use media with the Hui. The Hui not only have been disconnected from the outside world, but they also have been resistant to change. However, from the industrial influence of China, the Hui have begun to connect with mass media and are facing pressure to change.

In many developing countries where there are many reasons for resistance to change, mass media can be an effective tool to begin to lead the traditional society toward change.[17] In contrast with the traditional Hui, YEU-Hui are quite familiar with mass media. Their frequent contact with mass media information may cause some worldview change or create social gaps with other subculture groups among the Hui. It may even create new subculture groups and foster modern power and ability among them.

MEDIA DESCRIPTION

Using Schramm's principles, Theodore B. Peterson, Jay W. Jensen, and William L. Rivers contend that people generally select their media with two criteria: that which takes the least effort and that which carries the promise of reward.[18] People choose their channels of media based on their own preferences and situation. Understanding these characteristics can help Christian leaders to properly use media to maximize the YEU-Hui receptivity. The following study will introduce the characteristics of eight kinds of media. Part of the study is from the authors' personal observations and field research.

Print Media

Print media transmits the information by printed signals and includes books, newspapers, magazines, letters, mail, and tracts. Print has the longest media history and has largely influenced human beings. Ray Eldon Hiebert, Donald F. Ungurait, and Thomas W. Bhon reported that the first books appeared in 2400 BC on clay tablets about the size of shredded-wheat biscuits.[19]

---

17. Schramm and Roberts, *The Process and the Effects*, 758.
18. Peterson et al., *Mass Media and Modern Society*, 21.
19. Hiebert et al., *Mass Media V*, 23.

Traditionally newspaper has provided fast and trustworthy information to broad and wide layers of readers. Today, however, the fast speed of electronic media changes the popularity of newspaper. Now, its role is changing to "interpreting and analyzing the news," rather than "publishing news bulletins."[20] Journals and magazines specify their readership and deal with their own issues and concerns with a limited number of copies.

The role of printed media is slowly shrinking for two reasons. First, there is a low global literacy ratio. Among individuals over fifteen years of age, "more than one third are completely illiterate."[21] Second, people do not read because the continual growth of electronic media leads literates away from reading. Herbert V. Kelm illustrates the decline of readers in Europe and America:

> Europe is usually reported as over 95% literate. Yet over 40% of her adults are counted as "habitual non-readers or functionally illiterate." If traditional Bible study materials are not likely to be used by 40% of the people in a society counted to be industrial and 95% literate, what of target audiences in developing countries counted 80% illiterate.[22]

Field data research found that young Chinese urbanites use print media second only after the computer. The print media market is traditionally big and stable, even though the computer takes some of its position away—especially among youngsters who use the computer for news and information Thousands of books, journals, and newspapers pile up in bookstores and street shops. Paper media has many strong points in the Chinese Christian context: convenient to handle, able to be personalized, and easy to use in Christian meetings.

Television

Television is a very powerful form of media today. During the last fifty years, television has continually changed and improved its function through the use of satellites, cable boxes, low-power television, tele-text and video-text, videocassettes, videodiscs, and the Internet. Television has become "society's mass entertainer, mass informer, mass persuader,

---

20. Ibid., 71.
21. Kelm, "Bible as Oral Literature," 47.
22. Ibid.

and mass educator. It is a universal medium. . . . Television is the costliest of all the electronic media."[23]

Television provides tremendous opportunities for Christian evangelism. Therefore, Christian leaders need to conduct extensive research in order to provide an effective television ministry.

China has many broadcast channels, which are run by the government. Foreign channels are very limited and most domestic channels come through cable TV. Most of the programs do not handle religious material. Since 2000, government-driven campaigns are slowly replaced by society and family issues. The Chinese receive most of the world news that is not politically sensitive, but the freedom of speech is very limited.

Radio

Radio stimulates the listener's imagination and allows them to work while they listen. Radio is inexpensive, is a more "local medium," offers program selectivity that "can satisfy individual needs," and "has mobility."[24] It is good for imparting information and reinforcing a message. Radio has many good points for evangelism although it also has limitations. Radio can cross all kinds of barriers, can reach the nonliterate, has the potential to build a huge network of audiences, offers a personal reach, has a low cost in terms of price per person exposed, and keeps to the timing.[25]

Christian radio has contributed a great role, especially in developing and restricted countries. Christian broadcasters need to research the lifestyles and habits of their listeners in order to create the most ideal programs that hold the attention of the listeners.

China has many radio broadcast stations, and they are still run by the government just like the TV channels. Both TV and radio are part of very politically sensitive systems, so freedom of speech in China seems to be still far way, though the path is getting smoother. There are several Christian foreign radio broadcasts for China's inland audience, but they do not seem specially focused on the YEU-Hui. Based on the field research data, radio is the third favorite media of young urbanites. However, TV and radio programs that are focused on YEU-Hui and produced by foreigners seem to have many barriers: there are mechanical and political problems, and it's hard to develop an audience-targeted screening system.

23. Hiebert et al., *Mass Media V*, 215.
24. Ibid., 171.
25. Sundersingh, "Toward a Media-Based Translation," 139–42.

Films and Slides

After Thomas Edison invented the motion picture camera in 1880, the movie became a close friend in our lives. Though films and slides may have lost some viewers to video and TV, they still have their own roles. A motion picture can provide entertainment on big screen with wonderful sound effects.

There are many places to utilize movies in churches. Films can greatly enhance a message through the utilization of sound and powerful visual effects. Therefore, Christians need to develop more effective films for discipleship and evangelism by using professional techniques and research.

Many Chinese still go to the theater to watch movies, but relatively few of China's urbanites go to movie theaters, preferring the computer and DVDs instead. Furthermore, since the government strictly controls religious content in theater movies, it seems more relevant to copy Christian movies onto DVDs and online forums. The field data also reports that among the seven media priorities of young urbanites, going to the movies ranks only sixth.

Audio Cassette, CD, and MP3

People admire the versatility and functions of audiocassettes. They are simple, cheap, and very easy to use. Audiocassettes feature the dominant features of radio, such as decent sound quality, as well as some strong features of video, such as portability and practicality for personal use.

People can specifically design a cassette-based mission program for mission. This good point of cassette tape ministry enables us to make a program series with a long-term plan, even for those who are illiterate.

In many cases, the human factor is added to these audio media when people receive them. An "audio cassette usually has a friend or a personal contact as its distributor and hence it offers the possibility for an integrated strategy which includes the distributor in the plan."[26] To Chinese Muslims, evangelists cannot openly sell Christian materials, but they can distribute tapes from person to person through relationships.

In modern China, audio media is rapidly changing from cassette tape to CD and MP3. It is not difficult to find young people who put earphones in their ears on the street. Young Chinese often download audio files from

---

26. Ibid., 145.

the Internet. Therefore, these digital media cannot expect to have the human factor like cassettes had. The newly developed audio media are rapidly growing. PMPs (Portable Multimedia Players), PDAs (Personal Digital Assistant), and PSPs (PlayStation Portable) are good examples of these kinds of media, which can have video functions, as well.

Video and DVD

Although the video and DVD have a very short history, they influence our lives very much. In contrast to television, video and DVD are more personal and replayable. The continually dropping prices of video and DVD players allow a greater number of people to enjoy the equipment. In China, video is outdated, and most movies are distributed on DVD. Some people do not even need DVD players because they can watch programs through the Internet.

Christians can use video technology for education, entertainment, and evangelism. Søgaard describes the usability of Christian video as follows:

> There should be plenty of opportunities for using video in the church and in mission, but relevant programs are still difficult to find. Again, in the area of education we have seen the best productions, but there are also good videos produced for personal devotion and meditation. Many children's videos are on the market, including some sing-along programs. Christian performers have also entered the field of music video.[27]

Unlike film and tape, the digital media DVD can be copied limitlessly, as long as there is no licensing problem. In China, mission organizations allow the copying of many Christian materials freely, making DVDs and CDs quite easy and convenient to distribute. The biggest problem is that most of the content is directly translated from Western languages, and content that is especially designed for the YEU-Hui is almost nonexistent.

Drama, Dance, Music, and Painting

In ages past and even today, many religions have used drama, dance, music, and painting in ministry. Unfortunately, many Christians today regard these art forms as secular, allowing only a limited amount of

---

27. Søgaard, *Media in Church and Mission*, 158.

traditional religious music and stained glass into the church. However, Søgaard insists that Christians need to develop these instruments for greater usage.

> Today we are also encountering opposition to the use of drama in the church. In many cultures the original use of dance and drama has been related to the temples, but usually the church has taken an extreme position, not willing to recognize the validity in these forms of communication for today. There seems to be a certain amount of fear among Christians for using drama, a medium that has potential as an evangelistic and nurturing tool.[28]

Both the appropriate usage of mass media and the development of content are important factors for a Christian ministry that seeks to be receptor-oriented. A lot of new ideas and effort, as well as large financial investments, are also needed.

The Chinese government has used these media for advertising the communist party and for agitating people in their campaigns. It is common to see and hear campaigns on TV and the radio that use drama, dance, and music. Campaign paintings on the street and on walls are common and supported by the government. Those paintings show very large images of the faces of former leaders of modern China—Chairman Deng, Mao, or Jiang—along with a picture of the modern, developed China. Since 2000, the open door policy has brought private company advertisements that energetically use these media.

The official church prints calendars and sacred pictures for believers to hang on the walls of their houses. However, Christians in China have very limited freedom to use these media because many of their churches are nonofficial. Furthermore, field data also shows that young urbanites are not very much attracted to these media.

Computers and Internet

The application areas of computers are wide enough to cover and touch every corner of our lives. A computer's data storage capacity and processing speed are increasing extremely quickly. This digital media can copy files limitlessly while preserving original quality. Computer technology continually develops its function, and has become an integrated media.

---

28. Ibid., 200.

It is a storage tank of information, communication tool, personal office, and entertainment center.

Computers heavily influence Christian ministry. Christians can use CDs, as well as audio and visual programs to assist preaching and educating with Bible studies via the Internet. Global computerization has created many mission opportunities.

Today, the Internet can connect the entire world, including China. Computers and the Internet are not new technologies among intelligent Chinese Muslims. The most outstanding point of the Internet is that people can do two-way communication with many people. This two-way communication enables people to form virtual community and email networks and to easily download and upload files. An individual can open a personal broadcast or become a world superstar if he or she can attract enough people. As McLuhan said in his book title, the media represents the *Extensions of Man*; like other people in other parts of the world, Chinese urbanites seem to regard their computer and the Internet as a partner of their lives.[29]

MEDIA PREFERENCES AND THE YEU-HUI

Understanding YEU-Hui media and program preferences and availability is crucial in order to set up a mission strategy. According to the field research data, the most open group to new information among the YEU-Hui is E1 and E2, and the slower changing group is E3. A field research data summary of the E-Group's media and programs are compared here to a similar study that reports about the YEU-Han media tendency. This comparison study shows the similarities between the two groups in media preference and availability.

The first comparison was media preference. Depending on the amount of hours they used media, statistic programs gave each media different weights, grading them from 1 to 5. Since the sample numbers are different for the two groups, the total points were also different.[30]

Table 4 shows the results, which have two important points for strategist to use to set up mission strategy for the YEU-Hui: its similarity with the YEU-Han and its differences. First, as they approach the YEU-Hui, Christians can use media similar to that which is used by the YEU-Han.

---

29. McLuhan, *Understanding Media*.
30. Kim, "New Entrance Gate," 364.

The E1, E2, Non-E groups, and even the YEU-Han, showed almost the same priorities in their media preference. They almost all preferred the use of available computers, news publications and books, radios, and TV, including cable TV. Therefore, similar media influences both groups.

Table 4

YEU-Han and E-Group's Media Preference[31]

	Computer	News Publications, Books	Radio	TV, Cable	Records, Tapes	Movies	Play
E1	70	55	52	43	28	28	25
E2	95	90	67	76	40	35	33
Non-E	64	70	52	44	31	27	25
YEU-Hui total	229	215	171	163	99	90	83
YEU-Han	197	163	108	129	73	85	67

Second, the YEU-Hui trend is rapidly changing. Though print media is currently popular and easy to access, audio-visual media seems to be rapidly growing. Also, instead of watching outside entertainment like plays, operas, and musicals, they prefer personal and indoor media like computers, TVs, and DVDs.[32]

The second comparison between the YEY-Hui and the YEU-Han was about their media program and content preferences. Similar to the media comparison, the statistic program gave different weights to different priorities between 1 and 5. Table 5 shows the results of the comparison. Again, since the two sample sizes were different, the total possible points were not the same. Therefore, it's reasonable to simply compare the program items prioritized by the two groups.

Interestingly, all of the YEU-Hui and YEU-Han groups preferred similar programs. The top three preferences were equally DVD or computer movies, music, and soap operas. All of the four groups seem to spend a lot of hours watching movies through DVD and computer, and most of them can easily and inexpensively access computers in Internet

31. Ibid.
32. Ibid.

cafés. The price of MP3 players has dramatically decreased and many young people are privately listening to music on the street. Mission strategists need to be aware of these new trends.

Table 5

YEU-Han and E-Group Program Preferences

	DVD or Computer Movies	Music	Soap Operas	Concerts	Storytelling	Paintings and Photos	Operas, Musical	Plays
E1	69	65	40	28	11	14	8	2
E2	94	88	68	33	7	3	5	0
Non-E	62	72	43	28	11	8	4	0
YEU-Hui total	225	225	151	89	29	25	17	2
YEU-Han	169	173	122	57	31	21	11	15

Modern trends change YEU-Hui media and program preferences. Most of their preferences and needs are similar to those of the YEU-Han. The cheap prices at Internet bars enable the YEU to enjoy computers and the Internet. Though print media are currently easy to access, pictorial or audio-visual media use seems to be growing more rapidly. Also, instead of going out to watch plays, operas, and musicals, the new trend for program preference will be those that are loadable in personal mobile devices and other indoor media. For example, watching soap operas on a PMP and listening to gospel preaching on MP3s are no longer new and will become more popular. Young urbanites are attracted to new mobile and personal media. They seek to have and enjoy integrated multi-functional media such as cell phones, PMPs, PDAs, PSPs, MP3s, and MP4s.

SUMMARY

Understanding mass media and the target audience's situations and preferences will give crucial ideas for setting up mission strategy. Current YEU-Hui media trends and program preferences have several distinctive factors. Similar to the YEU-Han, the YEU-Hui prefer personal, indoor, mobile, digital, audio-visual, and quickly accessible media. This research result offers important ideas for the development of mission strategy for the YEU-Hui. Christian leaders need to develop a variety of content that may be loaded into personal media devices.

The content of the programs needs to touch upon YEU-Hui needs and favorite themes, which were researched in former chapters. At the center of this personal mobile media are the computer and Internet, which have a big influence upon YEU-Hui. Therefore, applying computer and Internet technology in missions is tremendously important in the modern world. Internet mission becomes a more strategic tool, especially in places like China or the Islamic world that do not allow freedom of religion, but where there are well-developed Internet facilities. It is necessary to research the feasibility of virtual community as a mission in creative access nations. Therefore, the next chapter studies Christian virtual community in China.

10

Christian Virtual Community in China

IN THE FORMER CHAPTER, a study of YEU-Hui media preferences indicated that computer, Internet, mobile, personal, and indoor media are the most strategic for communicating the gospel. At the center of these media are computers and the Internet. China's nonofficial church members have difficulty accessing the outside world, and they even have difficulty connecting among themselves. In this kind of creative access nation, building virtual community seems to be an alternative and supplementary tool to help local churches. The Internet is free from geographical limitations, can have multiple forms of communication, and can do two-way communication between a number of people. Therefore, the Internet can be a wonderful tool for forming virtual communities.

Along with studying virtual community theories, field research reports on the situation of China's Internet virtual communities can produce new ideas for mission strategy. The final goal is finding out the possibilities for a Christian approach to planting church through virtual community among the YEU-Hui. These findings and analysis provide the basal data for planning virtual community mission strategy.

DEFINING VIRTUAL COMMUNITIES

For an Internet-based virtual community approach, it is necessary to study the characteristics of both traditional and virtual community. Yijong Suh and Myungsoo Kang contribute a large portion of ideas to this area.[1]

---

1. Suh, *Internet Community*; Kang, *Dijitel Sidae Community Hualyong Junliak*.

Traditional vs. Virtual Community

In order to better understand the characteristics of virtual community, it is necessary to first study traditional community. Suh introduced four generations of traditional community research. The first generation began with Ferdinand Tönnies, who conceptualized modern community in 1967. In his book, *Gemeinschaft und Gesellschaft*, Tönnies characterized community as a group of people together without promotion of profit (*gemeinschaft*) and contrasted it with a society that promotes profits (*gesellschaft*).[2] Second, Robert MacIver conceptualized community as an integrated and continual society. According to Suh, MacIver compared and contrasted community with an association. MacIver regarded an association as a tentative, partial, and goal-oriented group, but a community is a naturally formed, continual, and integrated group. The third generation was understood as community from a socio-geographical view; Robert Ezra Park, E. W. Burgess, and Louis Wirth are major Chicago scholars for this generation. They saw community as a geographical neighborhood and developed urban anthropology. The fourth generation saw community as social network.[3]

Many scholars have studied the characteristics of traditional community. Robin Hamman summarizes four major factors of community: (1) a group of people (2) who share social interaction (3) and some common ties between themselves and the other members of the group, (4) and who share an area for at least some of the time.[4]

According to Kang, David A. Karp, G. Stone, and W. Yoels summarized that the three elements of community life are: (1) delineated by a geographically, territorially, or spatially circumscribed area; (2) seen as bound together by a number of characteristics or attributes held in common (values, attitudes, ethnicity, social class, etc.); and (3) engaged in some form of sustained social interaction.[5]

Kang summarized Joseph Gusfield's theory and extracted three community factors: shared consciousness of a group, shared rituals and traditions, and a sense of moral responsibility.[6]

---

2. Tönnies and Loomis, *Community & Society*.
3. Suh, *Internet Community*, 18–21.
4. Hamman, "Introduction to Virtual Communities."
5. Kang, *Dijitel Sidae Community Hualyong Junliak*, 41–42.
6. Ibid., 42.

What, then, are the characteristics of virtual community? Kang explains that virtual community has very similar characteristics to traditional community except that it is not limited by time and space. He summarized several scholars' views on virtual community. Howard Rheingold said that virtual community was a social association by human network where people can share feelings and continually discuss in the online space. Julian Farrior et al. described online community as a community like traditional and physical community in a virtual space. Anthony P. Cohen said it is a symbolically constituted community with meaningful symbols, a value of providing members identity in association, and a system of principles.[7]

Rheingold said, "Virtual communities are social aggregations that emerge from the Net when enough people carry on those public discussions long enough, with sufficient human feeling, to form webs of personal relationships in cyberspace."[8] He summarizes six characteristics of virtual community as instruments for connecting people, help coping the information overload, have drawbacks, easy to deceive, asynchronous, many to many medium.[9]

The concept of a virtual Internet community is a combination of traditional community and electronic space. Except for the fact that it is not limited by time and space, the virtual community is quite similar to the traditional community.

Sociological Analysis to the Virtual Community

What are the sociological characteristics of the virtual community? Kang summarized many scholars' sociological views about virtual communities. L. J. Lawrence said that having sustained social interaction, community standards, and membership rules are crucial factors for a virtual community. Rheingold said that virtual communities stress members' ideas, feelings, and mutual interests, rather than members' appearances and predestined factors. Muniz and O'guinn said that the sociological characteristics of virtual community are shared consciousness, rituals and traditions, and a sense of moral responsibility. Kang emphasizes that it is the motivations and attitudes of its members that make virtual

---

7. Ibid., 50–51.
8. Rheingold, *Virtual Community*, 5.
9. "Virtual Community," 118–22.

community a real community, not the characteristics of the media itself.[10] Virtual community has more interpersonal interactions among members than a virtual association. Virtual communities often interact with offline communities, and some offline communities expand their function into a virtual community.[11]

Virtual Community and Real Community

Though many people think that online relationships are relatively untrustworthy, irresponsible and weak, several scholars have tried to enlighten the positive points of virtual relationships.

According to Berry Wellman's summary, some of the negative views about online communication are that it can cause people to engage in cyber addiction, become antisocial and individualistic, or become socially maladjusted.[12]

However, there are positive voices from several scholars as well. Linda M. Harasim suggests that computer communication does not ignore other communication tools, nor does it start a totally new alternative. It only expands human communication zones. "Computer . . . increases our range of human connectedness and the number of ways in which we are able to make contact with others."[13]

Marc A. Smith and Peter Kollock said that in modern society the concept of community has changed from physical proximity to social networks. They analyzed that some unrealistic expectations toward real life can create negative opinions toward computer communication. They said, "Their comparison seems to be to an ideal of community rather than to face-to-face communities as they are actually lived. There is a great deal of loneliness in the lives of many city dwellers."[14] Wellman also summarized positive aspects of Internet communication. He pointed out the fact that, even before online communities appeared, the concept of community had already changed from physically closed neighborhoods to more integrated social networks. Thanks to personal media, communication tools, and increased mobility, people can sustain long-distance relationships even if they cannot maintain

10. Kang, *Dijital Sidae Community Hualyong Junliak*, 52–54.
11. Suh, *Internet Community*, 31.
12. Wellman, *Networks in the Global Village*, 344–48.
13. Harasim, *Global Networks*, 16.
14. Smith and Kollock, *Communities in Cyberspace*, 17.

face-to-face relationships.[15] This means that, though there is evidence of harm to human relationships, people use online communication to form and reinforce relationships.[16]

Wellmen seems to believe that online communities can lead a counter-trend to the contemporary privatization of community.

VIRTUAL COMMUNITY'S MODE OF COMMUNICATION

Suh has provided significant input regarding the virtual community mode of communication.[17] A virtual community's two major communication channels are a web page and offline activities.

An Internet web page has variety and integrated functions. For example, community members can share and discuss ideas simultaneously or not. They can share visual, audio, textual, and pictorial information. In order to have active interactions among members, web pages provide several kinds of functions.

First, forum boards have announcements and encourage members to share information. People bring their information, share resources, and get together in small groups in this web page.

Second, members can have multiple conversations through chatting functions. People can chat one-on-one, one-to-many, or many-to-many. Audio and video meetings on web pages enable members to share large amounts of information more actively.

Third, members contact each other by email. Members send or receive email, which enables them to have one-on-one or even group dialogue.

Fourth, another mode of communication within a virtual community is offline meetings. There are at least four types of offline meetings that can be considered virtual community activities: regular large meetings, thunder meetings (emergency or non-regular meetings), small group meetings, and individual meetings.

---

15. Wellman, *Networks in the Global Village*, 355.
16. Ibid., 350.
17. Ibid.

VIRTUAL COMMUNITY'S MEMBERSHIP STRUCTURE

Virtual communities have membership structure for maintaining their dynamics.[18] Communication channels and community culture are the mainframe of the membership structures.

According to chapter 5 in Suh's book *Internet Community Wa Hangook Sahue*, most virtual communities use four kinds of membership structures to maintain their dynamics: managing membership, community activities and members' proximity, membership interactions, and trust building.[19]

First, virtual communities manage their members. In most cases, the communities have at least two kinds of membership: the founder/maintainer and the members. To maintain its ethos and goal, communities usually have conditions for new members. Communities usually give unequal rights and areas of activity, and different levels of membership have different responsibilities.

Second, the characteristics of community activities and the proximity of the members affect the shape of the virtual community's membership structure. Depending on the type of activities, each community has a different membership structure. People choose different groups by their gender, age, education level, social group, cultural background, and so on.

Third, the variety of activities increases membership interactions. Virtual communities offer events, programs, and awards to encourage member participation.

Fourth, building trust is a crucial part of membership structure. Byunghui Shin and Jongho Lee said that there are two key areas of membership structure that require trust: (1) relationships between manager and members, and (2) relationships among members. Members can trust other members and the management of the community as the company opens community credit reports, has clear members' credit policy, has community policies, protects private information, and provides fair and proper services to different membership levels. Members can easily build trust when they feel that their manager provides three kinds of care: active member care, clear community policies and communications, and consistent and transparent policies and attitudes.[20]

---

18. Suh, *Internet Community*.
19. Ibid., 177.
20. Shin and Lee, *Eensaide Kumyuniti*, 79.

VIRTUAL COMMUNITY TYPES

There are several types of virtual communities. Suh introduces two different categorizations for virtual communities: by type and by goal.[21]

First, Suh divided virtual communities by their types into three categories: church, theater, and café. A church type of virtual community is leadership-centered community. In the church type of community, the leader's expertise and leadership is the key for community dynamics. Similar to a pastor who leads a church, the leader cares for and leads the community with leadership and expertise.

A theater-type of virtual community is where the members' interest and hobbies are centers of community dynamics. Members can enjoy their hobbies and develop their knowledge and skills. Offline activities are a core part of this type of virtual community.

Developing friendship is the center of the café type of virtual community. Horizontal relationship is crucial in this type, so the leader's role is simply as coordinator. Because their friendships naturally develop when the groups are homogeneous, these virtual communities are usually divided by age groups, home towns, and working status.

Second, Suh categorized communities into six kinds by their goals: hobbies, discussion, geography, community service, and general life issues.[22]

In a hobby community, the main reason members join their virtual community is to gain information about their hobby. For example, members share and discuss information, improve their skills, buy inexpensive products.

In a discussion virtual community, the main reason members join is to discuss common topics and gain knowledge. Campaigns against sexual violence, history discussions, and environmental concern groups are examples of this type.

Local virtual community is formed on the basis of similar offline backgrounds. Members enjoy friendship among themselves. Many of these communities are named after the members' hometowns.

Age communities are formed based on similar age groups. In this type of virtual community, they enjoy their homogeneousness, share experiences, ideas, and feelings.

---

21. Suh, *Internet Community*.
22. Ibid., 106–40.

Social and life service virtual communities consist of people who face similar situations and burdens.

DIRECTION FROM FIELD RESEARCH

Based on the previous theoretical study, field research was done on the virtual community situation in China. The key problem statement of this field report was the lack of understanding and lack of effectiveness of current Internet mission strategies for China and the Hui.

These problems have three research goals:

1. To address current Internet missions to China and the Hui.
2. To understand how Internet missions and virtual community strategy work in China and operate among the Hui.
3. To identify effective church-planting strategy through virtual community in China and the Hui.

Each of the goals has a research question:

1. What do the Internet missions to China and the Hui do?
2. How do Internet missions and virtual community mission strategy work in China and operate among the Hui?
3. What is an effective strategy for planting offline churches through virtual community?

Goals and Information Needed

The first research object had two major parts. Part A surveyed the big picture of China's general Internet situation. Part B researched the general situation of Internet missions and had two areas to research. First was analyzing whether the websites had an effective structure for producing offline community. The necessary information for this area were website goals, relevant circumstances of primary recipients, attraction for new and returning recipients, and virtual community feedback systems. The second area of part B was answering the question: "Do the websites actively work for building offline communities?" Information about their virtual community membership management system and their strategy for offline community was needed for this part.

The second objective was to address how Internet missions to China and the Hui operate. The data necessary for this objective were the effectiveness of the websites' mission strategy, and their development of the possibility for offline community.

The third research objective was to identify effective Internet mission strategies to China and the Hui. The necessary items of information were the identification of problems in current strategies for building offline community among the Hui, and its proper strategies.

Research Design and Sampling Plan

In order to gather the necessary information, there are four kinds of data collection methods: survey research, interview, participation observation, and case studies. The questionnaire in appendix B has ten questions. Rather than asking direct questions to participants, as traditionally done with questionnaires, researchers evaluated websites through a questionnaire. Therefore, the method was combined with a questionnaire and an interview. However, at this time, the samples were websites instead of people. For the case studies and participation observation, researchers joined an Internet community and participated in the community activities with an emic view.

In order to find an appropriate sampling of Christian websites, the researcher surveyed several web address lists. The lists on the *Global Missiology* website and on several other websites provided the beginning address lists for sampling. Additionally, the sending-base director of Hong Kong Frontiers' mission organization and three other missionaries in China helped develop the sampling. Finally, the researcher had sixty website addresses on the sample list. From these sixty addresses, the researcher screened appropriate samples through specific criterion, primarily that the site had a mission to Mainland China. It did not matter where the site manager was located, but it was expected that he or she would use simplified Chinese characters and have mission purposes.[23] Using these criteria, the researcher finally screened out twenty-six samples.

Data Collection and Data Processing

The questionnaire method used for data collection was self-administered. Before beginning the real research, two foreign Chinese conducted a pilot research test. After five respondents completed the pilot test questions, the researchers were able to reshape the questionnaire.

---

23. Mainland China currently uses only simplified Chinese characters.

Christian Virtual Community in China 175

The two foreign Chinese volunteers and the researcher regularly met for planning, screening samples, and developing questionnaires. They finally dismissed two questions regarding the number of site visitors and the community members' personal media usability. The reason was that every site had a different concept of visitors, members, and clicker numbers and records, making it difficult to fairly compare the number of visitors.

The researcher tabulated and typed answers into an SPSS (v.13.0) program for analyzing data. The SPSS categorized the samples into two groups: high tendency and low tendency toward virtual community sites. Microsoft Excel 2006 was used for further calculations in the next tabulation. Researchers spent three months doing library research and two months developing and answering questions, tabulating data, and writing and editing reports.

DATA REPORT TO CHINA'S CURRENT INTERNET USER SITUATION

Library research was the main method used to examine the current situation of Internet missions to China and the Hui.

In 2004 on the *eTForecasts* website, Egil Juliussen reported on the world's Internet demography and Asia's rapid growth in Internet use. According to the report, China would surpass Japan and become second to the United States in number of Internet users in 2004. The report claimed that in 2004 China was the second largest Internet country in the world.[24]

Then what is the current situation of the Internet and its users in China? In January of 2007, the China Internet Network Information Center (CNNIC) reported China's Internet demography. The report defined Internet users as "Chinese citizen aged 6 and above who averagely use the Internet at least one hour per week."[25]

---

24. Juliussen, "Internet User Forecast by Country."
25. CNNIC, "Statistical Survey Report," 3.

Part Two: Communication Principle and Strategy

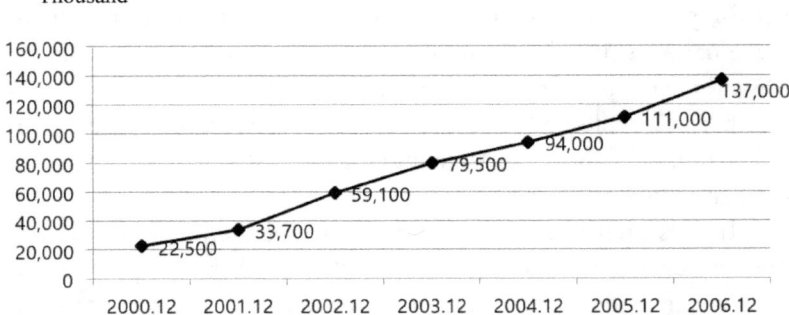

Number of Internet Users in Previous Survey[26]

Internet users in China totaled 137.0 million. The ninety-five percentage confidence intervals for the estimate were 133.62 million to 140.38 million. Figure 26 shows the rapid growth in the number of China's Internet users. About six times more members were using the Internet than were six years ago (22.5 million). The number of users had increased by 23.4 percent in the past year.

The number of computers in China with Internet connections was 59.4 million.[27] China had approximately four million domain names and 843,000 websites, which has increased to almost one million in the past year. These sites had 4.47 billion web pages, which increased by 86.3 percent to more than 6.5 billion in the past year.[28] Simplified Chinese characters were used in 95.4 percent of web pages, while 4.5 percent used traditional Chinese and only 0.1 percent used English.[29] As table 6 shows, the report found that Chinese web page content was dominated by text.

Table 6

The Percentages of Web Page Content Forms[30]

Text	Image	Audio	Video
70.2%	29.5%	0.0%	0.3%

26. Ibid., 24.
27. Ibid., 54.
28. Ibid., 27, 30, 33.
29. Ibid., 7.
30. Ibid.

CNNIC did demographic research of Chinese Internet users. Male percentages (58.3%) were slightly higher than female ones (41.7%). The age situation of Internet users is recorded in figure 27. More than half of them were less than twenty-four years old, and more than 70 percent were less than thirty years old, meaning that most users are quite young.

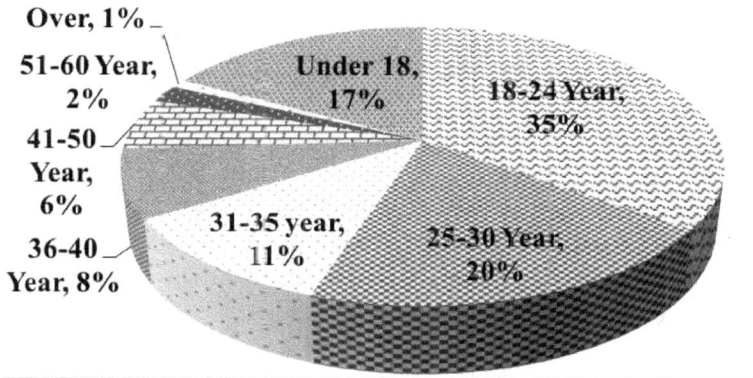

Internet Users' Age Situation[31]

Their marital status shows that 57.8 percent were unmarried, and 42.2 percent were married.[32] This means that many Chinese Internet users were relatively free from family responsibility. As they get married in a few years, these new families may be greatly influenced by the Internet information highway, and traditional family concepts may face tremendous changes.

Figure 28 shows the education levels of Chinese Internet users. More than half of them were high school students or lower. Considering that there was a strong trend toward education and that more than 70 percent of users were less than thirty, China's Internet users are definitely a young, educated group.

31. Ibid., 10.
32. Ibid., 11.

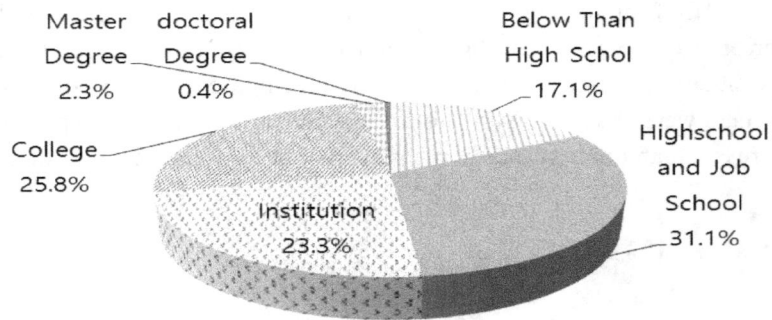

Internet User's Education Level[33]

Next, CNNIC reported China's occupation situation among Internet users (see figure 29). About 70 percent of users were students, school workers, and company workers. Considering that their average age was quite young and that many were jobless (7.2%), the freelancers group (9.6%) may also include people who were too young to have jobs yet.

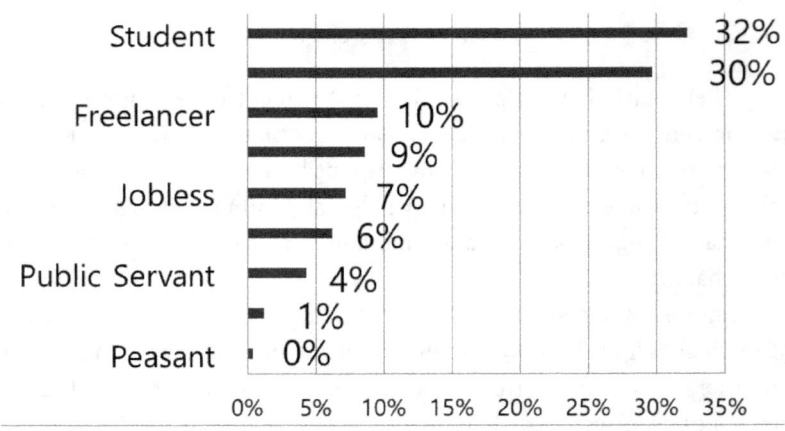

Internet User's Occupation Situation[34]

CNNIC also reported Internet users' geographical locations (see figure 30). According to mobile phone and Internet users' locations, about 83 percent of users lived in an urban setting.

33. Ibid.
34. Ibid., 47.

About 70 percent of their income was less than 2,000 Yuan, which is about 300 dollars.[35]

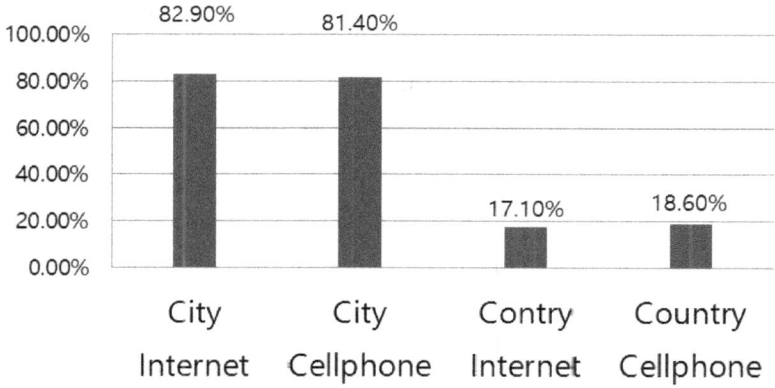

Internet and Mobile Phone Users' Location[36]

To summarize the data, the number of Internet users in China is rapidly growing. The main Internet users in China were urbanites and younger than thirty years old with more than a high school education. A very important finding is that the condition of this group was quite similar to that of the YEU group. Therefore, China's Internet users are automatically screened as part of the YEU group among the general Chinese population.

ANALYSIS OF CHINESE CHRISTIAN WEBSITE AND VIRTUAL COMMUNITIES

From the sixty original website addresses, the researcher screened samples by specific criteria. The websites needed to be oriented toward mission to Mainland China and written only in simplified Chinese characters. Some sites that simply had Christian articles, journals, and databases were not included since they did not seem to be mission-oriented. Sites with indirect evangelism methods were accepted as samples if the ultimate purpose was missions. Using these criteria, the researcher screened the list down to twenty-six samples.

35. Ibid., 45.
36. Ibid., 63.

Current Christian Websites

The first step of analyzing the sample involved categorizing them into two groups according to how actively they formed both on- and offline communities. Question 8 on the survey was multiple-choice, asking if the sites had virtual community functions and intentions. The high-tendency group consisted of those that checked more than four answers to these questions, and those who checked less than four were categorized into the low-tendency group.

Table 7

High and Low Tendencies for Forming Virtual Communities[37]

	Low Tendency Group				High Tendency Group				
Number of answers checked	0	1	2	3	4	5	6	7	Total
Doesn't seem to have plan for virtual community	5	3	0	0	0	0	0	0	8
Seems to have plan for virtual community	0	1	1	2	3	2	3	5	17
Totals	5	4	1	2	3	2	3	5	25

Table 7 shows the results that were calculated by the SPSS. Question 8 asked if the sites had a plan for building virtual community. Naturally, those that had plans for virtual community identified themselves by checking more answers and were categorized in the high tendency group. Based on the answers, twelve samples were categorized into the low group, and thirteen of them were in the high group.

The next comparison involved the goals of the sites and who their primary receptor groups were. Two questions contributed for this information: goal, and receptor groups. Since the high and low tendency sample numbers were not the same (thirteen and twelve), the numbers are expressed as percentages for equal comparison.

Table 8 shows the results of question 1, which asked about the goals of the website design. Among the high group samples, 46 percent seemed to seek to build virtual community, and 15 percent seemed to have a plan for offline community from the beginning. Lower group samples were very passive in forming offline community. Only 25 percent of the low group

37. Developed table from Kim, "New Mission Tool," 186.

had virtual community planning, and none of them had offline community plans. Therefore, planning for an offline community even before designing a website is crucial for developing on- and offline communities.

Table 8

Goal of Sites[38]

	Choices	High Tendency (%)	Low Tendency (%)
1(A)	Minister to missionaries	0	0
2(B)	Introduce the gospel	100	58
3(C)	Provide Christian information	62	83
4(D)	Build Chinese virtual community	46	25
5(E)	Build offline community	15	0
6(F)	Provide agents for offline community	0	0
7(G)	Other	0	8

Table 9 shows who the primary users of the sites were. Those from both high and low groups were generally Chinese. Specially, only thirty-one (17%) websites were designed to target young, educated, and urban Chinese. Even though these few sites were specifically targeting YEU groups, it should be considered that, according to the analysis of the CNNIC report, since Chinese Internet users are mainly young, urban, and educated, the users are automatically screened as part of the YEU group.

Table 9

Primary Recipients[39]

	Choices	High Tendency (%)	Low Tendency (%)
1(A)	Foreign missionaries	0	0
2(B)	Chinese all over the world	23	8
3(C)	Young, educated, and urban Chinese	31	17

38. Ibid.
39. Ibid.

	Choices	High Tendency (%)	Low Tendency (%)
4(D)	General Chinese Muslim	0	0
5(E)	Young, educated, and urban Chinese Muslims	0	0
6(F)	General Chinese in mainland	85	83

Table 10 lists the answers for question 3, which asked "In order to attract your primary recipients, how do you design your websites?" This question aimed to learn what kinds of cultural and social themes are used for screening out their primary receptor group from the general users.

Table 10

Cultural Theme of the Sites[40]

	Choices	High Tendency (%)	Low Tendency (%)
1(A)	No screening system	46	58
2(B)	Appropriate themes	46	33
3(C)	Appropriate education level	15	17
4(D)	Cultural situation	31	33
5(E)	Social situation (job, locality, preference)	15	8
6(F)	Ethnic group issues	0	0
7(G)	Touching felt needs	31	25
8(H)	Using special language	0	0
9(I)	Discussing their religion	0	0

A shocking result is that no matter how high or low the group tendency, about half of all sites said that they did not have any screening system. Some sites had a membership system and provided unequal services to the different membership levels, but still this is not the same as screening by cultural themes. People from any background can join if they just agree to the policy. This system cannot screen users. If the

40. Ibid.

site deals with special themes, tools, or programs, then only proper users joined, and this automatic screening system enabled the community to have homogenous groups

Sites generally did not have a cultural screening system for their users, except for the fact that consideration of social situation and ethnic issues in high tendency groups was slightly higher than in low groups.

Table 11 shows the results of question 4, which asked what kinds of method the site used for evangelism. This question aimed at learning how many of the sites directly introduced the gospel or used indirect methods as a stepping-stone. Most of the high tendency groups and more than half of the low tendency groups used direct methods. Approximately 38 percent of the high group tried to meet members' felt needs as they introduced the gospel.

Table 11

Evangelism Methods[41]

	Choices	High Tendency (%)	Low Tendency (%)
1(A)	Directly introduce	92	58
2(B)	Touching felt needs	38	25
3(C)	Cultural themes, common ground (filial piety, life issues, etc.)	8	0
4(D)	Others	8	25

Since most of sites seem to be designed for Christian believers, the sites were more likely to be information networks for Christians themselves, rather than primarily for introducing the gospel. Furthermore, most community members were Christians, rather than seekers or nonbelievers.

Question 12 refers to how many visitors and members the sites have, which is aimed at understanding the degree of activity on the sites. Answering this question was difficult because each site had a different concept of a visitor, and each one employed a different method of recording its traffic frequency. Also, most sites do not openly disclose their recent three-month traffic record.

41. Ibid.

Table 12 shows the results of question 6, which asked what kinds of attractions the sites offered their visitors. The high tendency group showed slightly higher percentages of multiple functions: web searching tools, weather forecasting, opportunities to locate old friends, cafés, blogs, and virtual communities.

Linking with other sites is a crucial function for advertising the site to new visitors. Seventy percent of the sites could link with other sites, but most of them were linked to other Christian sites, not secular ones. This means it may not be easy for both seekers and non-Christians to find these sites.

Most of the free downloadable content consisted of Christian materials—gospel songs, apologetics articles, the Bible—which few non-Christians would be interested in.

Though some of the websites introduced the gospel indirectly through secular professionalism, there were very few. Furthermore, none of the sites offered an online counseling system. The primary condition for forming virtual community is maximizing the Internet's two-way communication functionality. One interesting finding is that none of the low tendency groups had counseling or debate functions, but 54 percent of the high tendency groups did.

Table 12

Attraction to Newcomers[42]

		Choices	High Tendency (%)	Low Tendency (%)
1	(A)	Provide a variety of tools	62	25
2	(B)	Linked to other sites	77	75
3	(C)	Offer rewards	8	0
4	(D)	Free downloads	92	42
5	(E)	Online counseling/debates	54	0
6	(F)	Christian yellow pages	31	8
7	(G)	Updating secular/Christian news, events	31	42

42. Ibid.

	Choices	High Tendency (%)	Low Tendency (%)
8(H)	Provide more secular and professional materials (e.g., medical news and experts)	31	17
9(I)	Others	0	17

Table 13 shows the results of question 7, which asked how the websites were ready to receive feedback from recipients. Most of sites offered the managers' email address, phone number, and postal address.

Table 13

Feedback Systems[43]

	Choices	High Tendency (%)	Low Tendency (%)
1(A)	No functions	0	8
2(B)	Email, message	92	75
3(C)	Dialogue board	85	50
4(D)	Chatting	31	8
5(E)	Audio/video communication	0	0
6(F)	Provide contact information	85	58

Table 14 shows the results of question 9, which asked how the sites were ready to build offline communities. Unfortunately, most sites were not ready for an offline community. In fact, only one case proved ready to introduce people in person; however, even in this case, the strategy only offered a small amount of group management, rather than systematic church planting.

43. Ibid.

Table 14

Readiness for Offline Community[44]

	Choices	High Tendency (%)	Low Tendency (%)
1(A)	Do not provide services	92	100
2(B)	Persons are ready to contact	8	0
3(C)	Organization is ready to contact	0	0
4(D)	Local churches are ready to contact	0	0
5(E)	Others	0	0
6(F)	Provide contact information	0	0

Last, question 10 asks what kinds of media the online community members used. The goal was to learn about potential possibilities for forming offline community by understanding the members' frequency of personal media use. However, this information was unavailable because the communities did not clearly provide it.

SAMPLE CASE SITES

On some websites, researchers joined the community as members, which enabled them to make participant observations in the virtual community. The results of these observations lead to several cases of mission strategy, including several phenomena of development from online community into an offline community.

Appropriate Mission Strategy Cases

There were five cases that effectively and creatively communicated the gospel to their audiences. Most of them tried to meet the felt needs of their members and use expertise that could hold users' interests.

CASE 1: A CHRISTIAN LAWYER'S PERSONAL SITE

A Christian lawyer from Wenzhou provided online law consulting for free or at a low price on the website *Jidutufaluwang*.[45] In the middle of

---

44. Ibid.

45. Pronounced *jidutufaluwang*, which means "Christian Lawyer Website." The

such consulting, the lawyer introduced the gospel. Since the website is run by local Chinese and a professional lawyer, many people trusted him, and the gospel message seemed to be more effectively transmitted (*Christian Lawyer* website).

CASE 2: STUDYING ENGLISH AS THEY SHARE THE GOSPEL

At first, the website *Studying English*[46] seemed to be an English language study site, but there were several sections that hyperlinked to Christian sites. It meets the needs of those in YEU groups; therefore, it automatically screened a user's age and education level. Unfortunately, though this website provided the necessary potential conditions for forming virtual community, there was no attempt to form one (*Studying English* website).

CASE 3: VISUAL MEDIA-CENTERED EVANGELISM

The *Gospel Film* website was a very visual, media-centered site that appealed to the YEU group.[47] Furthermore, one encouraging thing is that, though it is in a preliminary situation, the site has already formed a virtual community. Members have shared responses to movies, DVDs, and sermons.

CASE 4: ACTIVATING VIRTUAL COMMUNITY THROUGH BLOG

The *Chinese Christian's Blog* website has facilitated the formation of virtual community among Chinese Christians by using a blog.[48] There were geographic districts, in which members chose their common concerns and topics. As the manager raised a topic, people shared their ideas by adding replies. Many repliers provided their personal web page address or personal communication media address. Blogs encouraged individuals to build their own personal, virtual community.

The *God Blog* website contained thirty-five district blogs in which many sub-blogs were provided.[49] For example, there were forty-six sub-blogs under the Beijing district. Individual members were able to suggest personal topics to share about within these sub-blogs.

---

website address is www.jdflw.com.
    46. The Studying English website address is www.abc111.com.
    47. www.gospelfilm.com.
    48. www.ccblog.net.
    49. www.god51.com/index.html.

Blogging is a tremendous system for building offline community in creative access nations since it enables geographical, sociological, and cultural proximity groups to get together. One problem found among blog users is that most of their relationship ties are weak and the level of conversations may be shallow and not serious. However, a blog can be a wonderful catalyst to further communication. Members, however, do strengthen their ties to each other by providing their personal email addresses, chat addresses, and phone numbers.

Case 5: Systemic Discipleship Course Using School Themes

The website *Christian Student Web* is decorated similarly to a school system. It offered several different reception gates for visitors.[50] There was a place for newcomers, and second-time visitors could choose a community by their real school level. There were several communities: middle school, high school, college, graduates, men's dormitory, girl's dormitory, and English corners. The next levels were quite similar to other sites. It offered daily Bible reading, boys' and girls' fellowship, new believers' corners, and so on. Even the title of membership levels and award systems were quite similar to real school in order to keep members familiar with the atmosphere. The titles are Principle, Teacher, Academic Advisor, Student Council, Homeroom Teacher, and Student of the Month.

From Online to Offline Cases

In several cases, the website members tried to develop themselves into offline communities from online community. People did not know each other before they met in their virtual spaces, and they tried to meet in offline spaces.

Case 6: Meeting at Offline Through an Online Community

There were links to local virtual communities on the website *Christian Student Web*. On this website, a seeker—using the screen name aaron918—wrote the following memo looking for a campus Christian community. There were six replies on the site, and table 15 introduces three of them after aaron918's question.

---

50. In Chinese, Christian Student Web is *jidujiaosueshung* (基督教学生网) [jeedoojyaosueshung], www.51sky.net.

Table 15

A Summary of Conversation on a Chinese Christian Website

(*Christian Student Web*)

Date	Identification	Conversation
September 9, 2006	Aaron918	Who knows of a Christian fellowship at Beijing Teachers' University? If it is impossible, any other nearby fellowship would be fine. Thank you. Help your sister please! Emmanuel!!
September 18, 2006	Yoyo	I know that!! I just came from Beijing, and there was a good Christian group at the Teacher's University.
February 2, 2007	214seven	I know. I know several brothers and sisters, and I can introduce them. My QQ chatting address is 316151968.
April 12, 2007	Can I long sustain	I am a member of the group. My QQ chatting address is 6197)378. You can contact me. Let's talk later.

When the Christian sites provide abundant information, effective network systems, and facilitation of relationships, members seem to be able to have active conversations.

Case 7: Manager Organizes Offline Meeting

Light of Spiritual Love is a private Christian website within China's Shenzhen City. The site had online community groups and offered an offline community meeting. Table 16 shows an announcement about changing the leader of the meeting.[51]

---

51. www.godislove.cn/forum_view.asp?forum_id=11&view_id=1867.

Part Two: Communication Principleand Strategy

Table 16

A Sample of Chinese Christian Website Bulletin

(*Light of Spiritual Love* website)

Time: Saturday 7:30–9:30 PM

Place: Shenzhen Linjiao Church Sunday school classroom

Recent News: June 15, 2005

Message: Thank God. Because of my class schedule, I cannot be the manager of our virtual group, and "Big Nature" sister will in charge of it. Please pray for her. . . . Her personal contact channels are as follows:

[Email, Phone Number, MSN Chat name]

Since meeting times and places are not perfectly fixed, please contact "Big Nature" sister before you come.

This is a good example of how the community develops from online to offline. It included the time and place of the regular meetings and a contact person's phone, email, and MSN address. The message added an alert that the place and time can be changed.

INTERPRETATION

The good news is that techniques for developing virtual community in China were far more developed than expected. In contrast to the fact that most Western and Korean church websites employ a one-way communication method—static pages, video sermon, and announcements—many Chinese Christian sites were equipped with hyperlinks connecting to a variety of functions. In addition to static pages, they offered forums, blogs, photo galleries, calendars, events, and many communication systems. These abundant two-way communication systems offered good fertilizer for forming online communities. Since many virtual community members are from Mainland China, the cultural themes and relational dynamics seem to be purely created by the Chinese, not by foreigners.

In order to build offline community among Chinese and the Hui, there are several areas that need to be developed for an Internet strategy.

First, many of the websites' goals were broad and unclear. Many of their primary receptor groups were general Chinese, and many sites did not have a screening system for their members.

Second, strategies for evangelism to non-Christians were very poor. Though they said their goal was to introduce the gospel, few of the sites met the needs of seekers and nonbelievers. Two-thirds of their methods were direct evangelism, and most of their data and documents were for the discipleship training of believers. Redesigning the site according to cultural themes will automatically screen for the target people.

Third, the sites need to offer a variety of services to attract users. The content and functions were too simple to be attractive. Additionally, most of their hyperlinks were linked with other Christian sites, not with secular sites. This disconnects the network from the secular world and reduces the chance of contact with non-Christians. As a result, the community can become a Christian ghetto.

Fourth, many of the websites' discipleship programs are too passive to hold users' attention. Similar to department store sites, they passively wait for visitors to choose them. With this approach, the site may not easily attract visitors to enter and stay.

Fifth, both the local church-initiated web management and offline community building were poor. Many domestic sites seemed to get help from foreign missions though they had an inland address. The key to the whole process of offline church planting, however, is the activity and involvement of local church members. The lack of local experts also seemed to be a serious problem.

Sixth, more systematic plans for building offline communities are important. So far, it seems that very few churches and individuals have successfully developed offline communities from online communities. It is necessary to educate and encourage local churches to take initiative in virtual community projects.

Seventh, only a few sites focused on the Hui, and those few need to change their communication style to become more receptor-oriented. There were only two samples that seemed to relate to mission and the Hui: the *Answering Islam* and *Walking to Arab World* websites. However, unlike their titles, these sites did not seem to be designed for mission to the Hui but for mobilizing and equipping Chinese Christians for mission to the Hui. There were several debates about Christian and Islam doctrines but no feedback system. Therefore, these two sites needed to clarify their goals as either mission to the Hui or mobilizing Christians.

SUMMARY

In creative access nations, building virtual community is a new alternative and supplementary tool to help local churches. The Internet is free from geographical limitations, and the opportunities for multiple forms of communication enable the formation of virtual communities. By these functions of virtual community, Christians can more effectively have receptor-oriented communication.

Internet mission is a proper alternative in a country where there is persecution, where there are not enough offline churches, and where there is a lack of Christian resources. Internet missions need to be culturally sensitive, strategic, and networkable with local churches, foreign missions, and other resources.

To be successful, Internet missions need to integrate with the local church's active evangelism and discipleship strategies. To recover from the shortcomings of current Chinese Christian websites, receptor-oriented attitudes, clearly defined goals, and receptors are necessary.

China is the second largest Internet country in the world, and the main users are young, educated urbanites; therefore, approaching the Hui through the Internet is a very strategic way to meet YEU-Hui.

Among several types and goals of virtual community, developing theater-type and hobby communities are strategic because they are easy to develop into offline communities. Chinese Christian websites are well developed and have a good potential for further development. Local churches and expatriates need to cooperate in website development and use the sites to plant future offline churches.

Virtual community for offline church can be a new alternative for planting churches among the YEU-Hui. Clarifying its process is another important step for planting receptor-oriented churches. The process should include designing and running the website, followed by the process of launching an offline church. The process of strategy will come in the next chapter.

11

Developing Strategies for Church Planting among the YEU-Hui

FOR SOME CHRISTIANS, THE issue of strategy sometimes conflicts with their theological understandings. They may ask questions like, "Why do we need a strategy? God is leading us, so why should we be depending on man-made tactics?" As we look to the Bible for answers to such questions, it is true that the Bible often tells readers to ask God for wisdom. For example, we can quote the following verse from the book of Isaiah, "Thus saith the LORD, the Holy One of Israel, and his Maker, Ask me of things to come concerning my sons, and concerning the work of my hands command ye me."[1] Actually, there is no conflict between these two positions. The text does not mean that we should ignore human wisdom, but God wants people to use their own wisdom empowered with his wisdom.

Two of the parables told by Jesus relate to the need for strategy. The parable of building a tower and the parable about a king who went to war with only ten thousand soldiers.[2] The story of Nehemiah is another good example regarding the need for strategy. Since Nehemiah prepared a full description of his strategy before he met king Artaxerxes, he could explain his plan and the necessary preparations.[3] The Bible continually respects people's wisdom and also asks individuals to use their own wisdom while respecting God's guidance. Edward R. Dayton and David A.

---

1. Isa 45:11.
2. Luke 14:28–32.
3. Neh 2:1–10.

Fraser describe Nehemiah as a skillful practitioner of "the art and science of getting things done with other people."[4]

Many biblical passages encourage the use of counseling, discussions, and strategies in order to achieve goals. One proverb says, "A wise man will hear, and will increase learning; and a man of understanding shall attain unto wise counsels."[5] Another proverb says, "For by wise counsel thou shalt make thy war: and in a multitude of counselors there is safety."[6]

Søgaard points out that there must be harmony between spiritual and rational things in order for strategies to develop. "The development of a strategy should involve the study of Scriptures, prayer, and relying on the work of the Holy Spirit, but it will also need data collection, research and analysis."[7]

Dayton reminds us that Christian mission needs a goal-centered strategy. He says that planning is a responsibility for any human who serves God.[8] He insists that many cases of failed Christian ministry are the direct result of poor planning.

DEFINING STRATEGY

Strategy is not a new issue in Christian mission; however, few Christians seem to have a clearly defined concept of strategy. When the Lord gives us his commission, he also provides us with his wisdom for assistance.

Robert J. Clinton has introduced what he calls "the bridging strategy" for defining strategy. He uses the term "here and there" and says that strategy involves choosing the best method of going from one situation, here, to another desired situation and goal, there. "Knowing the Now and the anticipated Then we are ready to devise a strategy to get from where we are Now to where we want to be Then."[9]

Viggo Søgaard describes strategy as follows:

> As a general definition of the term strategy, we can say that a strategy is an overall approach, plan, or way of describing how we will go about reaching our goal of solving our problem.

4. Dayton and Fraser, *Planning Strategies*, 21.
5. Prov 1:5.
6. Prov 24:6.
7. Søgaard, *Communicating Scripture*, p. 2 of ch. 19.
8. Dayton, *God's Purpose / Man's Plans*, 2.
9. Clinton, *Bridging Strategies*, 1.

> Strategy is a way to reach an objective, a kind of map of the territory to be covered in order to "reach from here to there."[10]

God wants us to use wisdom in designing and proceeding with the work. A poorly designed strategy wastes time, money, and manpower and causes unnecessary frustration. Søgaard therefore explains strategy as a concept of integrated terms:

> Strategy is a conceptual way of anticipating the future, guiding us in major decisions concerning alternative approaches and decisive action. In this way strategy helps us by providing a sense of direction and cohesiveness, focusing on the central issues of our task and philosophy of ministry.[11]

Dayton and Fraser define strategy as an overall way of reaching an objective. "Strategy looks for a range of possible 'means and methods' and various 'operations' that will best accomplish an objective.... It looks for a time and place when things will be different from what they are now."[12]

SELECTED THEORIES OF COMMUNICATION STRATEGY

In the following, several selected theories of communication strategy are presented. Each theory will provide theoretical support for specific aspects in the development of a new strategy for YEU-Hui.

Barriers and Bridges

For effective receptor-oriented communication, the speaker needs to overcome the cultural, social, and historical barriers that stand between the speaker and the audience. If the speakers retain those barriers, the barriers keep a distance and create a lot of noise within the communication. At the same time, understanding the audience's needs and contextualizing the message can be an effective bridge for a communicator.

To achieve the communication goal, the speaker needs to remove communication barriers that stand between the audience and the speaker. There are at least three areas that need to be considered when a Christian communicator removes these communication barriers so that effective

---

10. Søgaard, *Communicating Scripture*, p. 2 of ch. 19.
11. *Media in Church and Mission*, 56.
12. Dayton and Fraser, *Planning Strategies for World Evangelization*, 13–14.

communication bridges can be created. First, the Christian speaker needs to analyze if the audience is hostile or receptive to the gospel.[13]

Second, if the audience is hostile toward the gospel, the communicator needs to know the reasons, because these reasons for hostility can make the situation very complex and difficult. The reasons could be sociological, religious, doctrinal, political, or historical. As they analyze the reasons, Christian leaders need to develop long-term approaches to remove the barriers.

Third, a cross-cultural communicator's ethnocentric view or bias against the listeners can create barriers. Kenneth L. Pike said that an *etic* viewpoint is a behavior "as from outside of a particular system, and as an essential initial approach to an alien system."[14] Effective communication often asks cross-cultural workers to move away from the *etic* view.

After removing barriers, strategic bridge building between speakers and listeners is important. Again, there are three conditions for building an effective bridge in cross-cultural communication.

First, the bridge should maximize the speaker's strong points in order to get the most powerful impact.[15]

Second, the bridge should be culturally relevant. In many cases, people reject the gospel for cultural reasons. Missionaries need to change their ethnocentric views and be sensitive about cultural differences and use appropriate language and behavior. In other words, they need to adopt the mindset of receptor-oriented communication.

Third, the communicator should seek to understand and meet the receptors' needs. In every situation, individuals and communities have needs that they want to fulfill. Discovering those needs will be an important stepping-stone toward creating a communication bridge.

Among the needs that people have, some of them are necessary for survival. Abraham H. Maslow categorizes five kinds of needs: "physiological, safety, belongingness and love, esteem, self-actualization."[16] According to Engel, if people lack one of these, it becomes their need. "Each higher order of need will not function as a motivator until needs at the

---

13. Dayton and Fraser introduced "the resistance/receptivity scale" to help determine the attitude of the audience, utilizing a scale from strongly opposed to strongly favorable. Ibid., 129.

14. Pike, *Language in Relation to a Unified Theory*, 37.

15. Dayton and Fraser, *Planning Strategies*, 141.

16. Maslow, *Motivation and Personality*, 35–47.

lower levels are largely satisfied."[17] He also suggests that addressing felt needs can be a starting point for a spiritual decision. "A spiritual decision, or any other major decision for that matter, starts with a felt need for change."[18] Engel also points out that for those hostile to the gospel, "Much of the objection disappears when a felt need is viewed as the starting point for communication."[19]

This can be compared to the deep root of a plant. Deep under the felt needs, everyone has a real need that only a relationship with God can fulfill.[20]

Understanding the audiences' felt and real needs will enable the Christian cross-cultural communicator to build a strategic bridge. Engel explains the necessity of touching the real need and its relationship with felt needs:

> Felt needs cannot be ministered to unless underlying belief patterns are changed to bring them into accord with scriptural reality. This is a widely accepted contemporary principle of counseling. With the exception, of course, that only Christian counselors would add scriptural truth as being the basis of reality.[21]

There is an important relationship between these theories and the YEU-Hui situation. Let's consider the YEU-Hui receptivity to the gospel. The YEU-Hui, who are Islamic conservatives, may be more closed than the E-Group. Even the E-Group may have potential hostility toward the Han or outside influence. Such long-time and deep-rooted ethnic conflicts may represent the biggest hostility toward Han evangelists. Interestingly Hui ethnocentrism can sometimes be a bridge for foreign evangelists, because they prefer more contact with foreigners than do the Han people. The outsider's humble and incarnational attitude should be a bridge of communicating the gospel. Sometimes, Han and expatriates, who are seen as modernized to the YEU-Hui eye, become a bridge of communication with the E-Group as they are more open to outsiders. As researched in chapter 6, the E-Group's felt needs are quite similar to YEU-Han's. These needs are financial balance, love and married life, job

17. Engel, *Contemporary Christian Communication*, 112.
18. Ibid., 53.
19. Ibid., 117.
20. *Getting Your Message Across*, 91.
21. *Contemporary Christian Communication*, 118.

and social status, and acceptance. These common interests can build strong, widening bridges between the two YEU groups.

Diffusion of Innovation

Accepting a new trend and worldview by a group is called an innovation. Rogers primarily introduced the theory called diffusion of innovation. He describes the theory as "the process in which an innovation is communicated through certain channels over time among the members of a social system."[22] By the result of diffusion, societies have new behavioral and worldview changes, and this is called innovation. Each innovation has a different speed of diffusion. Roger introduces five characteristics of innovation: relative advantage, compatibility, complexity, trialability, and observability.[23]

The reality is that only a few innovations are successful. In his book *The Change Agent*, Lyle E. Schaller says, "Almost nothing new works."[24] Therefore, researching characteristics and bridges and barriers of successive innovation is needed.

The model presented by Rogers illustrates a process with five stages: knowledge, persuasion, decision, implementation, and confirmation. People experience these five stages to make the new information their own. Rogers's model explains communication as a process, and it can give communicators an idea of how to design communication step by step. However, Rogers's model does not always seem appropriate to the whole communication and diffusion process because the model is linear and sequential. People do not always change by new knowledge, and even when people change, their process is not always sequential. It may begin in the middle or go in an opposite direction. In other words, the elements of Rogers's model need to be considered, but the sequence may change.

Rogers's diffusion model still provides very helpful insights for the development of a YEU-Hui mission strategy. It seems that there are four areas that are appliable to YEU-Hui situation.

First, in order to receive the new innovation—becoming believers—the YEU-Hui need new knowledge, which needs to be perceived as better than their old worldview. The new ideas need to be seen as more relative in advantage, compatibility, complexity, trialability, and observability

---

22. Rogers, *Diffusion of Innovations*, 5.
23. Ibid., 15–16.
24. Schaller, *Change Agent*, 55.

than was their old idea.[25] New knowledge can be communicated not only through personal contact, but also through the use of personal media.

Second, this new idea—Christianity and the gospel—require continual persuasion from outside and inside of the YEU-Hui. For this, the gospel needs to be seen as culturally relevant, convenient and available, and transferred through proper means and methods.

Third, YEU-Hui needs a special pivotal situation for decision-making. Traditionally for Asians, the human factor deeply contributes to making important decisions, like whether to believe in Christ. To YEU-Hui, receiving Christ as their savior may be influenced when a trusted person encourages them.

Fourth, an implementation process is crucial. Though the YEU-Hui may have decided to change their worldview, without having an implementation process they may turn back to their original lives. Especially, the YEU-Hui who live under high community pressure, or those who, when faced with big ethnic issues in China might easily turn back, will benefit from the implementation stage. Through fellowship, testimony, word, and answering prayer, the YEU-Hui will continually find confirmation that their new belief is true.

Rogers introduced four elements of a successful diffusion of innovation: innovation, communication channel, time, and the social system. It has already been mentioned above that the new idea needs to be a true innovation, which is perceived as being better than the old idea or approach.

Communication is essential for social change and for diffusion of innovation, the process has several different steps, and different communication channels have different effectiveness in each step. Rogers characterizes communication channels as being mass or interpersonal media.[26]

Rogers categorizes three kinds of time concepts that involve the diffusion of innovation: innovation, innovativeness, and an innovation's rate of adoption.

Diffusion of innovation takes place within a social system. Social systems are consistent with their own structures. Those structures are patterned arrangements of the units in a system, and members of the system have stability and regularity. This social structure can be a major bridge or barrier to the diffusion of innovations in the system. Social

---

25. Ibid., 15–16.
26. Ibid., 18.

norm is another factor involved in diffusion. Norms are the established behavior pattern. They define a range of tolerable behavior and serve as a guide or standard for the behavior of members of a social system.[27]

Rogers's four elements of the diffusion of innovation are useful when strategists set up strategies for missions with the E-Group in YEU-Hui. First, introducing the gospel among the YEU-Hui is innovation itself, because the gospel brings a new worldview. For successful innovation, the gospel should be introduced as a relatively advantageous worldview, use forms compatible with YEU-Hui society, and be conveniently approachable to seekers. By the result of this innovation, new YEU-Hui believers need to prove their changed lives among the nonbelievers in the YEU-Hui community. For this, the new believer community needs to live as salt and light among the nonbelievers.

As Rogers pointed out, using mass and interpersonal channels for introducing the gospel is necessary. Unfortunately, because of the government's strict control of mass media, using the airwaves to introduce the gospel is very limited. However, because YEU-Hui people are familiar with using personal media and the Internet, receiving the new innovation through such media is quite relevant. The development of proper content that can be used in both personal media and the Internet, along with a distribution strategy, is necessary. Local churches can play a key role for these mass and interpersonal channels.

It seems that there are many innovators and early adopters in the YEU-Hui. As one field report found, those in the E-Group are quite open to new information, have many contacts with people who give new information, and have a large number of common situations and interests with outsiders.

The YEU-Hui social system and social norms make it relatively easy to diffuse new information because they have a fairly good communication infrastructure in the city. The newly formed self-esteem among urbanites and the urban atmosphere that encourages new achievements serve to catalyze the diffusion of new information. However, diffusion to the whole Hui is a different situation because there is a huge generational, geographical, and cultural gap between YEU-Hui and the general Hui.

---

27. Ibid., 26.

Issues in Developing a Virtual Community into an Offline Church

When Christians plant churches in creative-access nations through virtual communities, they need to set up some criteria for the community even before they start the project in order to successfully plant an offline church later. Chapter 10 summarized five factors for building offline communities: community type, community goal, geographical distance, proximity, and leadership.

First, community type affects the possibility of building offline relationships. Suh found that theater-types of communities have the highest probability of forming offline communities because they invite to offline meetings. For example, baseball fans need baseball games, where they get together to cheer at the stadium. These theater-type activities promote cohesiveness between members and naturally build trustworthiness in offline relationships.[28]

Second, the goal of a community affects the possibilities for forming offline communities. Suh found that hobby communities easily develop into offline communities for two reasons. First, members participated in the specific hobby before joining the virtual community. Second, once members join, the community characteristics naturally lead them to joining its offline community, as expanded meetings. Therefore, Suh found that the camera and photo community, Yodel song club, baseball clubs, and vegetarian clubs are easily developed to offline communities.[29]

Third, geographical distance is a factor in forming an offline community. Online community managers need to geographically categorize their members, making it easier when they develop offline community.

Fourth, the proximity of members' backgrounds affects possibility for forming offline community. Similar culture, ethnicity, education level, social class, age, and gender make it easier to find common grounds among members.

Fifth, a community leader's skills in leadership affect the possibility of forming offline community. The leader needs to have creativeness and passion, clear vision and sacrifice, and good relationship abilities.

In order to build an offline community, YEU-Hui's virtual community should not be just for discussion or sharing information, but rather it should be a community that connects activities and develops offline

---

28. Suh, *Internet Community*, 111–12.

29. Ibid., 162–66.

contacts. For example, sports, hobby, and practice-oriented communities may seem quite relevant. This offline-oriented virtual community automatically screens for similar geographic members. The role of urban Han churches is quite important as the community forms offline, and details about the role of the local church will follow later.

Two-Dimensional Strategy and Decision Model

Søgaard also introduces strategy as a process. He introduces two factors that contribute to people's attitude toward Christ: cognitive and affective factors. The cognitive dimension is knowledge and the affective dimension consists of attitudes or feelings.[30] He illustrates the process on a scale that can be used for strategy development as illustrated in figure 33.

This scale addresses the receptor's current spiritual situation as well as the desired goal, and Søgaard calls the process a journey. He explains the scale as follows:

> The journey towards spiritual maturity becomes a journey from one's present position towards "the upper right hand corner" of the model.... Most likely, this will not be a straight line ... but it will fluctuate between cognitive and affective change.[31]

Søgaard suggests a totally integrated program for developing a strategy based on his chart. In the integrated program, he suggests using different programs and media in each stage of the strategy. The illustration in figure 32 shows the use of the scale to develop a complete ministry program to reach a group of young people in Denmark.

> The group is located at approximately 7 on the cognitive dimension and -5 on the affective dimension. A church has established a youth club as a contact ministry.... There a testimony is given, and a trust relationship is established.... The leader of the club conducts a Bible study in his home and interested youth are invited to attend.... The nearby church has occasional youth rallies.... Such evangelistic rallies will provide a definite challenge to accept Christ.[32]

---

30. Søgaard, *Media in Church and Mission*, 64.
31. Ibid., 65.
32. Ibid., 71.

Developing Strategies for Church Planting among the YEU-Hui

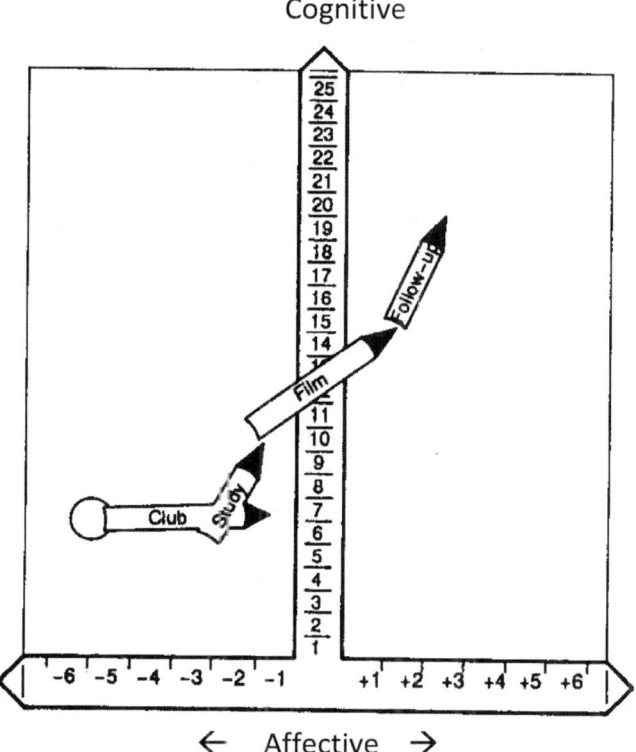

Søgaard's Two Dimensional Model with All
Media Penetration Project Example[33]

This illustration in figure 32 is an urban case, and it is a similar situation to YEU-Hui. Søgaard's scale can apply not only to urban cases, but also to rural situations and can apply to many different social classes. A detailed application of Søgaard's theory to YEU-Hui mission will follow in the next section.

Søgaard usually locates non-Christian receptors at the lower-left side of his scale, and sets a goal for the receptor. He points out that each of the receptors needs their own relevant process as Christians help them to move into a spiritually mature situation.

33. Ibid., 73.

DEVELOPING STRATEGIES

By integrating previous theories and collected data, a new criterion is identified that is useful for developing church-planting strategies among the YEU-Hui. As it was described in the purpose statement of this dissertation, this newly developed model will identify conceptual issues for the development of receptor-oriented communication strategies among young, educated, urban Hui Muslims in China's northwestern cities in order to achieve culturally relevant churches.

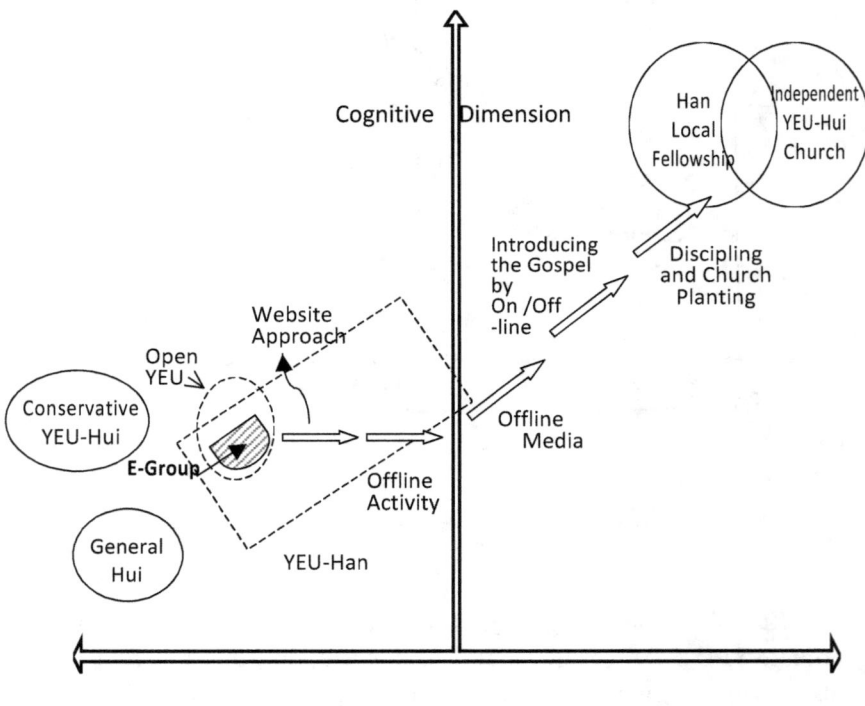

Overall Mission Strategy and Søgaard's Two Dimensional Model

Søgaard's two-dimensional model offers a beginning point for the development of a new strategy model. Because the model involves a process, it can be integrated with other previous process models to develop a receptor-oriented communication strategy to be implemented among the YEU-Hui. Søgaard's model clearly helps church planters address the current YEU-Hui situation and their final goal. By this process model, researchers and practitioners can design each ministry step, effectively choosing the proper methods and constructively evaluating the process through feedback.

Figure 33 shows a full picture of a local church-driven online and offline church-planting strategy for the YEU-Hui. The circles and squares in figure 33 represent several subculture groups that are comparable or related to the YEU-Hui. Those groups are conservative YEU-Hui, open YEU-Hui, general Hui, and YEU-Han. Compared to the general Hui who have only limited information about the gospel and negative feelings toward it, the YEU-Hui, who have conservatives and open groups, may have more information. However, though they have similar information, open groups have more positive associations with Christianity than conservative groups do. The Han-YEU are broadly located on the scale because they have varied backgrounds and information channels. Usually the Han-YEU are no more hostile toward the gospel than are the Hui. Among the open YEU-Hui, there is an E-Group, which is the most strategic group of this research. The E-Group members' attitudes toward the gospel are quite similar to those of the YEU-Han. The former field data report defined the E-Group as the most open to new information. The ideal Han and YEU-Hui churches are located in the upper-right area. They have the same level of spirituality. The local church and its initiatives are crucial to this whole project. The Han Chinese church needs to contribute to this project rather than rely on expatriate drives.

The five arrows in figure 33 show an integrated ministry plan to the YEU-Hui's E-Group. The plan starts from the current situation and finishes with the stage of having independent YEU-Hui churches. The five steps between these two situations are website approach, offline activity, offline media contact, introducing the gospel online and offline, and discipleship and forming an offline church. As the stages go up, more accessible and prepared YEU-E are screened. Here are details of the five stages.

The first step is website approach. The website is designed to meet receptors' needs. From this first step, the local church role is crucial. Not only is an online first contact approach very helpful, but also starting with offline contact and using online as a supplementary tool is good as well.

Since many of the YEU-Hui are familiar with Internet bars, accessing the Internet is very convenient in China. As the people develop a positive attitude toward the gospel, the offline team can develop personal relationships. Virtual community facilitators can arrange global resources to help lubricate the offline team's personal relationships with the YEU-Hui seekers.

The website should necessarily be designed with diversified functions. Having hypermedia in the website is recommended for building community rather than just static pages because the hypermedia website can include blogs, discussion tables, and forums, offering many kinds of opportunities for communication. Additionally, hypermedia websites can facilitate the creation of many small communities, so that they can independently meet each social group's unique needs. Such small groups are also relatively safe when persecution comes.

When web design teams plan the first stages of their websites, it is important to keep the final picture in mind—an offline church. In the first stage, the most important issue is how to make the site easy to access and attractive to the primary receptor group.

This website needs to have three elements: links with appropriate sites, the opportunity to touch felt needs, and the cooperation of interpersonal networks. It is important to advertise and provide links at non-Christian sites frequently visited by the intended target audience.

International teamwork is important for virtual community projects. Even before the website is designed, web designers, supporters, foreign churches, communication experts, ethnographers, and sociologists need to share ideas and plan the whole process together. Though the local church drives the effort, expatriate roles are not diminished, but rather changed. Expatriates can provide foreign networks, resources, and expertise to those in need through the websites. Sometimes, expatriates provide good ideas that they have learned about from either cases of other foreign virtual communities or converts from other Islamic cultures. Expatriates can provide human, technical, and material resources for the project, if necessary.

Next, sites should connect with the receptor group's needs, not just purely introduce the gospel. To accomplish this, web designers, communication experts, ethnographers, socio-anthropologists, and local church leaders need to have cooperation. Ethnographers and socio-anthropologists need to address appropriate cultural themes, first. The second step is aligning and mobilizing Christian experts who can touch their needs. For example, medical doctors from America, family counselors from Hong Kong, legal advisors from inland China, pastors from

Korea, and community development experts from Singapore may contribute to meeting their needs. Of course, translators are needed for such an international project.

Finally, local churches in China need to participate in this process from the first step. It seems that current Chinese websites are receiving direct and indirect foreign aid, and sometimes the whole process of Internet ministry seems to be driven by foreign churches. However, the new suggestion for a healthy, indigenous Internet ministry is a local church-driven, virtual community model.

Chinese church members will use the site and introduce their local people. This strategy mixes interpersonal communication and mass media communication. As Elihu Katz and Engel state, new information effectively spreads when mass media is combined with interpersonal networks.[34]

As mentioned in chapter 10, in order for the virtual community to develop into offline activities, theater-style and hobby-oriented communities are recommended.

Among the several sample sites in the field research mentioned in chapter 10, our campuses, baseball clubs, and English conversation opportunities with natives are good examples of this. Among the Hui target group, introducing Christian medical websites will facilitate the relationship between offline agents and the Hui. The agent may visit the Hui family and comfort the sick family, working between virtual contacts and the web medical experts in America. The family may heavily depend on the information that the Christian agent brings from the web, and the agent can be salt and light during the process of medical counseling offline.

The second step of the five-step process is offline activity. At this offline activity, the local church participates in the virtual community's offline activities. For this, the local church needs to prepare an offline team beforehand. The offline team members have already participated in virtual activities as community members, so some E-Group members and offline team members are already familiar with each other. In their offline activities, people may increase their affections positively by playing sports, singing songs, or receiving counseling. Offline members may then introduce themselves as Christians. Through this, though their cognitive scale on Søgaard's scale may not have changed, this offline contact may move E-Group's affections in the right direction.

34. Katz, "Social Itinerary," 793; Engel, *Contemporary Christian Communication*, 134.

The third step is the offline media stage. Offline members give printed media, DVDs, or MP3 files to personally contact E-Group members after most of their relationships have already matured. When offline members hand over these personal media, naturally the human factor is involved in the level of reception. Especially in an Asian context, the person who gives this media is more important than what is in it. Offline people may watch a DVD together or hold a meeting with E-Group members where they share about books they've read.

The forth step is introducing the gospel online and offline. For the E-Group members who have arrived at this stage, the church needs to prepare other websites. Of course, the offline team's role at this stage is more crucial than before. The offline team introduces the E-Group members to a totally different website. The second site's contents include introducing the gospel and spiritual encouragement. Most of people who receive Jesus Christ as their savior do so at this stage. As a result, the Han and the Hui believers can form cell groups.

As people connect more with and grow in the gospel, contextualization factors become more important. The gospel website needs to be introduced in culturally appropriate ways. Well-combined personal touches through offline contact and in virtual space will encourage the new believers' spiritual growth. In contrast to current department store style database and static pages, the new sites need to have more active two-way functions for communicating with E-Group members.

The fifth stage is online and offline discipleship. By this step, the E-Group members who have arrived at the fourth step can begin discipleship. At this stage, the offline members from the Han church need to slowly step back and support the church formed purely by the E-Group members. As it was introduced in chapter 7, this new contextual church practices the new identity of believers, has a culturally appropriate worship style, prayer, and praise style, and has a way of interpreting the Bible. The final goal of this stage is to let the YEU-Hui have their own indigenous church.

Figure 34 shows a flow chart of the whole process. It is a local church-driven church-planting diagram. It shows how online and offline ministries are combined to plant an offline church.

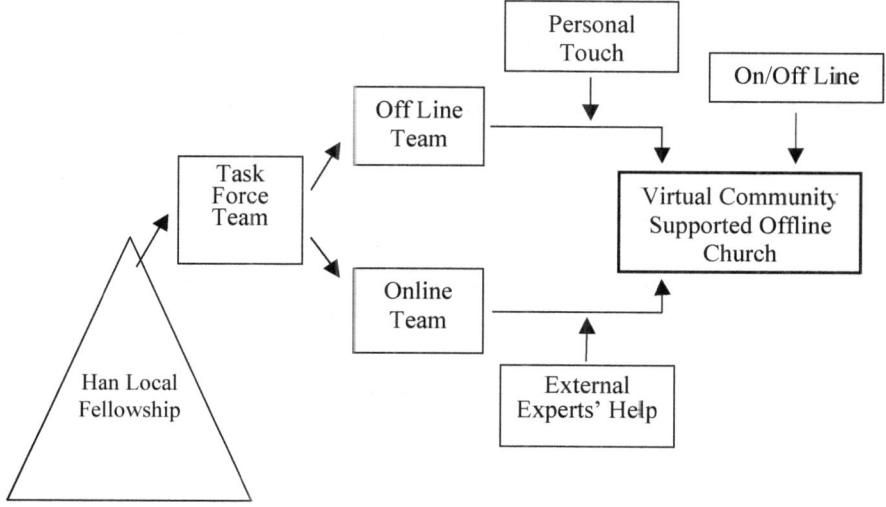

Local Church-Driven Virtual-Supported Offline Church-Planting Model

This new strategy suggestion identifies conceptual issues for the development of receptor-oriented communication strategies among young, educated, urban Hui Muslims in China's northwestern cities, in order to plant culturally relevant churches.

SUMMARY

Strategy involves choosing the best method of going from the current situation to a desired situation. Strategy looks for a range of possible means and methods and various operations that will best accomplish an objective.[35]

The Bible supports the need for strategy and shows successful examples of children of God who developed strategies to lead their ministries. Therefore, Christians need to have strategies in place to avoid wasting the resources that God gave us and to anticipate future results of the projects. Having a strategy exercises a Christian's servanthood and testimony.

Selected theories of the communication strategies, which were related to the goal of this study, were reviewed. Identifying YEU-Hui situational bridges and barriers is crucial for laying a communication strategy. The view held by Engel and his coworker, as well as by Rogers, on strategy is an information process. This lays a theoretical foundation

---

35. Dayton and Fraser, *Planning Strategies*, 13–14.

for developing a new mission strategy to reach the YEU-Hui. Engel's CDP introduced a spiritual decision as a process of information. Though there maybe some exceptions, Rogers's five stages in the innovation decision process gave strategists the idea that the people have confirmation stage through sequential process. For planting an offline church from a virtual community, the website and church-planting team should bear in mind the five criteria of a website: community type, goal, distance, proximity, and leader. Søgaard's two-dimensional model is good for ministry to YEU-Hui because it shows us how to guide YEU-Hui's affection and cognitive movement. Søgaard's scale is a process model, and can integrate with other models in order to design the strategy.

New criteria for a church-planting model among the YEU-Hui that are developed out of a virtual community are summarized. By this newly developed strategy, conceptual issues for the development of receptor-oriented communication strategies among young, educated, urban Hui Muslims in China's northwestern cities are identified in order to plant culturally relevant churches.

Using all the background studies, theoretical studies, and field data, a new set of mission strategies to the YEU-Hui are developed. Through this, the mission world can have new missiological impact, enabling Christians to expand missiological ideas. With this new strategy, a mission to the YEU-Hui will be more effectively receptor-oriented. The next chapter will discuss what these issues are, what Christians need to do, and how the mission world needs to be changed.

12

Propositions for Receptor-Oriented Communication Strategies for the YEU-Hui

THE PRECEDENT STUDIES AND the analysis of theories have given new missiological insights regarding the development of mission strategies for reaching the Hui. Through the precedent theories, field research, and background studies, we have been able to identify crucial issues that can lead to effective ways for using receptor-oriented communication to introduce the gospel to the Hui. Following the approach of Rogers in his diffusion of innovation theory, these insights are presented as a series of missiological propositions

> Proposition 1: YEU-Hui is an emerging social group that is open to change.

YEU-Hui is a generation with multiple identities. The YEU-Hui worldview has at least two layers, similar to an onion. Islamic factors, historical factors, ethnicity, and their relationships with other peoples have formed the inner circle of their worldview. The outer layer has been mainly formed after the open door policy, which was introduced in China in 1970.

The YEU-Hui have traditional culture in a deeper part of their worldview, but this post-Cultural Revolution generation has had tremendously different experiences than their parents.

Among the whole Hui people group, the YEU group is more highly receptive to new information. Urban juncture, proximity, and common space and time with other people groups provide the YEU-Hui opportunities to change. Their urban situation, the consumer revolution, the impact of modernization, the influence of global networking, and their media preferences all propel the YEU-Hui to change.

In spite of this openness, not all the YEU-Hui change or show a similar rate of change. Since, different subgroups of YEU-Hui have different change rates and directions, mission strategists need to find the most receptive subgroup, as they introduce the gospel.

> Proposition 2: Modernization strongly impacts the YEU-Hui, and this begs Christians to introduce the gospel primarily to the YEU-Hui.

The five main characteristics of modernization—urbanization, secularization, globalization, pluralization, privatization—make a big impact on the YEU-Hui. As a result, YEU-Hui have two main tendencies: conservatism and liberalism. The YEU-Hui conservatives are quite different from mid-Eastern ones. YEU-Hui are devoted to ethnic ideology rather than religious activities, and their felt needs, networks, and preferences are quite similar to the YEU-Hui liberalists and the YEU-Han. Therefore, there does not seem to be a need for different mission strategies for these two groups. Because of their receptivity to new information, these two subgroups will actively lead new innovation.

> Proposition 3: The impact of modernization challenges cross-cultural workers to do inter-status mission rather than a whole people group approach.[1]

Traditionally, many Christian missionaries have seen people groups as closed systems and homogeneous groups, so many mission strategies are similar, no matter what the first receptor's social class is. However, most of the groups have many social classes, and the whole people group is a mosaic of subculture groups. Each subgroup has a different level openness to change. Therefore, a social class approach that is initiated by other people groups who have similar proximity, experiences, and openness is more strategic. This approach has two strong points. First, it helps Christian expatriates contact social classes who have higher receptivities within the people group. Second, it helps mission leaders have an idea of mobilizing proximate Christian social group in different people, for reaching the

---

1. Kim, "'Us' or 'Me'?," 95–96.

target social group who are unreached. These two strategic points are the biggest reasons for regarding the YEU-Hui as a strategic group. The YEU-Hui's proximity to and communication with a majority group increase their ethnic assimilation. This assimilation and increased personal abilities encourage the YEU-Hui toward having interethnic communication with those of a different status and generation.

This new phenomenon challenges missiologists to understand the impact of modernization, which leads several special classes within the people groups to move away from tradition and toward international common ground. In this adaptation process, the locals have to either voluntarily or forcefully adapt to modernization. That means the locals move into the middle point between tradition and global trends. In many people groups, there are some social groups who are faster at adopting new fashions. Therefore, inter-status mission is strategic, as other similar social classes of people groups introduce the gospel to the locals who have moved out. An inter-status mission is an important strategy, and a good example is the mission to YEU-Hui from YEU-Han.

> Proposition 4: The impact of modernization gives the YEU-Hui a new self-consciousness and new abilities, which provides a certain amount of positive circumstances to evangelism.[2]

The impact of modernization gives the Hui middle-class three abilities—resources, opportunities, and mobility. With these abilities they have also created the "my life mentality." These new abilities and accompanying fresh mentality allow individuals to hold multi-ID, and have multi-faces. These identities provide great power and energy to the Hui middle-class.

The urban secondary networks are generally weak ties. Those ties ask for limited contribution and sacrifice to the network, and guarantee that individuals have a large amount of freedom of choice and self. The newly formed "my life mentality" enables YEU-Hui individuals to make choices according to their personal preferences without much community pressure. As characteristically objective thinkers, this choice of freedom provides an important meaning in regard to evangelism. The traditional social hurdles to reaching the YEU-Hui are now relatively lower as they receive the gospel. Now, the YEU-Hui satisfies the strategic condition of being a group of innovators and early adopters of innovation.

2. Ibid.

Proposition 5: The YEU-Hui's unbalanced development between the primary and secondary networks will be a major challenge to the YEH-Hui when they hear the gospel. For this, Christians need to understand Asian values and relationships when they introduce the gospel.[3]

The impact of modernization causes the YEU-Hui secondary units to grow faster but their primary networks remain relatively tied with tradition. This differentiation may create inter-network and intergenerational conflicts. Because of this, the primary network will be a major challenge when the YEU-Hui receive the gospel. Opportunities for the YEU-Hui to hear the gospel may increase, but the religious and ethnic persecution from kin will remain. Therefore, to allow for the YEU-Hui to consistently grow in the gospel, the mission senders need to understand Asian values and communication styles.

Proposition 6: Cultural symbols, lifestyles, and rituals show that the Hui's primary cultural themes are power and pride.

Concerning cultural symbols, the Hui emphasize power and pride, and the Bible provides a divine answer to this. It was found that their *qingzhen* (请真) is a representative cultural symbol of this power and pride. Therefore, using a biblical message of power and pride is recommended while communicating the gospel. The Bible communicator needs to emphasize that *qingzhen* is not just their naturally developed cultural theme; it is a divinely given theme, for God planned to save the Hui since ancient times. The study developed seven messages that can be used in the process of developing a contextualized message.

Proposition 7: Critical contextualization theory is biblical, effective, and appropriate for a future YEU-Hui church.

Among the several tools of contextualization, this study concludes that critical contextualization seems to be an effective tool for understanding the meaning of cultural symbols and then suggesting new biblical forms to express the meaning. The method enables Christians to express symbols and signs to the YEU-Hui in an effective way. Through

3. Ibid.

this critical contextualization, Christians can recombine dynamically equivalent Christian messages, and can design guidelines for the future YEU-Hui church.

> Proposition 8 Starting from where the YEU-Hui feel familiar is the key of designing contextualized church.

The contextualization process needs to start by thinking about what the YEU-Hui feel familiar about. Since the YEU-Hui are quite influenced by the impact of modernization, their initial step in the contextualization process of church development seems not to be quite different from that of the general YEU-Han. This is a quite different contextualization approach from the precedent theory of "reusing common pillars," or "Christian *umma*." These two approaches are trying to find the common ground between the two traditional religions. However, a new approach involves initiating communication with which both the communicators and receptors are familiar. This spirit of communication, finding commonness in trends and preferences needs to be strongly considered as the YEU-Hui set up the identity of believers, a worship style, an administration structure, relationship within the community, and a strategy. Worship style, rituals, a discipleship program, social practices, and church systems also need to be able to be communicated and culturally appropriate among the YEU-Hui.

> Proposition 9: The Bible provides a strong foundation for receptor-oriented communication and strategy.

The Bible provides many important examples of communication processes. God's communication methods are incarnational and receptor-oriented. Just like Jesus humbly identified with and learned from Jewish culture, cross-cultural communicators need to maintain humble and teachable attitudes. The church is not only a vehicle for carrying the gospel; the church itself is a medium of the gospel. Today, Jesus works and communicates with us in this way, as he did with his disciples. Jesus wants Christians to follow this receptor-oriented style of communication when they communicate the gospel to the world.

> Proposition 10: Both mass and interpersonal communication need to be receptor-oriented in order to be effective.

There are certain differences between the theories of mass communication and interpersonal communication, but both of them need to be receptor-oriented in order to be effective. For this receptor-oriented communication, the communicator needs to share feedback with the receptor multiple times, because the process of communication is creating understanding. Added to this, programs and strategies that are well designed by experts are necessary in mass communication.

The need for receptor-oriented communication is even more crucial in cross-cultural communication. The cross-cultural communicator needs to identify the receptor's culture, frame of reference, language, forms of expression, and emotions.

> Proposition 11: Virtual community is a practical alternative approach to plant an offline church in creative access nations.

The Internet is free from geographical limitations, and its opportunities for multiple forms of communication are wonderful tools for forming virtual communities. Traditional mission approaches to creative access nations, where there is religious persecution, were accomplished through radio or literature. Since it's difficult to establish two-way communication through those media, such ministries had many limitations. The development of virtual space communication can provide a more effective approach to reach unreached people in these countries.

The virtual community approach in creative access nations is suggested because its two-way communication can network members, offer care to people, and communicate the gospel. This approach provides community, information, global resources, personal care, practical help, and the future possibility of offline meetings. In this way, the virtual community becomes an extension of the local church.

A virtual community project may not be possible if persecution by the government is too strict, there is poor infrastructure, or there is very low usability. However, China's current situation is quite good for developing Internet ministries, and Internet cafés provide easy access to the YEU-Hui, so this virtual community approach is an excellent new alternative to earlier mission approaches.

> Proposition 12: For planting offline church from virtual community, local church involvement from the early stage is the key.

Running virtual communities alone may not be ideal for missions to the YEU-Hui. Planting offline churches is the goal, and the virtual community project plays a significant role in this. One of the most important roles in this whole project is the local church's involvement from the early stage. Unfortunately, many websites are presently running without church connections, so the community cannot introduce offline fellowship when seekers want to join. The church needs to be involved with designing the websites and preparing offline teams for discipleship training in offline activities. Foreign resources should not be excluded, but should serve the local churches' new online and offline communities with their resources from within and outside of China.

> Proposition 13: The E-Group is a very strategic entrance group for reaching the YEU-Hui and the whole Hui.

The E-Group (entering group) is a sociocultural group among the YEU-Hui. From the field data, among the Hui, the E-Group is the group most open to modernization and change. That is why, strategically, they should be the first group that is introduced to the gospel.

The results of the field research data defines E-Group members as the YEU-Hui who have more than three years of urban residence, have more than ten years of work and schooling, spend more than one hour in daily contact with outside media, go to mosque only on special occasions, and have fewer than four out of ten Muslim friends.

Three scales were developed as tools to find members of the E-Group. These scales are: M (modernization), MM (more modernization), and Q (*qingzhen*). Among them, the MM-Scale is the most effective tool to measure each YEU-Hui individual's openness. It consists of four factors that contribute to YEU-Hui modernization: urbanization, secularization, globalization, and religious pluralization. Therefore, I suggest using the MM-Scale to determine any YEU-Hui individual's openness to the new information, meaning the gospel.

Proposition 14: The Han and YEU-Hui media and program preferences are similar on the surface level, but cultural consideration is needed for deeper level programs with the Hui.

Quantitative data collection results show that YEU-Hui media use, issues, and felt needs are not much different from those of the YEU-Han people. They prefer media content that can be enjoyed in private and convenient places. Though many current people are still using print media, new audio-visual and mobile personal media will soon become more popular. Preparing audio and visual content that is manageable to use in personal media is greatly needed for reaching those in the E-Group.

Reusing the Han church's content and programs are possible in the first stage of YEU-Hui church planting, but an increased consideration of the traditional Hui culture is needed as the new church grows. They cannot be regarded as the same group; they have different cultural and historical backgrounds. Therefore, they need to develop their own curriculum as the discipleship program goes deeper. The curriculum should touch their needs and cultural themes. Developing new programs and content that deal with power and pride using audiovisual media is needed.

Proposition 15: The development of an integrated mission strategy to reach the YEU-Hui is a process and a realistic possibility.

A new suggested mission strategy is introduced. A process model is quite effective for designing a mission strategy to reach the YEU-Hui. Among the several process models, the two-dimensional model can integrate other models, precedent theories, and collected data.

By locating the E-Groups' current situation and spiritual goals, and then identifying the five steps between the two situations, a process model mission strategy can appropriately be designed to reach the YEU-Hui.

13

Future Challenges

THIS DISSERTATION RESEARCHES THE young, educated, and urban group only in its Hui research. However, the impact of modernization on the YEU within the larger Islamic societies reveals similar trends and characteristics. Not only is this so in the Islamic world, but YEU groups in other traditional societies also seem to have similar trends. Therefore, there is a great need for research among this YEU group, which is cause for great excitement as we develop missiology and mission strategy for the twenty-first century.

Though modernization causes many problems, God brings opportunity even from within the problems. The impact of modernization allows the YEU-Hui to have dialogue with Christians, and Christian should not disregard this God-given opportunity and challenge. The challenges are of two kinds. The first challenge is that this new trend requires new missiology and mission strategy. The traditional receptor-oriented communication relied on the idea that the receptors do not change, but, instead, speakers need to hold the receptor-oriented premise in mind. The new missiology should answer how to do receptor-oriented communication with YEU members who move away from their traditions. The new missiology needs to work out how to contextually communicate the gospel with members of this two-layer worldview generation.

The second challenge is that the paradigm of mission to Muslims is changing from traditional "go" mission to round-table mission. Modernization required Christians not only to go to mission fields, but also to meet in the middle of YEU groups who are ready to talk, visit our places, and observe our lives. The YEU are at our door, but are we ready to welcome them? Are we ready to show these people our fruits of the Holy

Spirit? There must be missiological preparation in order to meet these people it the middle zone of their two-layer worldview, and this will be a big challenge and opportunity in twenty-first-century missions.

Future missiology asks us to research and develop at least five areas for the YEU-Hui. First, continually developing culturally appropriate media content is necessary. The receptor's preferences are quickly changing to mobile, online based, personal, and audio-visual media. Having proper content for introducing the gospel is important.

Second, further research about YEU-Hui behavioral patterns—job preference, female daily life cycles, childhood education preferences, etc.—are urgent. Few Christians know about YEU-Hui life patterns after they graduate from high school. Without this data, the development of the next mission strategy will be greatly limited.

Third, a new paradigm of missionary training is important. Current missionary training for mission to Muslims does not much seem to consider new trends in the Islamic world, but is rather focused on traditional Muslims. Developing this YEU-Hui focused training program is necessary for both expatriates and locals.

Fourth, more research on the cultural themes of power and pride are needed. For this research, further biblical study, cultural study, and field data are needed.

Fifth, researching the warnings about modernization is necessary. The main direction of this research concerns using some of the benefits of modernization for evangelism. However, unconditional acceptance of this modernization within evangelism may create another extreme: secularism and syncretism. This study does not consider the by-products or philosophical reviews of modernization. Adding these studies will keep the balance of future strategy to the YEU-Hui.

God gives us challenges and opportunities in the mission to the YEU-Hui in the twenty-first century. We as Christians need to walk in the light and keep researching the world, because missiology is introducing eternal truth to an ever-changing world.

APPENDIX A

Questionnaire to YEU-Hui and Their Media Preference

Greetings! Thank you very much for helping with this research. We are an advertising company, and this research serves the purpose of improving service to our customers by understanding their needs. This survey is anonymous. So, feel free to answer. Thank you again for your time for this research.

1. Please introduce yourself. Gender: (1) Male (2) Female
2. Your age: (___)
3. How long have you been in the capital city of the province?
   A. (___) less than 1 year
   B. (___) 1–3 years
   C. (___) 3–10 years
   D. (___) more than 10 years
4. Which people group are you a part of? (_____) people
5. In what situation are you living within the city? Please check V.
   A. (___) majority people schools' dormitory
   B. (___) majority town
   C. (___) 30%–50% Muslim-populated town
   D. (___) more than 50% Muslim-populated town

6. What is your education level?
    A. (__) less than high school
    B. (__) high school experienced
    C. (__) college or higher than college
7. Which of the following sentences best describe your diet rule?
    A. (__) only eat *ahong* killed meat that has the *qingzhen* mark
    B. (__) only eat in *qingzhen* restaurant or in a Hui house.
    C. (__) can eat mass-produced food (McDonald's or Coke) or can go to foreign restaurants
    D. (__) can eat at a Han restaurant, but cannot eat pork
    E. (__) can eat pork anywhere
8. Do you want to live in a big city after your marriage? (Yes / No), If yes, please check all of your reasons
    A. (__) abundance of information and material
    B. (__) for Job opportunity and self development
    C. (__) for children's education and family happiness
    D. (__) Other: please explain _____.
9. If you had to choose only one, what would be your choice? Please write the reason.
    A. (__) I must enroll them into a minority school, because _____.
    B. (__) I do not necessarily need to enroll them into a minority school because _____.
    C. (__) I will enroll them to majority school because _____.
    D. (__) Other: please explain _____.
10. How often do you go to mosque?
    A. (__) more than once in a week
    B. (__) more than once in a month
    C. (__) only for special meetings or ceremonies
    D. (__) rarely

11. How many hours do you watch, listen to, or read world news or Western culture in a week (through Internet, TV, DVD, soap operas, movies, etc.)?
    A. (__) almost none
    B. (__) less than 1 hour
    C. (__) 1–3 hours
    D. (__) more than 3 hours

12. How much do Western and Hong Kong fashions and styles influence your own style, fashion, consumption habits, or mentality?
    A. (__) very much
    B. (__) some
    C. (__) little
    D. (__) very little

13. How long have you studied and worked in majority's school and company?
    ( ) years

14. Among your 10 closest friends, how many of them are Muslims?
    A. (__) none
    B. (__) between 1–4
    C. (__) between 5–9
    D. (__) all 10

15. If you need advice from someone while making an important decision (like family problems, romance issues, or business), with whom do you counsel?
    Please add priority number for each choice (__).
    A. (__) religious leader,
    B. (__) father or mother
    C. (__) your friend
    D. (__) I always decide my problem by myself.
    E. (__) other: please explain _____.

16. If you did any shameful act (fail exam or business, religious or ethical problem), which group would you be most afraid would find out?

    Please add priority number for each choice (___).

    A. (___) family members and relatives
    B. (___) schoolmates and company coworkers
    C. (___) neighbors
    D. (___) religious leaders
    E. (___) teachers or leaders
    F. (___) other: please explain (_)

17. Tell me the truth! Which of these are most important to you? Please choose three.

    A. (___) money
    B. (___) elevating social position, fame
    C. (___) romance (girl-friend) and marriage/ family
    D. (___) job opportunity
    E. (___) contribution to society (serving society)
    F. (___) recognition from others
    G. (___) personal and people's religious revolution
    H. (___) my people's ethnic up-rise (economically, socially)
    I. (___) China's up-rise (economically, socially)

18. If you had to choose between the benefits of modernization (new education, technology, economic growth, social system) and your own religious purity, which would you choose?

    A. (___) I would sacrifice modernization for saving my religious purity.
    B. (___) I would choose the benefits of modernization over my religious purity.

19. What do you think about the influence of Western culture?
    A. (__) I believe that my people's tradition is threatened by the Western culture.
    B. (__) I believe that we need to resist the outside culture for protecting my tradition.
    C. (__) I think we can have both of Western culture and tradition.
    D. (__) I prefer Western culture more than our tradition.
    E. (__) I am not so much interested my people's tradition.
20. Please write the amount of time each week that you are in contact with the following media (except for textbooks or supplementary books for your school study).
    A. printed news papers, journals, books: (__) hours in a week
    B. TV or cable TV: (__) hours in a week
    C. radio: (__) hours in a week
    D. computer (Internet video, DVD, VCD, Internet cafe): (__) hours in a week
    E. theater (__) hours in a week
    F. audio cassette: (__) hours in a week
21. Please give a priority number (__) for each type of program that you most prefer.
    (__) music
    (__) soap operas
    (__) movies, DVD, computer movie, etc.
    (__) concerts
    (__) operas
    (__) story telling
    (__) drama
    (__) dance
    (__) music
    (__) paintings and pictures

22. Tell me what was the most make your heart moving or influence my life and minded program.

    A. Please write the title. _____.
    B. Why? _____.

23. If you have any program that deals with "power and pride" for your people on TV/DVD/radio/journals, will it be attractive to Muslim youngsters?

    A. (__) yes, it will be very attractive
    B. (__) somewhat
    C. (__) we are not interested in the theme

24. If you have the following titles in any of your media, do you think your high school graduates Muslim youngsters love to watch or think that it is meaningful theme? Please check in the blank.

		very good	good	not attractive
A	pride as a minority people in China	(__)	(__)	(__)
B	for an eternal power and pride (meaninglessness of secular power and pride)	(__)	(__)	(__)
C	the true fame that lasts, and does not go away	(__)	(__)	(__)
D	about forgiveness and embracement, father's heart	(__)	(__)	(__)
E	about eternal honor and shame	(__)	(__)	(__)
F	big brother who wipes out our shame	(__)	(__)	(__)
G	the power (attraction) of weakness	(__)	(__)	(__)

Thank you very much.

APPENDIX B

Questionnaire for Chinese Chrisitan Websites

1. What is the goal of your Internet site? (Select one or more appropriate answers.)
   A. (__) To mobilize and help Christians who are interested in mission to China.
   B. (__) To introduce the gospel to Chinese who are interested in the gospel.
   C. (__) To help Mainland Chinese Christians have more information.
   D. (__) To facilitate Mainland Chinese Christians having virtual fellowship.
   E. (__) To build offline fellowship (church) by way of the Internet.
   F. (__) We have specific groups, churches, and individuals in China, and they are actively using the site for forming offline community.
   G. (__) Others: _____.
2. Who are your primary target recipients? (Select one or more appropriate answers.)
   A. (__) non-mainland Chinese Christian workers who minister to Chinese
   B. (__) Chinese all over the world
   C. (__) Young, educated, and urban Chinese
   D. (__) General Chinese Muslims in China

E. (__) Young, educated, and urban Chinese Muslims

F. (__) Any Mainland Chinese

3. In order to attract your primary recipients, how do you design your websites? How does your site screen out primary recipients among the general recipients? (Select one or more appropriate answers.)

   A. (__) We do not have a recipient screening system. We welcome anyone who is interested in our site.

   B. (__) We consider what are appropriate themes to the primary recipients.

   C. (__) We consider their appropriate education level.

   D. (__) We consider their cultural situation.

   E. (__) We consider their social situation (job, geographical difference, preference).

   F. (__) We consider what our targeted ethnic group is.

   G. (__) We consider their felt needs.

   H. (__) We consider their language (other than Chinese).

   I. (__) We consider their main religion.

4. How does your site introduce the gospel or your message? (Select one or more appropriate answers.)

   A. (__) We directly introduce the gospel.

   B. (__) We try to touch their felt needs (ex. English or computer).

   C. (__) We deal with cultural themes and common ground with non-Christian target groups (ex. Filial piety, friendship, the goal of life success, ethnic issues).

   D. (__) Others: _____

5. How many visitors and members does your site have?

   We have _____ visitors, _____ since year/month.

   We have _____ members, _____ since year/month.

If you have a membership system, please fill out the number of participants in the following blanks.

	Last One Month	Between the last one to two months	Between the last two and three months
Number of visitors	____	____	____

6. In order to make your site attractive to primary recipients, what kinds of functions and services does your site provide? (Select one or more appropriate answers.)
   A. (__) We provide more than one service function other than just introducing the gospel. (ex. search functions, weather forecasting, meeting old friends, cafés, blogs, virtual community)
   B. (__) Our site is linked with other secular or Christian sites so that visitors easily visit us and connect to us to other sites.
   C. (__) We send free materials and gifts.
   D. (__) We provide free downloadable materials (gospel songs, Bible study materials, or secular programs)
   E. (__) We provide online counseling/debate forums.
   F. (__) We provide domestic churches and Christian organizations' online/offline addresses
   G. (__) We provide updated secular news and events.
   H. (__) We provide (not directly related to the gospel but) professional materials and access to related experts.
   I. (__) Others: _____.
7. What kinds of feedback systems do you have? (Select one or more appropriate answers.)
   A. (__) We do not provide any feedback system.
   B. (__) email/voting/suggestion
   C. (__) dialogue board
   D. (__) chatting system
   E. (__) audio/video communication
   F. (__) provide contact phone/mailing address

8. How does your site facilitate the development of virtual community among its members? (Select one or more appropriate answers.)
    A. (__) We provide virtual community, blogs, cafés, free board system
    B. (__) We provide sites for geographically close people to contact each other
    C. (__) We have evaluation system to provide different membership levels
    D. (__) We provide Abata, Nicknames, an identification system, and a mascot in our virtual community
    E. (__) We provide a cyber money/gift system
    F. (__) We provide clear community policies
    G. (__) We provide updated information
    H. (__) We provide experts to fill members needs and suggestions for the community's direction
    I. (__) We organize offline meetings
    J. (__) None of above
9. Do you provide any offline (face-to-face) contact information?
    A. (__) No, we do not provide services for face-to-face meeting.
    B. (__) We provide a contact person (the person is our related one).
    C. (__) We refer to related organizations in China.
    D. (__) We provide further church contact information.
    E. (__) Others
10. What percentage of participants release the following communication channels for further contact?
    A. (__) phone number
    B. (__) email address
    C. (__) chatting address (ex: QQ) or in site chatting
    D. (__) physical mail address
    E. (__) text message
    F. (__) personal home page
    G. (__) others
    H. (__) Our site does not have communication for SUCH purpose.

APPENDIX C

Pearson Correlation Coefficient and Each M-Factors Contribution to MM-Scale

The following are the definitions of Pearson Correlation(r), and Significance.

> **Pearson Correlation(r):** In statistics, the Pearson product-moment correlation coefficient (sometimes referred to as the MCV or PMCC) (r) is a common measure of the correlation between two variables X and Y. When computed in a sample, it is designated by the letter "r" and is sometimes called "Pearson's r." Pearson's correlation reflects the degree of linear relationship between two variables. It ranges from +1 to -1. A correlation of +1 means that there is a perfect positive linear relationship between variables. A correlation of -1 means that there is a perfect negative linear relationship between variables. A correlation of 0 means there is no linear relationship between the two variables. Correlations are rarely if ever 0, 1, or -1. If you get a certain outcome it could indicate whether correlations were negative or positive.[1]
>
> **Significance:** The significance level of a test is a traditional frequentist statistical hypothesis-testing concept. In simple cases, it is defined as the probability of making a decision to reject the null hypothesis when the null hypothesis is actually true (a decision known as a Type I error, or "false positive determination")
>
> > Significance < 0.05: there is co-relationship between factor and value.
> >
> > Significance < 0.01: they have strong co-relationship.

1. See *Wikipedia*, s.v. "Statistical Significance."

Significance> 0.05: weak relationship, and cannot be used[2]

N: Number of Cases

Table 21 shows the degree of correlation of two variables by the Pearson number.

By the definition of Pearson correlation each of five modernization factors' contribution to M-Scale are listed in table 21.

Table 17
Each M-Factors Contribution

Factors		M-Number	Value
Urbanization	Pearson	1	0.579
	Significance		0.000
	Number	90	90
Secularization	Pearson	1	0.692
	Significance		0.000
	Number	90	90
Globalization	Pearson	1	0.527
	Significance		0.000
	Number	90	90
Pluralization	Pearson	1	0.555
	Significance		0.000
	Number	90	90
Privatization	Pearson	1	0.367
	Significance		0.000
	Number	90	90

---

2. Ibid.

APPENDIX D

Analyzing E-Group's Background

Table 18
E-Group and Residence Period

		Residence Period				
		below 1 year	1~3 years	3~10 years	above 10 years	Total
E-Group	E1	2	8	3	11	24
	E2	2	11	12	6	31
	Non-E	4	7	6	7	24
Total		8	26	21	24	79

Table 19
E-Group and Residence Environment

		Residence Environment				
		More Than 50% of Hui	30-50% of Hui	Area of the Majority	Dormitory of the Majority School/Company	Total
E-Group	E1	2	1	3	18	24
	E2	4	0	5	22	31
	Non-E	2	2	5	15	24
Total		8	3	13	55	79

Table 20
E-Group and Working and Schooling Period

		Working and Schooling Period					
		Below 5 Years	5~10 Years	10~15 Years	15~20 Years	above 20 Years	Total
E-Group	E1	2	3	7	8	4	23
	E2	7	3	11	3	3	28
	Non-E	6	3	8	6	0	23
Total		15	9	26	17	7	74

(Missing 5)

Table 21
E-Group and Mosque Attendance

		Mosque Attendance				
		more than once a week	more than once a month	only on special occasions	don't go	Total
E-Group	E1	0	0	12	12	24
	E2	0	3	19	9	31
	Non-E	4	2	8	10	24
Total		4	5	39	31	79

Table 22
E-Group and Contact with Western Culture

		Contact with Western Culture				
		almost none	less than 1 hour a week	1-3 hours a week	more than 3 hours a week	Total
E-Group	E1	1	2	8	13	24
	E2	8	6	8	9	31
	Non-E	8	3	6	7	24
Total		17	11	22	29	79

Table 23
E-Group and Influence of Western and Hong Kong Fashion

Influence of Western and Hong Kong Fashion

		very little influence	comparatively little influence	comparatively big influence	very big influence	Total
E-Group	E1	2	15	4	3	24
	E2	8	16	5	1	30
	Non-E	13	8	2	0	23
Total		23	39	11	4	77

(Missing 2)

Table 24
E-Group and Muslim Friends

Muslim Friends

		8-10 people	5-8 people	1-4 people	none	Total
E-Group	E1	0	3	19	2	24
	E2	0	10	21	0	31
	Non-E	10	7	7	0	24
Total		10	20	47	2	79

APPENDIX E

Background Analysis: Conservatives versus Liberal and Open E-Groups

Table 25
Residence Environment of the Two Groups

	Conservatives		LOE-Group	
	frequency	percent	frequency	percent
Living in more than 50% of the Hui area	4	8.7	6	11%
Living in 30-50% of the Hui area	1	4.3	1	2%
Living in the majority area	2	13.1	8	15%
Living in majority school dormitory	18	73.9	40	73%
Total	25	100.0	55	100%

Table 26
Urban Preferences among the Two Groups

	Conservatives		LOE-Group	
	frequency	percent	frequency	percent
I don't want to live in big city	2	8%	4	7%
I do want to live in big city	23	92%	51	93%
Total	25	100%	55	100%

Table 27
Reasons for Urban Preference among the Two Groups

	Conservatives		LOE-Group	
	frequency	percent	frequency	percent
City provides abundant material	8	32	16	29%
City provides job and self-development opportunity	12	48	26	47%
City provides child education and family happiness	5	19	12	22%
other reasons	0	0	1	2%
Total	25	100%	55	100%

Table 28
Child Education among the Two Groups

	Conservatives		LOE-Group	
	frequency	percent	frequency	percent
I will enroll my children to ethnic school system	0	0%	1	2%
I will not necessarily enroll them to ethnic school	15	60%	31	57%
I will choose other choices	6	24%	12	22%
I will enroll my children to majority school system	4	16%	10	19%
Total	25	100%	54	100%

(Missing 1)

Table 29
Mosque Attendance among the Two Groups

	Conservatives		LOE-Group	
	Frequency	percent	frequency	percent
I go to mosque more than once a week	0	0%	0	0%
I go to mosque more than once a month	1	4%	3	5%
I go to mosque only on important occasions	14	56%	31	56%
I don't go to mosque	10	40%	21	38%
Total	25	100%	55	100%

Table 30
Contact with Global Media among the Two Groups

	Conservatives		LOE-Group	
	Frequency	Percent	frequency	percent
I contact global news very little	5	20%	9	16%
I contact global news less than 1 hour a week	4	16%	8	15%
I contact global news 1-3 hours a week	7	28%	16	29%
I contact global news more than 3 hours a week	9	36%	22	40%
Total	25	100%	55	100%

Table 31
Influence from Western and Hong Kong Fashion among the Two Groups

	Conservatives		LOE-Group	
	Frequency	percent	frequency	percent
very little influence	5	20%	10	19%
comparatively little influence	14	56%	31	57%
comparatively big influence	5	20%	9	17%
very big influence	1	4%	4	7%
Total	25	100%	54	100%
				(Missing 1)

Table 32
Muslim Friends among the Two Groups

	Conservatives		LOE-Group	
	frequency	Percent	frequency	percent
8-10 of my ten close friends are Muslim	0	0%	0	0%
5-8 of my ten close friends are Muslim	8	32%	13	24%
1-4 of my ten close friends are Muslim	16	64%	40	73%
none of my ten close friends are Muslim	1	4%	2	4%
Total	25	100%	55	100%

Bibliography

Achor, Shirley. *Mexican Americans in a Dallas Barrio*. Edited by Achor Shirley. Tucson: University of Arizona Press, 1978.
Adeney, David H. *China, the Church's Long March*. Ventura: Regal, 1985.
Aikman, David. "The Reason Is Christianity." Adapted from a speech delivered at Chinese House Church Missions and Evangelism: In Commemoration of the 200th Anniversary of Robert Morrison's Arrival in China. *China Ministry Report* 162–63 (2007–8) 1–8.
Allen, Roland. *Missionary Methods: St. Paul's or Ours?* Grand Rapids: Eerdmans, 1962.
———. *The Spontaneous Expansion of the Church: And the Causes Which Hinder It*. English ed. Grand Rapids: Eerdmans, 1962.
Anderson, John D. C. "The Missionary Approach to Islam: Christian or 'Cultic.'" *Missiology: An International Review* 4 (1976) 283–300.
Anderson, Nels. "Aspects of Urbanism and Urbanization." In *Urbanism and Urbanization*, edited by Nels Anderson, 1–6. Leiden: Brill, 1964.
Andrew, G. Findlay. *The Crescent in North-West China*. London: China Inland Mission, 1921.
Antoun, Richard T. *Understanding Fundamentalism: Christian, Islamic, and Jewish Movements*. Walnut Creek, CA: AltaMira, 2001.
Ayubi, Nazih N. M. *Political Islam: Religion and Politics in the Arab World*. English ed. London: Routledge, 1991.
Bailey, Kenneth E. *The Cross and the Prodigal: The 15th Chapter of Luke, Seen through the Eyes of Middle Eastern Peasants*. St Louis: Concordia, 1973.
Baker, Hugh D. R. *Chinese Family and Kinship*. New York: Columbia University Press, 1979.
Beavans, Stephen B. *Models of Contextual Theology*. Maryknoll: Orbis, 2000.
Berlo, David K. *The Process of Communication an Introduction to the Theory and Practice*. San Francisco: Rinehart, 1960.
Bethmann, Erich W. *Bridge to Islam: A Study of the Religious Forces of Islam and Christianity in the near East*. London: Allen & Unwin, 1953.
Borsch, Frederick Houk. *Power in Weakness: New Hearing for Gospel Stories of Healing and Discipleship*. Philadelphia: Fortress, 1983.

Bourque, Susan Carolyn, and Kay B. Warren. *Women of the Andes: Patriarchy and Social Change in Two Peruvian Towns*. Ann Arbor: University of Michigan Press, 1981.

Box, Harry. "Communicating Christianity to Oral, Event-Oriented People." DMiss thesis, Fuller Theological Seminary, 1992.

Braswell, George W. *Islam: Its Prophet, Peoples, Politics, and Power*. Nashville: Broadman & Holman, 1996.

Brislen, Mike. "A Model for a Muslim-Culture Church." *Missiology: An International Review* 24 (1996) 355–67.

Brock, Charles. *Indigenous Church Planting*. Neosho, MO: Church Planting International, 1994.

———. *The Principles and Practice of Indigenous Church Planting*. Manila, Philippines: Baptist Center, Southern Baptist Mission, 1980.

Bromiley, Geoffrey William. *The International Standard Bible Encyclopedia*. Rev. ed. 4 vols. Grand Rapids: Eerdmans, 1979.

Broomhall, Marshall. *Islam in China: A Neglected Problem*. New York: Paragon, 1966.

Brown, Colin. *The New International Dictionary of New Testament Theology*. Grand Rapids: Zondervan, 1975.

Burgoon, Michael, and Michael Ruffner. *Human Communication*. New York: Holt, Rinehart and Winston, 1978.

Buttrick, George Arthur. *The Interpreter's Dictionary of the Bible: An Illustrated Encyclopedia*. New York: Abingdon, 1962.

Chen, Nancy N. *China Urban: Ethnographies of Contemporary Culture*. Durham, NC: Duke University Press, 2001.

Clinton, J. Robert. *Bridging Strategies: Leadership Perspectives for Introducing Change*. Altadena, CA: Barnabas, 1992.

Cloer, Clayton Parnell. "Samuel Zwemer: A Model of Muslim Contextualization." PhD diss., Mid-America Baptist Theological Seminary, 2000.

CNNIC. "Statistical Survey Report on the Internet Development in China." China Internet Network Information Center, July 13, 2007.

Conn, Harvie M. *Eternal Word and Changing Worlds: Theology, Anthropology, and Mission in Trialogue*. Phillipsburg, NJ: P&R, 1984.

———. "Urbanization and Its Implications." In *Muslim and Christians on the Emmaus Road*, edited by John D. Woodberry, 61–83. Monrovia, CA: MARC, 1989.

Davis, Deborah. *The Consumer Revolution in Urban China*. Studies on China 22. Berkeley: University of California Press, 2000.

Dayton, Edward R. *God's Purpose / Man's Plans: A Workbook*. Monrovia, CA: MARC, 1974.

Dayton, Edward R., and David Allen Fraser. *Planning Strategies for World Evangelization*. Rev. ed. Grand Rapids: Eerdmans, 1990.

DeSilva, David Arthur. *Despising Shame: Honor Discourse and Community Maintenance in the Epistle to the Hebrews*. Dissertation Series / Society of Biblical Literature 152. Atlanta: Scholars, 1995.

Dewey, Richard. "The Rural-Urban Continuum." Chapter 9 of *Urban Man and Society: A Reader in Urban Sociology*, edited by Albert N. Cousins and Hans Nagpaul, 78–82. New York: Knopf, 1970.

Dillon, Michael. *China's Muslim Hui Community: Migration, Settlement and Sects*. London: Curzon, 1999.

———. *China's Muslims*. Images of Asia. New York: Oxford University Press, 1996.

Dyrness, William A. *Invitation to Cross-Cultural Theology: Case Studies in Vernacular Theologies*. Grand Rapids: Zondervan, 1992.

Eames, Edwin, and Judith Granich Goode. *Anthropology of the City: An Introduction to Urban Anthropology*. Englewood Cliffs, NJ: Prentice-Hall, 1977.

Ekvall, Robert B. *Cultural Relations on the Kansu-Tibetan Border*. Chicago: University of Chicago Press, 1939.

Engel, James F. *Contemporary Christian Communication*. Nashville: Nelson, 1979.

———. *Getting Your Message Across*. Mandaluyong: OMF Literature, 1989.

Entwisle, Barbara, and Gail E. Henderson, eds. *Re-Drawing Boundaries: Work, Households, and Gender in China*. Berkeley: University of California Press, 2000.

Evans, Craig A., and Stanley E. Porter. *Dictionary of New Testament Background*. Downers Grove: InterVarsity, 2000.

Findlay, G. Andrew *The Crescent in North-West China*. London: China Inland Mission, 1921.

Fischer, Claude S. *To Dwell among Friends: Personal Networks in Town and City*. Chicago: University of Chicago Press, 1982.

———. *The Urban Experience* 2nd ed. San Diego: Harcourt Brace Jovanovich, 1984.

Flanagan, William G. *Contemporary Urban Sociology*. Cambridge: Cambridge University Press, 1993.

Fletcher, Joseph. "Brief History of the Naqahbandiyya in China." Unpublished manuscript. Harvard University, 1977.

Freedman, David Noel, et al., eds. *The Anchor Bible Dictionary*. New York: Doubleday, 1992.

Gans, Herbert J. "Urbanism and Suburbanism as Ways of Life: A Re-evaluation of Definitions." In *Human Behavior and Social Processes: An Interactionist Approach*, edited by Arnold Marshall Rose, 507–21. Boston: Houghton Mifflin, 1962.

Gao, Zhanfu. "民族教育于甘肅少數民族地區的補貧問題 (Minzu Jiaoyu Yu Gansu Xiaoshu Minzu Diqu De Fupin Wonti)." *Journal of Gansu Minzu Yanjiu* (甘肅少數民族研究) 52 (1997) 35–42.

Gillette, Maris Boyd. *Between Mecca and Beijing: Modernization and Consumption among Urban Chinese Muslims*. Stanford: Stanford University Press, 2000.

Gilliland, Dean S. "Context Is Critical in 'Islampur' Case." *EMQ*, October 1998, 415–17.

———. "Doing Theology in Context." Class syllabus, MT510. Fuller Theological Seminary. Pasadena, CA, 2001.

———. *Pauline Theology & Mission Practice*. Jos Plateau State, Nigeria: Albishir Bookshops, 1983.

———. *The World among Us: Contextualizing Theology for Mission Today*. Dallas: Word, 1989.

Gladney, Dru C. *Ethnic Identity in China: The Making of a Muslim Minority Nationality*. Case Studies in Cultural Anthropology. Orlando: Harcourt Brace, 1998.

———. *Making Majorities: Constituting the Nation in Japan, Korea, China, Malaysia, Fiji, Turkey, and the United States*. East-West Center Series on Contemporary Issues in Asia and the Pacific. Stanford: Stanford University Press, 1998.

———. "Qingzhen: A Study of Ethnoreligious Identity among Hui Muslim Communities in China." PhD dissertation, University of Washington, 1987.

Glazer, Nathan, and Daniel P. Moynihan. "Beyond the Melting Pot." In *Urban Man and Society: A Reader in Urban Sociology*, edited by Albert N. Cousins and Hans Nagpaul, 203–20. New York: Knopf, 1970.

———. *Beyond the Melting Pot: The Negroes, Puerto Ricans, Jews, Italians, and Irish of New York City*. Cambridge: MIT Press, 1963.

Goldsmith, Martin. "Parabolic Preaching in the Context of Islam." *Evangelical Review of Theology* 4 (1980) 218–22.

Goldthorpe, John H., and Keith Hope. *The Social Grading of Occupations: A New Approach and Scale*. Oxford: Clarendon, 1974.

Green, Joel B., et al. *Dictionary of Jesus and the Gospels*. Downers Grove: InterVarsity, 1992.

Greenway, Roger S. *Discipling the City: A Comprehensive Approach to Urban Mission*. 2nd ed. Grand Rapids: Baker, 1992.

Greenway, Roger S., and Timothy M. Monsma. *Cities: Missions' New Frontier*. Grand Rapids: Baker, 1989.

Gulick, John. *The Humanity of Cities: An Introduction to Urban Societies*. Granby, MA: Bergin & Garvey, 1989.

Hai, Xuewang. "Tradition and Rule of Linxia Baifang (Linxia Baifang Huizu Fungsu Guilue)." *Journal of Gansu Minzu Yanjiu* 2 (1992) 57–64.

Hamman, Robin. "Introduction to Virtual Communities." *Cybersociology: Magazine for Social-Scientific Researches of Cyberspace*. November 20, 1997. http://www.cybersociology.com/files/2_1_hamman.html.

Hannerz, Ulf. *Exploring the City: Inquiries toward an Urban Anthropology*. New York: Columbia University Press, 1980.

———. *Soulside: Inquiries into Ghetto Culture and Community*. New York: Columbia University Press, 1969.

Harasim, Linda M. *Global Networks: Computers and International Communication*. Cambridge: MIT Press, 1993.

Hattaway, Paul. *Operation China: Introducing All the Peoples of China*. Colorado Springs: GMI, 2000.

Hawthorne, Gerald F., et al. *Dictionary of Paul and His Letters*. Downers Grove: InterVarsity, 1993.

Heberer, Thomas. *China and Its National Minorities: Autonomy or Assimilation?* Armonk, NY: Sharpe, 1989.

Hertig, Paul. "The Messiah at the Margins: A Missiology of Transformation Based on the Galilee Theme in Matthew." PhD diss., Fuller Theological Seminary, 1995.

Hertz, Ellen. *Face in the Crowd: The Cultural Construction of Anonymity in Urban China in China Urban: Ethnographies of Contemporary Culture*. Durham, NC: Duke University Press, 2001.

Hesselgrave, David J. *Communicating Christ Cross-Culturally: An Introduction to Missionary Communication*. Grand Rapids: Zondervan, 1978.

Hiebert, Paul G. "Critical Contextualization." *International Bulletin of Missionary Research* 11 (1987) 104–12.

———. *Cultural Anthropology*. 2nd ed. Grand Rapids: Baker, 1983.

———. "Cultural Differences and the Communication of the Gospel." In *Perspectives on the World Christian Movement: A Reader*, edited by Ralph D. Winter and Steven C. Hawthorne, 373–83. Pasadena: William Carey Library, 1999.

———. "Form and Meaning in Contextualization of the Gospel." In *The World among Us: Contextualizing Theology for Mission Today*, edited by Dean S. Gilliland, 101–20. Dallas: Word, 1989.

Hiebert, Paul G., and Eloise Hiebert Meneses. *Incarnational Ministry: Planting Churches in Band, Tribal, Peasant and Urban Societies*. Grand Rapids: Baker, 1995.

Hiebert, Paul G., et al. *Understanding Folk Religion: A Christian Response to Popular Beliefs and Practices*. Grand Rapids: Baker, 1999.

Hiebert, Ray Eldon, et al. *Mass Media V: An Introduction to Modern Communication*. New York: Longman, 1988.

Hiro, Dilip. *Holy Wars: The Rise of Islamic Fundamentalism*. New York: Routledge, 1989.

Hitching, Bob. *McDonalds, Minarets and Modernity: The Anatomy of the Emerging Secular Muslim World*. Sevenoaks, UK: Spear, 1996.

Hodges, Melvin L. *The Indigenous Church: Including the Indigenous Church and the Missionary*. Rev. ed. Springfield, MO: Gospel, 1953.

Hoffman, Lisa. *Guiding College Graduates to Work: Social Constructions of Labor Markets in Dalian in China Urban: Ethnographies of Contemporary Culture*. Durham, NC: Duke University Press, 2001.

Horrie, Chris, and Peter Chippindale. *What Is Islam?* London: Star, Allen, 1990.

Huffard, Evertt W. "Thematic Dissonance in the Muslim-Christian Encounter: A Contextualized Theology of Honor." PhD diss., Fuller Theological Seminary, 1985.

Humble, Arnold Leon. "Power as a Cultural Theme in Java: Its Interaction with Harmony." DMiss thesis, Fuller Theological Seminary, 1993.

Huntington, Samuel P. "The Clash of Civilizations?" In *Globalization and the Challenges of a New Century: A Reader*. Bloomington: Indiana University Press, 2000.

Israeli, Raphael. *Muslims in China: A Study in Cultural Confrontation*. Scandinavian Institute of Asian Studies Monograph Series 29. London: Curzon, 1980.

Jankowiak, William. "Urban Chinese: Family Life in a Communist Society." In *Urban Life: Readings in Urban Anthropology*, edited by George Gmelch and Walter P. Zenner, 335–52. Prospect Heights, IL: Waveland, 1996.

Johnson, Bonnie McDaniel. *Instructor's Manual to Accompany Communication The Process of Organizing*. London: Allyn and Bacon, 1977.

Johnstone, Patrick J. St G., et al. *Operation World*. Rev. ed. Waynesboro, GA: Gerrards Cross: Authentic Lifestyle, 2005.

Jorgensen, Knud. "The Role and Function of the Media in the Mission of the Church: With Particular Reference to Africa." PhD diss., Fuller Theological Seminary, 1986.

Juliussen, Egil. "Internet User Forecast by Country: Leading Countries by Internet Users." eTForecasts, http://www.etforecasts.com/products/ES_intusersv2.htm. Accessed May 17, 2007. Link no longer working.

Kang, Myungsoo. *Dijitel Sidae Community Hualyong Junliak* [Strategy for community building in the digital age]. Kyung Gee, Korea: Korea Academic Information, 2006.

Karris, Robert J. *Jesus and the Marginalized in John's Gospel*. Zacchaeus Studies, New Testament. Collegeville: Liturgical, 1990.

Katz, Elihu. "The Social Itinerary of Technical Change: Two Stories of the Diffusion of Innovation." *Human Organization* 20 (1961) 70–82.

Kearney, Michael. *World View*. Chandler & Sharp Publications in Anthropology and Related Fields. Novato, CA: Chandler & Sharp, 1984.

Kelly, Daniel P. "Receptor Oriented Communication: An Approach to Evangelism and Church Planting among the North American Indians." DMiss thesis, Fuller Theological Seminary, 1982.

Kelm, Herbert V. "The Bible as Oral Literature in Oral Societies." Lecture from the course titled "Communication with Non-Literates" (MB542), Fuller Theological Seminary, Pasadena, CA, 2000.

Kim, Enoch J. "A New Entrance Gate in Urban Minorities: Chinese Muslim Minority, the Hui People Case." *Missiology: An International Review* 39 (2011) 353–71.

———. "A New Mission Tool in Creative Access Nations: Christian Virtual Community in China." *International Journal of Frontier Missiology* 27 (2010) 183–88.

Kim, Enoch Jinsik. "'Us' or 'Me'? Modernization and Social Networks among China's Urban Hui." In *Longing for Community: Church, Ummah, or Somewhere in Between?*, edited by David Greenlee, 89–96. Pasadena: William Carey Library, 2013.

Kincaid, D. Lawrence, and Wilbur Schramm. *Fundamental Human Communication.* Honolulu: East-West Communication Institute, 1975.

Kotter, Herbert. "Changes in Urban-Rural Relationship in Industrial Society." In *Urbanism and Urbanization*, edited by Nels Anderson, 21–29. London: Brill, 1964.

Kraemer, Hendrik. *The Communication of the Christian Faith*. Philadelphia: Westminster, 1956.

Kraft, Charles H. *Anthropology for Christian Witness*. Maryknoll: Orbis, 1996.

———. *Christianity in Culture: A Study in Dynamic Biblical Theologizing in Cross-Cultural Perspective.* Maryknoll: Orbis, 1979.

———. *Communicating the Gospel God's Way*. Pasadena: William Carey Library, 1980.

———. *Communication Theory for Christian Witness*. Maryknoll: Orbis, 1997.

———. "Dynamic Equivalence Churches in Muslim Society." In *The Gospel and Islam: A 1978 Compendium*, edited by Don M. McCurry, 114–42. Monrovia, CA: MARC, 1979.

———. "The Incarnation, Cross-Cultural Communication, and Communication Theory." *EMQ*, fall 1973, 277–84.

Kraft, Charles H., Dean S. Gilliland. *Contextualizing Communication in the World among Us: Contextualizing Theology for Mission Today.* Dallas: Word, 1989.

Kruse, Colin G. *The Second Epistle of Paul to the Corinthians.* Tyndale New Testament Commentaries. Grand Rapids: Eerdmans, 1987.

Kurzman, Charles. *Liberal Islam: A Sourcebook.* New York: Oxford University Press, 1998.

Lawrence, Carl, and David Wang. *The Coming Influence of China.* Rev. ed. Artesia, CA: Shannon, 2000.

Lawrence, Louise Joy. *An Ethnography of the Gospel of Matthew: A Critical Assessment of the Use of the Honour and Shame Model in New Testament Studies.* Teubingen: Mohr Siebeck, 2003.

Lawton, John. "Muslim in China: An Introduction." *Aramco World* 36 (1985) 20–29.

Lee, Jung Young. *Marginality: The Key to Multicultural Theology.* Minneapolis: Fortress, 1995.

Leslie, Donald. *Islam in Traditional China: A Short History to 1800.* Belconnen, Australia: Canberra College of Advanced Education, 1986.

Lewis, Oscar. "Urbanization without Breakdown a Case Study." *Scientific Monthly* 75 (1952) 31–41.

Lingenfelter, Sherwood. *Transforming Culture: A Challenge for Christian Mission.* 2nd ed. Grand Rapids: Baker, 1998.

Lipman, Jonathan N. "The Border World of Gansu, 1895–1935." PhD diss., Stanford University, 1981.

Lipman, Jonathan N. "Ethnic Violence in Modern China: Hans and Huis in Gansu, 1781–1929." In *Violence in China*, edited by Jonathan N. Lipman and Steven Harrell, 71–73. Albany: State University of New York, 1950.

———. *Familiar Strangers: A History of Muslims in Northwest China*. Studies on Ethnic Groups in China. Seattle: University of Washington Press 1997.

Lu, Hsiao-Peng. *China, Transnational Visuality, Global Postmodernity*. Stanford: Stanford University Press, 2001.

Luzbetak, Louis J. *The Church and Cultures: New Perspectives in Missiological Anthropology*. Maryknoll: Orbis, 1988.

Lyon, David. *Postmodernity*. Concepts in Social Thought. 2nd ed. Minneapolis: University of Minnesota Press, 1999.

Ma, Tong. *Zhongguo Yishiland Jiaopai Yu Menhuan Zhidu Shilue* [A history of Muslim factions and the Menhuan system in China]. Yinchuan: Ningxia People's Publishing Society, 1983.

Mackerras, Colin. *China's Ethnic Minorities and Globalisation*. London: Routledge, 2003.

———. *China's Minority Cultures: Identities and Integration since 1912*. New York: Oxford University Press, 1995.

Mann, Susan. "Re-Drawing the Boundaries at Work on the Meaning of Work (Gongzuo)." In *Re-Drawing Boundaries: Work and Household, and Gender in China*, edited by Barbara Entwisle and Gail Henderson, 33–50. Berkeley: University of California Press, 2000.

Maslow, Abraham H. *Motivation and Personality*. New York: Harper & Row, 1970.

McLuhan, Herbert Marshall. *Understanding Media: The Extensions of Man*. 4th ed. London: MIT Press, 1964.

Mogensen, Mogens Stensbµk. "Contextual Communication of the Gospel to Pastoral Fulbe in Northern Nigeria." PhD diss., Fuller Theological Seminary, 2000.

Monshipouri, Mahmood. *Islamism, Secularism, and Human Rights in the Middle East*. Boulder, CO: Rienner, 1998.

Moore, Joan W., et al. *Homeboys: Gangs, Drugs, and Prison in the Barrios of Los Angeles*. Philadelphia: Temple University Press, 1978.

Muller, Roland. *Honor and Shame: Unlocking the Door*. Philadelphia: Xlibris, 2000.

Muniz, Albert M., Jr., and Thomas C. O'Guinn. "Brand Community." *Journal of Consumer Research* 27 (2001) 412–32.

Nevius, John Livingston. *The Planting and Development of Missionary Churches*. 4th ed. Philadelphia: Presbyterian and Reformed, 1958.

Neyrey, Jerome H. *Honor and Shame in the Gospel of Matthew*. Louisville: Westminster John Knox, 1998.

Nida, Eugene A. *Signs, Sense, Translation*. Roggebaai, Cape Town: Bible Society of South Africa, 1984.

Nida, Eugene Albert. *Message and Mission: The Communication of the Christian Faith*. New York: Harper, 1960.

Park, Robert Ezra. "The City: Suggestions for Investigation of Human Behavior in the Urban Environment." In Park et al., *The City*, 1–46.

Park, Robert Ezra, et al., eds. *The City: Suggestions for Investigation of Human Behavior in the Urban Environment*. Chicago: University of Chicago Press, 1925.

Parker, Simon. *Urban Theory and the Urban Experience: Encountering the City*. New York: Routledge, 2004.

Parratt, John. *A Guide to Doing Theology*. London: SPCK, 2000.

Parshall, Phil. *Beyond the Mosque: Christians within Muslim Community*. Grand Rapids: Baker, 1985.
———. "A Contextualized Approach to Muslim Evangelization." DMiss thesis, Fuller Theological Seminary, 1980.
———. "Danger! New Directions in Contextualization." *EMQ*, October 1998, 404–10.
———. *Muslim Evangelism: Contemporary Approaches to Contextualization*. Waynesboro, GA: Gabriel, 2003.
Peterson, Theodore, et al. *The Mass Media and Modern Society*. New York: Holt, Rinehart and Winston, 1965.
Pike, Kenneth L. *Language in Relation to a Unified Theory of the Structure of Human Behavior*. The Hague: Mouton, 1967.
Pillsbury, Barbara L. "Cohesion and Cleavage in a Chinese Muslim Minority." PhD diss., Columbia University, 1973.
Rheingold, Howard. "Virtual Community." In *The Community of the Future*, edited by Frances Hesselbein, 115–22. New York: Jossey-Bass, 1998.
———. *The Virtual Community: Homesteading on the Electronic Frontier*. Reading, MA: Addison-Wesley, 1993.
Rippin, Andrew. *Muslims: Their Religious Beliefs and Practices*. 2nd ed. New York: Routledge, 2001.
Roberts, Bryan R. *Organizing Strangers: Poor Families in Guatemala City*. Austin: University of Texas Press, 1973.
Rogers, Everett M. *Diffusion of Innovations*. 5th ed. New York: Free Press, 2003.
Schaller, Lyle E. *The Change Agent*. Nashville: Abingdon, 1972.
Schimmel, Annemarie. *Mystical Dimensions of Islam*. Chapel Hill: University of North Carolina Press, 1975.
Schramm, Wilbur. *Mass Media and National Development: The Role of Information in the Developing Countries*. Stanford: Stanford University Press, 1964.
Schramm, Wilbur, and Donald F. Roberts, eds. *The Process and the Effects of Mass Communication*. Chicago: University of Illinois Press, 1965.
Shaw, R. Daniel. *Transculturation: The Cultural Factor in Translation and Other Communication Tasks*. Pasadena: William Carey Library, 1988.
Shin, Byunghui, and Jongho Lee. *Eensaide Kumyuniti* [Inside community]. KyungGee, Korea: Angraphics, 2006.
Sinclair, Daniel. *A Vision of the Possible: Pioneer Church Planting in Teams*. Waynesboro, GA: Authentic, 2005.
Smalley, William A. "Cultural Implications of an Indigenous Church." *Practical Anthropology* 5 (1958) 51–65.
Smith, Donald K. *Creating Understanding: A Handbook for Christian Communication across Cultural Landscapes*. Grand Rapids: Zondervan, 1992.
Smith, Marc A., and Peter Kollock. *Communities in Cyberspace*. London: Routledge, 1999.
So, Ying Lun, and Anthony Walker. *Explaining Guanxi: The Chinese Business Network*. New York: Routledge, 2006.
Søgaard, Viggo B. "Applying Christian Communication." PhD diss., Fuller Theological Seminary, 1986.
———. *Communicating Scripture*. Reading, UK: Bridge House, 2001.
———. *Media in Church and Mission: Communicating the Gospel*. Pasadena: William Carey Library, 1993.
Steffen, Tom A. *Passing the Baton: Church Planting That Empowers*. Rev. ed. La Habra, CA: Center for Organizational & Ministry Development, 1997.

Suh, Yijong. *Internet Community Wa Hangook Sahue* [Internet community and Korean society]. Seoul: Hanwool, 2002.

Sundersingh, Julian. "Toward a Media-Based Translation: Communicating Biblical Scriptures to Non-Literates in Rural Tamilnadu, India." PhD diss., Fuller Theological Seminary, 1999.

Tenney, Merrill C. *Pictorial Bible Dictionary*. Nashville: Southwestern, 1975.

Tenney, Merrill C., and Steven Barabas. *Zondevan Pictorial Encyclopedia of the Bible*. Grand Rapid: Zondervan, 1975.

Tibi, Bassam. *The Challenge of Fundamentalism: Political Islam and the New World Disorder*. Updated ed. Berkeley: University of California Press, 2002.

Tönnies, Ferdinand. *Community & Society*. Translated by Charles P. Loomis. East Lansing: Michigan State University Press, 1957.

Travis, John. "The C1 and C6 Spectrum." *EMQ* 34 (1998) 407–8.

———. "Must All Muslims Leave 'Islam to Follow Jesus'?" *EMQ* 34 (1998) 411–15.

Travis, John, and Anna Travis. "Factors Affecting the Identity That Jesus-Followers Choose." In *From Seed to Fruit: Grobal Trends, Fruitful Practices, and Emerging Issues among Muslims*, edited by J. Dudley Woodberry, 193–205. Pasadena: William Carey Library, 2008.

Unger, Merrill F., and William White. *Nelson's Expository Dictionary of the Old Testament*. Nashville: Nelson, 1980.

Verderber, Rudolph F. *Communicate!* 9th ed. Belmont, CA: Wadsworth, 1993.

Voll, John O. "Pluralism and Islamic Perspectives on Cultural Diversity." In *Cultural Diversity and Islam*, edited by Abdul Aziz Said and Meena Sharify-Funk, 119–28. New York: Colombia University, 2003.

Voll, John Obert. *Islam: Continuity and Change in the Modern World*. Contemporary Issues in the Middle East. 2nd ed. Syracuse, NY: Syracuse University Press, 1994.

Wagley, Charles, and Marvin Harris. *Minorities in the New World: Six Case Studies*. New York: Columbia University Press, 1958.

Wagner, C. Peter, and Donald A. McGavran. *Understanding Church Growth*. 3rd ed. Grand Rapids: Eerdmans 1991.

Walsh, Brian J., and J. Richard Middleton. *The Transforming Vision: Shaping a Christian World View*. Downers Grove: InterVarsity, 1984.

Wang, Chien-ping. *Concord and Conflict: The Hui Communities of Yunnan Society*. Lund Studies in African and Asian Religions 11. Stockholm: Almqvist & Wiksell, 1996.

Watson, David. *I Believe in the Church*. London: Hodder and Stoughton, 1978.

Webber, Robert. *God Still Speaks: A Biblical View of Christian Communication*. Nashville: Nelson, 1980.

Weber, Max. *The Theory of Social and Economic Organization*. Translated by A. M. Henderson and Talcott Parsons. Edited and introduction by Talcott Parsons. New York: Oxford University Press, 1947.

Wellman, Barry. *Networks in the Global Village: Life in Contemporary Communities*. Boulder, CO: Westview, 1999.

Wen, Jun. "*Ershishijijiushiniandaizhongguominzurenkoudebiandong Jianping* (20世纪90年代中国各民族人口的变动 简评)." [In Chinese]. *Minzu Yanjiu* (民族研究) 3 (2006) 2.

Whyte, Martin King, ed. *China's Revolutions and Intergenerational Relations*. Michigan Monographs in Chinese Studies. Ann Arbor: Center for Chinese Studies, University of Michigan, 2003.

Whyte, Martin King, and William L. Parish. *Urban Life in Contemporary China*. Chicago: University of Chicago Press, 1984.
Winter, Ralph D. "Going Far Enough: Taking Some Tips from the Historical Record." In Winter et al., *Perspectives on the World Christian Movement*, 509–24.
Winter, Ralph D., et al., eds. *Perspectives on the World Christian Movement: Reader*. 3rd ed. Pasadena: William Carey Library, 1999.
Winters, Clyde-Ahmad. *Mao or Muhammad: Islam in the People's Republic of China*. Asian Studies Monograph Series. Hong Kong: Asian Research Service, 1979.
Wirth, Louis. *The Ghetto*. Chicago: University of Chicago Press, 1956.
———. "The Problem of Minority Groups." In *The Science of Man in the World Crisis*, edited by R. Linton, 347–72. New York: Columbia University, 1945.
———. "Urbanism as a Way of Life." *American Journal of Sociology* 44 (1938) 1–24.
Woodberry, J. Dudley. *Current Trends in Islam*. Pasadena: Fuller Theological Seminary, 2002.
———. "The Fullness of the Time for the Muslim World: 9/11 as Its Herald." In *Islam and Grantmaking in the Middle East*, 3–15. Naples, FL: The Gathering, 2002.
———. *Muslims and Christians on the Emmaus Road*. Monrovia, CA: MARC, 1989.
Woodberry, J. Dudley, and Shah Ali. "South Asia: Vegetables, Fish and Messanic Mosque." In Winter et al., *Perspectives on the World Christian Movement*, 680–82.
Worden L. Robert, et al., eds. *China: A Country Study*. Washington, DC: Library of Congress, 1988.
World Bank. "Urban Population (% of Total)." 2017. China section. https://data.worldbank.org/indicator/SP.URB.TOTL.IN.ZS.
Wright, Charles Robert. *Mass Communication: A Sociological Perspective*. 3rd ed. New York: McGraw-Hill, 1986.
Zhang, Li. "Contesting Crime, Order, and Migrant Spaces in Beijing." In *China Urban: Ethnographies of Contemporary Culture*, edited by Nancy N. Chen, 201–22. Durham, NC: Duke University Press, 2001.
Zho, Muzhi. *Urbanization: Theme of China's Modernization* (城市化： 中国现代化的主旋律). [Place unknown]: Hunan People's Publishing, 2000.

Index

acculturation, 26, 34
Achor, Shirley, 40–41
adaptation, 122, 213
Adeney, David H., 114
ahong, 17, 48, 66, 129, 222
Aikman, David, 115
Allen, Roland, 116
Anderson, John D. C., 122
Anderson, Nels, 37
Antoun, Richard T., 21
Arabization, 27–28, 31, 41
assimilation, 11, 29–32, 34, 213
audience sovereignty, 148
authority, 15, 22, 84–85, 105
Ayubi, Nazih, 59

Bailey, Kenneth Ewing, 95–96
Baker, Hugh D. R., 41–43
Beavans, Stephen B., 106–7
Beijing, 10, 27–28, 37–38, 47, 55, 58, 60, 187, 189
Berlo, David K., 143
Bethmann, Erich W., 17
Bhon, Thomas W., 156
Borsch, Frederick Houk, 102
Bourque, S. C., 84
Box, Harry, 146–47, 157
Braswell, George W. Jr., 122
Brislen, Mike, 17
Brock, Charles, 116

Bromiley, Geoffrey W., 81, 84–85, 102
Broomhall, Marshall, 10
Brown, Colin, 83–86
Burgoon, Michael, 147
Buttrick, George Arthur, 81

Chairman Deng, 54, 56–57, 161
Chairman Mao, 42–44, 47, 54, 56–57, 140
channel, 2–4, 11, 35, 52, 60, 74, 103, 121, 143–45, 147, 149–51, 156, 158, 170–71, 190, 198–200, 205, 230
Chinese Muslim, 1, 3, 5, 13–15, 27, 114, 119, 128, 159
Chippindale, Peter, 14
Christian umma, the, 120, 215
church planting, 2–4, 104, 108, 114–21, 125, 173, 185, 191, 193, 195, 197, 199, 201, 203–5, 207–210, 218
Clinton, Robert J., 194
Cloer, Calyton Parnell, 107
CNNIC (China Internet Network Information Center), 175, 177–78, 181
Cohen, Anthony P., 168
communication, 184–85, 187–88, 190–92, 195–200, 206–7, 209–211, 213–16, 219, 229–30

communication, *cont.*
   cross-cultural, 3–4, 16, 53, 110, 113, 115, 141–42, 144, 147, 150–52, 196–97, 215–16
   principles, 116, 135–36, 138–40, 150, 156, 168
   process, 22, 24–25, 28, 31, 36, 80, 90–91, 104–8, 120–21, 123–24, 126–28, 131, 140–45, 147, 149–51, 154–56, 161, 174, 191–92, 198–99, 202–210, 213–16, 218
   receptor-oriented, 148
community, 5–6, 11–12, 14, 17–19, 26–30, 35, 40–41, 45–54, 58–59, 61, 87–88, 91, 93, 95–97, 99, 104, 109, 111–12, 115, 118, 120–22, 128–30, 141, 162, 165–75, 177, 179–81, 183–92, 199–202, 205–7, 209–210, 213, 215–17, 227, 229–30
   offline, 169–70, 172–74, 180–81, 185–86, 188–92, 201–2, 204–210, 216–17, 227, 229
   virtual, 6, 39, 85, 124, 162, 165–73, 175, 179–81, 184, 186–88, 190–92, 201–2, 205–210, 216–17, 227, 229–30
compositional theory, 34
computer, 6, 58, 145, 157, 159, 161–66, 169, 176, 225, 228
Confucianism, 11
Conn, Harvie M., 106, 108
conservatives, 31–32, 38, 44, 64, 72, 80–81, 89, 97–98, 100, 104, 199, 260, 274, 283
consumer revolution, 58, 212
contextualization, 4, 78, 80, 105–6, 108–111, 113, 119–20, 123, 131, 208, 214–15
critical contextualization, 80, 107–8, 214–15
critical mass, 37–38
Cultural Revolution, 4, 11, 26–27, 43–44, 54, 57, 114, 211
culturally relevant church, 1–3, 6, 204, 209–210
culture, 6, 10, 15–17, 25–26, 29–39, 41, 45–46, 58, 74–76, 78, 88–90, 94, 96–98, 102, 107–112, 114, 117, 119, 122, 125, 131, 138–39, 146, 148, 150–51, 153, 156, 161, 171, 202, 206, 211, 215–16, 218, 223, 225, 234
cultural appropriateness, 119
cultural forms, 108, 113, 146

Davis, Deborah S., 58
Dayton, Edward R., 194–95
deSilva, David A., 98–99
determinism, 53
Dewey, Richard, 35
diffusion of innovation, 59, 198–200, 211
Dillon, Michael, 12
Dyrness, William A., 115

Eames, Edwin, 53–54, 58, 62–63, 67
E-Group, 82–83, 91, 95–98, 100–104, 207, 260, 267–68, 274, 277–78, 289–90
   members, 101, 104, 274, 277–78, 289
Ekvall, Robert, 15
Engel, James F., 142, 177, 183, 190, 258–61, 276, 280
Entwisle, Barbara, 60
eTForecasts, 226
Evans, Craig A., 109

Farrior, Julian, 168
feedback, 142–43, 145, 147, 155, 173, 185, 192, 205, 216, 229
felt needs, 61, 74, 76, 109–110, 116, 125, 145–49, 182–83, 186, 197, 206, 212. 218, 228
filial piety, 43–45, 48, 53, 183, 228
Findlay, Andrew G., 55
Fischer, Claude S., 34–35, 42
Flanagan, William G., 41
Fraser, David A., 194–96, 209
fundamentalism, 21, 27–28

Gans, Herbert J., 34
Gao, Zhanfu, 11
gedimu, 11–12, 14–15, 17, 19
ghetto, 24, 38–41, 56, 58, 61, 68, 191

Gillette, Maris Boyd, 9–10, 26–28, 47, 58
Gilliland, Dean S., 106–7, 109, 113
Gladney, Dru C., 1, 12–15, 17–18
Glazer, Nathan, 34
globalization, 22, 24–25, 31, 68–69, 212, 217, 232
Goldsmith, Martin, 125
Goldthorpe, J. H., 85
gongbei, 13
Goode, Judith Granich, 38, 46, 49
Green, J. B., 84
Greenway, Roger S., 24–25
Gulick, John, 37, 40

Hai, Xuewang, 17
Hamman, Robin, 167
Hannerz, Ulf, 40, 52
Harasim, Linda M., 169
Hattaway, Paul, 1, 9, 119
Hawthorne, General F., 102
Heberer, Thomas H., 29
Hertig, Paul, 87
Hertz, Ellen, 57
Hesselgrave, David J., 142–43
H-H ratio, 122–23
Hiebert, Paul G., 16, 80, 107–9
Hiebert, Ray Eldon, 156, 158
Hiro, Dilip, 23
Hitching, Bob, 21, 24–25, 58–59, 68
Hodges, Melvin L., 116
Hoffman, Lisa, 56–57
homogeneous unit principle, 117
honor and shame, 88, 90–91, 94–95, 98, 100–101, 111, 226
Hope, K., 85
Horrie, Chris, 14
house church, 111, 114–15, 119
Huffard, Evertt W., 83, 87, 89–90
Huhhot, China, 44
Humble, Arnold L., 102
Huntington, Samuel P., 24

Ikhwan al-Muslim, 12, 15
indigenous, 11, 105, 109, 114, 116–19, 131, 207–8
information processing, 149
innovation, 59–60, 198–200, 210–13

Internet, 5, 39, 50–51, 58, 157, 160–75, 181, 184, 191–92, 200, 205, 207, 216, 223, 225, 227
 blog, 184, 187–88, 206, 229–30
 missions, 173, 175, 192
inter-status mission, 212–13
Israeli, Raphael, 26, 29

Jahriyya, 13, 15
Jankowiak, William, 44
Jensen, Jay W., 156
Johnson, Bonnie McDaniel, 145
Johnston, Patrick, 114
Jorgensen, Knud, 16, 139, 142

Kaizhaijie, 128
Kang, Myungsoo, 212–15
Karp, David A., 167
Karris, Robert J., 87–88
Katz, Elihu, 207
Kearney, Michael, 16
Kelly, Daniel P., 143, 148
Kelm, Herbert V., 157
Khubrawiyya, 15
Khubrawiyya menhuan, 13
Khufiyya, 13
Kim, J. Enoch, 10, 19, 42, 45–47, 50, 53–54, 60, 62, 120, 162, 180, 212
Kincaid, Lawrence, 147
kinship, 42–44, 82
Koch, Bruce A., 117
Kollock, Peter, 169
Korbanjie, 17
Kotter, Herbert, 34–35
Kraemer, Hendrik, 137
Kraft, Charles H. 16, 88, 106, 108–9, 138–41, 146–48
Kruse, Colin, 102
Kuerbangjie, 128
Kurzman, Charles, 23

Lanzhou, China, 38, 46
Lawrence, Carl, 115
Lawrence, Louise Joy, 84
Lee, Jongho, 171
Lee, Jung Young, 87
Leslie, Donald, 12
Lewis, Oscar, 34

liberalism, 212
Lingenfelter, Sherwood, 119
Linxia, 13, 17
Lipman, Jonathan N., 92
local church-driven church planting, 209
Lyon, David, 22

Ma, Tong, 15
Mackerras, Colin, 30–31
Mandryk, Jason, 114
Mann, Susan, 44
marginal group, 86–88, 92, 103, 125
Martin, Ralph P., 102
Maslow, A. H., 196
McLuhan, Marshall, 153–54, 162
media revolution, 28, 58
Meneses, E. H., 109
menhuan, 13, 15, 17
Middleton, J. Richard, 16
Mingxin, Ma, 13
minkaohan, 55–56
minkaomin, 55
minzu, 4, 9–10, 19
modernization, 4, 20–36, 38–42, 44, 46–49, 51, 53, 55–57, 61, 65, 68–73, 77–80, 93, 120, 131, 144, 212–15, 217, 219–20, 224, 232
Mogensen, Mogens Stensbaek, 146–47
Mohammed, 17
Monshipouri, Mahmood, 23
Monsma, Timothy M., 24
Moore, Joan W., 40
Moynihan, Daniel P., 34
MP3, 152, 159, 164, 208
M-Scale, 68–71, 77, 232
Muller, Roland, 90–91, 100–101, 110
Muslim background believer, 5, 112
Muslim dressed Christian faith, 120

Nevius, John L., 116
New Teaching, 12
New-new Teaching, 12
Neyrey, Jerome H., 94–95
Nida, Eugene A., 139, 152

Old Teaching, 12

Parish, William L., 45, 47
Park, Robert Ezra, 33, 167
Parratt, John, 108
Parshall, Phil, 109–110, 113, 120, 130
Peterson, Theodore B., 156
Pike, Kenneth L., 196
Pillsbury, Barbara Kinne Kroll, 40–41, 80
pluralization, 30–31
Porter, Stanley E., 82, 206
postmodern, 21–22, 55, 58
power, 14, 18–21, 25, 27, 31, 37, 44, 46, 58–59, 74, 77, 80–81, 83–86, 88, 91–94, 101–4, 121, 125, 130, 137, 140, 155–57, 159, 213–14, 218, 220, 226
pride, 17–20, 37, 80–84, 86, 91–93, 101, 103, 121, 125, 130, 214, 218, 220, 226
primary social unit, 42
printed media, 145, 157, 208
privatization, 24–25, 31, 58, 68–70, 170, 212, 232
proximity, 28, 50–51, 169, 171, 188, 201, 210–13

Qadariyya, 13
Qing Dynasty, 11, 13–14, 26–27, 42
qingzhen, 13–14, 17–18, 65–66, 101, 103–4, 121, 214, 217, 222
Q-numbers, 67
Q-Scale, 65–69, 77

Ramadan, 17, 128
Reid, Daniel G., 102
Rheingold, Howard, 168
Rivers, William L., 156
Roberts, Bryan R., 34
Roberts, Donald F., 142–43, 149, 154–56
Rogers, Everett M., 59–60, 198–200, 209–211
Ruffner, Michael, 147

Schaller, Lyle E., 198
Schimmel, Annemarie, 13
Schramm, Wilbur Lang, 142–43, 147, 149, 154–56

secondary social unit, 57, 62–70, 73, 79, 146, 284–85
self-theologizing, 45–46
Shaw, R. Daniel, 107
Shin, Byunghui, 171
signals, 16, 151–53, 156
Silk Road, 10–11, 14, 19
sinification, 26–27, 29, 31, 32
Smalley, William A., 117
Smith, Donald K., 21–22, 179, 194, 198
Smith, Marc A., 15–16, 141, 152, 155
social networks, 17, 33, 41–42, 47–48, 60, 78169
Søgaard, Viggo, 135–37, 141–42, 144, 152, 160–61, 194–95, 202–4, 207, 210
Steffen, Tom A., 116
Stone, G., 167
subculture, 29, 31–33, 35, 37–39, 48, 52–54, 109, 122, 156, 205, 212
Suh, Yijong, 166–67, 169–72, 201
Sundersingh, Julian, 137, 158
Sunni Muslims, 12
syncretism, 107–8, 113, 220

three-self, 109, 114, 116
Tienou, Tite, 107
traditionalist, 23
Travis, Anna, 112
Travis, John, 112–13

Ungurait, Donald F., 156
unit of integration, 37
urban
    anthropology, 15, 36–38, 46, 49, 167
    components, 46–47, 49–51, 143
urbanism, 33–37, 48, 53

urbanization, 24–25, 28, 31, 33–34, 36–37, 40, 51, 56 68–69, 74, 212, 217, 232
Uyghur, China, 10, 31

Verderber, Rudolph F., 141, 143
Voll, John Obert, 23, 28

Wagley, Charles, 30–31
Wahhabism, 15
Walker, Anthony, 43
Walsh, Brian J., 16
Wang, David, 114–15
Wang, Jianping, 26
Watson, David, 111, 123, 129
Webber, Robert E., 135–36, 138
Weber, Max, 85
Wellman, Barry, 169–70
Wen, Jun, 43
White, William, Jr., 82–83, 85
whole people group approach, 212
Whyte, Martin King, 44, 47
Winter, Ralph D., 113, 117
Winters, Clyde-Ahmad, 26
Wirth, Louis, 29–30, 33–34, 39, 167
Woodberry, J. Dudley, 21–23, 112, 120
worldview, 5, 10, 15–16, 19–20, 41, 51, 63, 79–80, 110, 131, 144, 155–56, 198–200, 211, 219–20
Wright, Charles R., 154

Xian, China, 38, 46
Xidaotong, 15

Yoels, W., 167
Yunnan Province, China, 11, 26

zaishengjie, 128
Zho, Muzhi, 36

www.ingramcontent.com/pod-product-compliance
Lightning Source LLC
Chambersburg PA
CBHW051517230426
43668CB00012B/1646